Colleen

Leadership:
Building High-Performance Buying and Selling Teams

Gregory A. Garrett
and
William C. Pursch

National Contract Management Association
800-344-8096
www.ncmahq.org

Printed in the United States of America
ISBN 0–9700897–2–4

Contents

Selected Interviews

The views expressed in these interviews are the sole opinions and ideas of the interviewees, and do not necessarily reflect the positions of the authors of this book or the interviewee's organization, company, or government agency.

Forms

Tables

Figures

Foreword

My hat's off to Gregory A. Garrett and William C. Pursch for writing a practical, informative, and compelling book about leadership specific to the buying and selling business communities. This is an extraordinary book. It takes an insightful view of how and why leadership is essential to successful business transactions. Garrett and Pursch have developed unique leadership surveys, self-assessment tools, best practices, and case studies focused on building high-performance buying and selling teams.

I really like how the authors blended the key leadership competencies and organizational leadership levels of mastery into an integrated model. Another plus is the simple yet highly effective Six Steps to Success© (S3) leadership process. The S3 leadership process helps business professionals focus their thinking, words, and actions to build leaders and achieve team excellence with integrity.

Two unique aspects of this book are the personal stories and interviews. The authors have skillfully woven into the fabric of the book their personal stories of leadership and 14 interviews with buying and selling business leaders. The interviews alone are worth the price of the book. The interviews provide candid assessments of buying and selling leadership shortfalls and success stories. The interviewees represent U.S. federal government agencies, government contractors, and commercial companies, that collectively buy and sell billions of dollars of products, services, and integrated solutions.

If you are interested in learning how to improve your buying or selling performance results, then this book is a must read! In fact, everyone who is involved in buying or selling complex products, services, and solutions should read this book, especially those in senior leadership positions.

Sincerely,
Neal Couture, CPCM
Executive Director
National Contract Management Association

Preface

This book provides the reader unique insights into what it takes to successfully lead the buying and selling of products, services, and integrated solutions. No other book ever written about leadership has clearly focused on how to build high-performance buying and selling team leaders. Our intent is to provide practical and highly effective tools, best practices, case studies, personal stories, and engaging interviews of buying and selling business leaders to help your organization improve performance.

Our approach is simple yet effective. Chapter 1 paints the picture of the two biggest leadership challenges faced in both the public and private business sectors: (1) an aging buying and selling workforce, whose leaders have not consistently achieved high-performance results, and (2) the lack of a quality buying and selling leadership pipeline in most organizations. Thus, the need for developing great buying and selling business leaders is both real and significant!

Chapter 2 uses a visual model to address the leadership competencies and leadership levels that one must master to become a successful buying or selling team leader. The buying and selling leadership levels and competencies model contains five specialized skill areas (SSAs) and seven levels of organizational mastery that one must attain to achieve the highest level of business success.

Chapter 3 introduces the Six Steps to Success (S3) leadership process, which can be effectively used by any business professional to improve individual leadership and team performance. The best practices and personal stories in this chapter make the S3 leadership process highly relevant to members of the buying and selling business communities.

Chapters 4 through 9 provide in-depth discussions of each step in the S3 leadership process. Each chapter provides numerous best practices, personal stories, and selected interviews to highlight what challenges you will face and how others have worked to overcome the obstacles and achieve excellence with integrity.

Chapter 10 introduces benchmarking survey tools that you can use to evaluate overall organizational performance or maturity level in buying or selling products, services, and solutions.

In addition, the book contains these value-added appendices:

A. The U.S. Government Accountability Report, *Framework for Assessing the Acquisition Function at Federal Agencies* (September 2005), GAO-05-218G

B. Glossary of Key Terms

This book provides a comprehensive, practical, and compelling guide to help every buying and selling organization, in both the public and private sectors, achieve excellence with integrity through leadership!

Sincerely,
Gregory A. Garrett, CPCM, C.P.M., PMP
William C. Pursch, Ph.D., CPCM

Dedications

"A teacher affects eternity; he can never tell where his influence stops."

—Henry Adams

Gregory A. Garrett

I dedicate this book to my family, friends, mentors, and former bosses—the good, the bad, and the really awful. I have learned what to do and what not to do from each of you.

On a more serious note, I dedicate this book to three extraordinary gentlemen. First, my father, Otis Garrett, for his absolute confidence in me. He has instilled in me the belief that I can do anything that I set my heart and mind to achieve! My father is my rock of support, whom I always count on.

Second, I would like to dedicate this book to my friend, mentor, former boss, and "second-father"—my coauthor, Dr. William C. Pursch. Dr. Bill, as I call him, has supported my professional development for 20 years and has opened many doors for me. I am blessed to have Dr. Bill as my colleague.

Third, I dedicate this book in memory of my friend, mentor, and contract management guru, the late W. Gregor Macfarlan. Greg Macfarlan spent his life in pursuit of knowledge, always working to make a positive difference in the lives of others.

William C. Pursch

I dedicate this book to my best friend, my wife Lenore, who has been the "wind beneath my wings," and to the memory of our beautiful daughters, Wendy and Heidi, who gave us great joy.

I also want to acknowledge the following leaders and mentors who set the example for me during my career:

Colonel Clifton A. Horn, U.S. Army, retired, and Lt. Colonel Thomas E. Snyder, U.S. Army, retired, who encouraged me to pursue a career in contract management, and who were my bosses at the U.S. Army Procurement Agency Europe, in Frankfurt, Germany. I could not have wanted better guidance and oversight; it was a pleasure to go to work.

Colonel Russell C. Hastler, U.S. Air Force, retired, who was the director for procurement and manufacturing for the Aeronautical Systems Division, Air Force Systems Command at Wright-Patterson Air Force Base, Ohio, who helped me understand Air Force procurement policies and supported me in my National Contract Management Association (NCMA) endeavors.

Colonel Larry L. Smith, U.S. Air Force, retired, who was the dean of the School of Systems and Logistics, Air Force Institute of Technology, and who supported me when I was elected national president of the NCMA and was my boss when I was chairman of the Department of Contract Management.

Each of these officers practiced every step of the S3 leadership process and helped me along the way in my career in contract management.

Acknowledgments

We would like to thank the following individuals for their friendship, guidance, knowledge, and inspiration in the research, writing, editing, formatting, technical reviews, and interviews for this book.

- Steve B. Boshears, Col., U.S. Army (Ret.), CPCM
- Neal J. Couture, CPCM
- Kenneth L. Dixon, CPCM
- Steve Hill
- Dennis Knapp, PMP
- Gregory C. Landon
- Gail A. Parrott, CFCM
- Gary L. Poleskey, Col., USAF (Ret.), CPCM
- Rene G. Rendon, Lt. Col., USAF (Ret.), CPCM, C.P.M., PMP
- Linda F. Rivera
- Paul R. Rosengrant
- Charles Rumbaugh, Esq.
- Philip E. Salmeri, CPCM
- Janice Smets
- Ron Smith, CPCM, C.P.M.
- John E. Stuart, Col., USAF (Ret.)
- Lenn Vincent, RADM, USN (Ret.)
- Rita L. Wells

A special thanks to Barbara Hanson for her continued outstanding administrative support and to the NCMA editorial and design staff for their excellent work.

NCMA editorial and design staff:

- Amy Miedema, Director of Communications
- Kurt Lindblom, Acting Editor
- Kerry McKinnon, Assistant Editor
- Tabetha Jones, Senior Graphic Designer
- Ioana Condrut, Freelance Graphic Designer

Introduction

In a world of constant change, increased outsourcing, and highly demanding customers, the need for on-time delivery of quality products, services, and solutions is at an all-time high. Thus, society, our government, and companies all demand the creation of high-performance buying and selling teams to ensure flawless business execution at fair and reasonable prices.

This book provides the reader unique insights into what it takes to successfully lead the buying and selling of products, services, and integrated solutions. No other book ever written about leadership has clearly focused on how to build high-performance buying and selling team leaders. Our intent is to provide practical and highly effective tools, best practices, case studies, personal stories, and engaging interviews of buying and selling business leaders to help your organization improve performance.

When viewed as a whole, this book provides a comprehensive, practical, and compelling guide to help every buying and selling organization, in both the public and private sectors, achieve excellence with integrity through leadership!

Sincerely,
Gregory A. Garrett, CPCM, C.P.M., PMP
William C. Pursch, Ph.D., CPCM

Chapter 1

The Leadership Gap in Buying and Selling

"Leadership means setting an example. When you find yourself in a position of leadership, people follow your every move."

—Lee Iacocca

Introduction

Are successful buying and selling team leaders made or born? Increasingly, that is the question facing both the government and industry. According to recent U.S. federal government reports from the Office of Personnel Management (OPM), 75 percent of top civil service executives are older than 50 and nearly half are older than 55. According to numerous industry surveys, from the Institute of Supply Management (ISM) and others, the private sector is facing similar challenges. Soon these senior executives will retire and will be replaced.[1] Yet some would say that the fact that many buying and selling business executives are soon to retire is not necessarily bad, because many are doing a mediocre or poor job.

However, tight budgets in both the government and industry have taken a real toll on the leadership pipeline in most organizations. Many organizations have reduced their training efforts to develop new leaders. Our experience and research indicate that leaders should be developed at every level of an organization. Leaders can thrive with different styles. Yet there are certain core characteristics and specific competencies that leaders at every level must possess to be successful. Some of the core characteristics include integrity, energy, passion, vision, dedication, concern for customers, and concern for team members. But leadership is much more than just personality traits.

The world we live in is changing at an ever-increasing rate. Likewise, business paradigms are shifting significantly for organizations and for individuals. Downsizing, outsourcing, horizontal supply-chain relationships, globalization, and increased pressures to achieve high-performance results are affecting nearly everyone—especially business leaders. Within the buying and selling communities, organizations are struggling to advance from classic stovepipe structures to talent-based integrated project teams. With the power of tremendous communication technologies, individuals are now challenged to overcome the overwhelming daily e-mails, voice mails, and instant messages, to establish focused priorities and to ensure flawless execution.

The world of business is also evolving from a focus on large-scale manufacturing to a focus on professional services, often integrated with customized products, both hardware and software. This dramatic paradigm shift in business, coupled with the aging executive workforce, is resulting in a greater need to develop talent—hiring, training, retaining, and creating business leaders. Unfortunately, many organizations in both the public and the private business sectors are now being led by individuals who know what needs to be done but are not able to get it done. Thus, we live in a world with a significant leadership gap, especially in the leadership of large buying and selling organizations, in both the public and the private business sectors.

Said differently, today at every level of most organizations we have far too many managers, including micro managers, just-plain-worthless managers, wanna-be-your-friend managers, stab-you-in-the-back managers, and clearly clueless managers—and far too few true leaders. We all know a true leader when we work for one or see one in action. True leaders are people of action, who recognize that talk is important but results are what counts. True leaders do what is right, at the right time, for the right reason. True leaders take the time to build high-performance teams, thus creating leaders along the way. True leaders enjoy coaching and helping others focus on what is important for the organization and for the individual, both in the long term and in the short term.

This chapter focuses on the new performance-based buying and selling environment, leadership as the key to business success, things leaders of buying and selling organizations should know and do, the leadership gap in buying and selling, the importance of filling the gap by developing a leadership pipeline, and two successful leadership case studies. This chapter establishes the tone for the rest of the book by painting a big picture of the challenges we face in business and the critical need for true leadership at every level of each buying and selling organization.

The New Performance-Based Buying and Selling Environment

The mantra of business today is flawless execution, whether buying or selling products or services. Every organization in both the public and the private business sectors is trying to increase its velocity of business (the speed with which it meets customers' needs), while reducing costs and simultaneously ensuring that it is providing quality products or services to meet or exceed customer expectations. There is no question that the performance bar has been raised in all aspects of business. Some customers have such incredibly high performance expectations that achieving them may seem impossible. Yet what often appears impossible today becomes the performance norm tomorrow or in the not so distant future.

Clearly, in both the public and the private business sectors, we are witnessing increased use of outsourcing and performance-based contracts. Today, more than ever, buyers require customized integrated solutions to their business challenges. Often these customized solutions require multiple suppliers, each with multiple functions, to team up to seamlessly deliver solutions composed of hardware, software, and professional services. All these forces are transforming the marketplace, while posing greater risks to both parties.

Sellers are being asked to agree to increasingly demanding performance-based contracts with specific product performance requirements and service-level agreements, often with significant penalties for failure to perform. Buyers are also taking greater risks, because they are increasingly outsourcing their capabilities to other parties, thus losing some direct control over their success or failure. Business is becoming more electronically enabled, less personal, more regulated, and highly interdependent. Thus, the world we live in and the forces of emerging technologies, growing customer demands, and increased government regulations are shaping a new performance-based supply environment.

In the public business sector, composed of federal, state, and local government agencies, it is clear that all agencies are adopting more commercial buying practices in a quest to reduce acquisition cycle-time, reduce expenses, and increase customer satisfaction. Similarly, the private business sector is moving to create better, more defined, and effectively implemented business processes. Especially, in the wake of the Sarbanes-Oxley Act, private sector companies are struggling to increase speed to market, improve profitability, and increase customer confidence and loyalty. It is apparent that the public and private business sectors are in many ways converging through technology and regulations, resulting in two distinct paths: the increased use of electronic tools to rapidly procure simple off-the-shelf products and services, and the increased use of large, complex, performance-based deals.

Leadership Is the Key to Business Success

Achieving high-performance buying and selling results is a real and significant challenge. The old ways of doing business do not work in today's electronically enhanced, "business at the speed of thought" world. Thus, in both the public and the private business sectors, most organizations are fighting to survive and to find a way to thrive. Many buying and selling organizations now realize that the most important factor for achieving success is developing great talent. Likewise, many organizations know that the most valuable aspect of talent, which they must possess at every level of their organization, is leadership. Said simply, leadership makes the biggest difference between consistent success and repeated failure.

What Leaders of Buying and Selling Organizations Should Know and Do

The Contract Management Senior Executive Assessment Tool (CMSEAT) was developed in 1993 by Garrett Consulting Services, a Virginia-based international consulting practice, to aid organizations in both the public and the private business sectors in achieving improved performance results on their contracts and related projects. The CMSEAT focuses on what senior executives who are responsible for the success of their organization's contract management—whether buying or selling products, services, or solutions—should know and do to optimize business results.[2]

The CMSEAT was developed as a simple tool to quickly assess the level of contract management support provided by senior executives. It has evolved with changes in business processes and emerging technologies. As of August 2005, more than 6,000 individuals from more than 150 organizations in both the public and the private business sectors have completed the CMSEAT. Approximately 5,800 people surveyed were buying or selling business professionals, below the level of senior executive. Approximately 200 people who completed the survey were senior executives, thus conducting a self-assessment. They have commented that the tool is an easy, quick, comprehensive, and demanding survey and assessment of what senior executives should know and do to ensure success in buying and selling products, services, and solutions.

The CMSEAT is composed of two parts. The first part is a 50-question checklist survey **(Form 1-1),** divided into 10 sections of what senior executives should know and do. The second part is a quick analysis tool **(Form 1-2)** that allows organizations and individuals to compare and contrast results so that they can identify areas that require increased executive attention and support to improve business results. The CMSEAT is based on the premise that in every organization senior executives play a vital role in the successful transaction of products, services, and solutions. Thus, senior executives in an outsourcing environment should be held to a high standard of what they know and do to ensure that their organizations have a proactive ethical business culture that consistently achieves customer satisfaction through professional contract management.

Form 1-1 CMSEAT Survey: Your Opinion Counts

Please provide your assessment for each of the questions below. Use the scale of 1 to 5, in which 1 is poor, 2 is needs improvement, 3 is satisfactory, 4 is good, and 5 is excellent. This survey can be used as a self-assessment or an assessment tool for individuals in your organization. Place a check in the appropriate box.

1.0 Role in Business Conduct Issues

What senior executives should know and do

1.1	Create a clear vision, mission, and goals for the buying and selling teams	❐1 ❐2 ❐3 ❐4 ❐5
1.2	Establish lines of authority—who's in charge of what?	❐1 ❐2 ❐3 ❐4 ❐5
1.3	Create lines of communication—how to get work done	❐1 ❐2 ❐3 ❐4 ❐5
1.4	Facilitate communication methods and structure—make sharing information easy	❐1 ❐2 ❐3 ❐4 ❐5
1.5	Set performance-based expectations for the buying and selling teams	❐1 ❐2 ❐3 ❐4 ❐5
1.6	Ensure escalation processes are developed—when problems arise, people know whom to contact	❐1 ❐2 ❐3 ❐4 ❐5
1.7	Ensure that an employee feedback and performance evaluation process is conducted regularly	❐1 ❐2 ❐3 ❐4 ❐5

1.0 Role in Business Conduct Issues, continued

1.8 Create a shared reward and recognition process .... ❑1 ❑2 ❑3 ❑4 ❑5

1.9 Create and follow a code of conduct........ ❑1 ❑2 ❑3 ❑4 ❑5

2.0 Role in Creating Buying and Selling Teamwork

What senior executives should know and do:

2.1 Communicate effectively the organization's vision and the buying and selling teams' roles .... ❑1 ❑2 ❑3 ❑4 ❑5

2.2 Understand stakeholder expectations and conflicts .... ❑1 ❑2 ❑3 ❑4 ❑5

2.3 Encourage respect and business-like interaction among all buying and selling team members .... ❑1 ❑2 ❑3 ❑4 ❑5

2.4 Ensure that reward and incentive structures acknowledge buying and selling teams' performance .... ❑1 ❑2 ❑3 ❑4 ❑5

2.5 Look for and encourage buying and selling managers to provide evidence of teamwork with users, customers, supporting organizations, and suppliers........ ❑1 ❑2 ❑3 ❑4 ❑5

3.0 Role in Establishing a Common Buying and Selling Vocabulary and Process

What senior executives should know and do:

3.1 Understand and use the correct buying and selling terminology .... ❑1 ❑2 ❑3 ❑4 ❑5

3.2 Demonstrate an understanding of the buying and selling process through actions .... ❑1 ❑2 ❑3 ❑4 ❑5

3.3 Fund and support development of a glossary of common buying and selling terminology used in the industry, organization, and contracts .... ❑1 ❑2 ❑3 ❑4 ❑5

3.4 Ensure the development of a consistent buying and selling process or methodology with appropriate automated enterprise wide tools for buying and selling............................ ❐1 ❐2 ❐3 ❐4 ❐5

3.5 Insist that all team members faithfully use the approved buying and selling process and terminology.. ❐1 ❐2 ❐3 ❐4 ❐5

4.0 Role in Oversight of Contract and Project Planning

What senior executives should know and do:

4.1 Ensure that time and money to plan is provided... ❐1 ❐2 ❐3 ❐4 ❐5

4.2 Require an internal contract kick-off meeting to review the plan with all appropriate parties .... ❐1 ❐2 ❐3 ❐4 ❐5

4.3 Review selected contracts.............................. ❐1 ❐2 ❐3 ❐4 ❐5

4.4 Establish executive management milestones reviews.. ❐1 ❐2 ❐3 ❐4 ❐5

4.5 Define the business aspects that executives need to review and approve contracts............ ❐1 ❐2 ❐3 ❐4 ❐5

4.6 Establish consistent performance-based metrics for contracts and related projects ..... ❐1 ❐2 ❐3 ❐4 ❐5

5.0 Role in Oversight of Opportunity and Risk Management

What senior executives should know and do:

5.1 Encourage everyone to identify potential opportunities and risks.................................. ❐1 ❐2 ❐3 ❐4 ❐5

5.2 Require that tailoring of procedures and templates be accompanied by risk assessment.. ❐1 ❐2 ❐3 ❐4 ❐5

5.3 Require and review opportunity and risk assessments throughout the buying and selling process.. ❐1 ❐2 ❐3 ❐4 ❐5

5.0	**Role in Oversight of Opportunity and Risk Management, continued**	
5.4	Require the planning and execution of approved risk mitigation and opportunity enhancement actions	❒1 ❒2 ❒3 ❒4 ❒5
5.5	Stay cognizant of the high risks and the progresstoward mitigation	❒1 ❒2 ❒3 ❒4 ❒5

6.0	**Role in Commitment to Contract Changes Management** *What senior executives should know and do:*	
6.1	Ensure the contract changes management process is well defined and used on all contracts	❒1 ❒2 ❒3 ❒4 ❒5
6.2	Be an advocate of contract changes, as appropriate	❒1 ❒2 ❒3 ❒4 ❒5
6.3	Constructively challenge informal contract changes at your internal reviews with team members..	❒1 ❒2 ❒3 ❒4 ❒5
6.4	Constructively challenge the effectiveness of the contract changes management process at program reviews...	❒1 ❒2 ❒3 ❒4 ❒5

7.0	**Role in Contract Visibility Management** *What senior executives should know and do:*	
7.1	Ensure that corporate information systems benefit the buying and selling teams and provide the teams with detailed information necessary to manage their contracts..............	❒1 ❒2 ❒3 ❒4 ❒5
7.2	Share as much organizational information as possible	❒1 ❒2 ❒3 ❒4 ❒5
7.3	Eliminate barriers to sharing information	❒1 ❒2 ❒3 ❒4 ❒5

7.4	Create a method for exchange of lessons learned between contracts and related projects	❒1 ❒2 ❒3 ❒4 ❒5

8.0 Role in Business Management

What senior executives should know and do:

8.1	Ensure that all contracts are properly planned	❒1 ❒2 ❒3 ❒4 ❒5
8.2	Receive status reports on all major contracts and related projects	❒1 ❒2 ❒3 ❒4 ❒5
8.3	Do not allow activity reports to substitute for status reports	❒1 ❒2 ❒3 ❒4 ❒5
8.4	Do not substitute paper optimism for intelligent, perceptive judgment	❒1 ❒2 ❒3 ❒4 ❒5
8.5	Verify that the reported status is consistent with contract results	❒1 ❒2 ❒3 ❒4 ❒5
8.6	Focus on corrective actions in status meetings	❒1 ❒2 ❒3 ❒4 ❒5
8.7	Ask how they can help the corrective action process	❒1 ❒2 ❒3 ❒4 ❒5
8.8	Ensure that they are not a bottleneck to required resources	❒1 ❒2 ❒3 ❒4 ❒5

9.0 Role in Development of the Buying and Selling Culture

What senior executives should know and do:

9.1	Ensure that managers have the correct organizational and buying and selling vision	❒1 ❒2 ❒3 ❒4 ❒5
9.2	Understand managers and their leadership styles, and provide training or counseling to correct deficiencies	❒1 ❒2 ❒3 ❒4 ❒5

10.0 Role in Support of Contract Corrective Actions *What senior executives should know and do:*	
10.1 Publicize expectations that contracts be technically compliant, completed on time, and as much under budget as possible...........	❒1 ❒2 ❒3 ❒4 ❒5
10.2 Require the use of action item registers to drive corrective actions to closure	❒1 ❒2 ❒3 ❒4 ❒5

Form 1-2 CMSEAT Quick Analysis Tool (What Senior Executives in Buying and Selling Should Know and Do!)

- Count the number of checked boxes (☑) on the previous pages **(Form 1-1)** with a rating of 4 or 5.
- Buying and Selling Senior Executive Assessment:

Excellent:	45 to 50	❒
Good:	39 to 44	❒
Average:	34 to 38	❒
Needs improvement:	28 to 33	❒
Poor:	27 or below	❒

The Leadership Gap in Buying and Selling

With an average response rate greater than 40 percent, the following statistically valid results were obtained.[3]

Buying and Selling Senior Executive Assessment:

Excellent	=	2%
Good	=	18%
Average	=	39%
Needs improvement	=	25%
Poor	=	16%

When we considered the results of the CMSEAT and numerous other surveys of the buying and selling communities **(Table 1-1),** it becomes crystal clear to us that most senior executives do not effectively lead their buying and selling organizations to consistently achieve high-performance business results.

Table 1-1 Other Surveys of the Buying and Selling Communities
☑ Institute of Supply Management, Center for Advanced Purchasing Studies, Cross-Industry Benchmarking Results (2004)
☑ Nextance Corporation, Contract Management Organizational Assessment (2002)
☑ National Contract Management Association and Contract Management Institute surveys (2000 and 2001)

Well over 90 percent of the organizations surveyed via CMSEAT have the opportunity to improve their buying and selling performance. In fact, more than 40 percent of the buying and selling organizations surveyed need significant improvement. Assuming these senior executives are qualified for their positions in terms of education, experience, and knowledge, there is a large gap between knowing what to do and doing it.

Creating an effective buying or selling organization is a complex process. It is difficult to instill an ethical and performance-based culture. Exceptional business managers may institute sound practices despite the prevailing culture. Most business managers take their guidance from the prevailing culture. Thus, an unsupportive or misinformed senior executive will generally lead to ineffectual buying and selling practices.

Buying and selling organizations that routinely execute business successfully usually have a well-understood and practiced contract management culture backed by strong, knowledgeable, senior executive support!

Filling the Gap by Developing a Leadership Pipeline

There are far too many managers and far too few true leaders. The demand for leadership talent at all levels of organizations, especially at the senior levels, greatly exceeds the current supply. There are clear indicators of this manager versus leader imbalance everywhere. Just about every major government agency and many large corporations are attempting to hire "stars" to lead their organizations. Newspapers such as the *Wall Street Journal* carry news about organizations bringing in top executive talent from outside their company—and increasingly from outside their industry—to provide a fresh perspective.

Clearly, what is needed is an approach that will permit organizations to develop great talent from within, rather than competing for outside talent. More and more organizations, in both the public and the private business sectors, are instituting leadership succession plans and talent development programs, thus creating leadership pipelines within their organizations to fill the leadership gap.

To create a leadership pipeline, one must understand the natural hierarchy of work that exists in most organizations. According to Ram Charan, Stephen Drotter, and James Noel, coauthors of *The Leadership Pipeline*,

> In a large, decentralized business organization, this hierarchy takes the form of six career passages or pipeline turns. The pipeline is not a straight cylinder but rather one that is bent in six places.

Charan, Drotter, and Noel's pipeline is illustrated in **Figure 1-1.** Each of the passages represents a change in organizational position—a different level and complexity of leadership where a significant turn has to be made. These turns involve a major change in job requirements, demanding new skills, time applications, and work values.[4]

Three of the biggest challenges that most organizations encounter when creating a leadership pipeline are the following:

1. Promoting people to manage others, simply because they were good individual performers
2. Promoting people to the next level or passage who have not mastered their current level
3. Promoting people on the basis of non-performance-related aspects (because they are available, because of who they know, because of where they went to school, because of some quota requirement, etc.)

In fact, extensive research and experience shows that it is quite common to find 30 percent or more of people in leadership positions operating at levels far below their assigned position.[5] Fortunately, a few highly successful organizations focus on leadership development. Two companies are widely considered to be world class at developing great talent—General Electric (GE) and Citigroup.

Figure 1-1 Critical Career Passages in a Large Business Organization

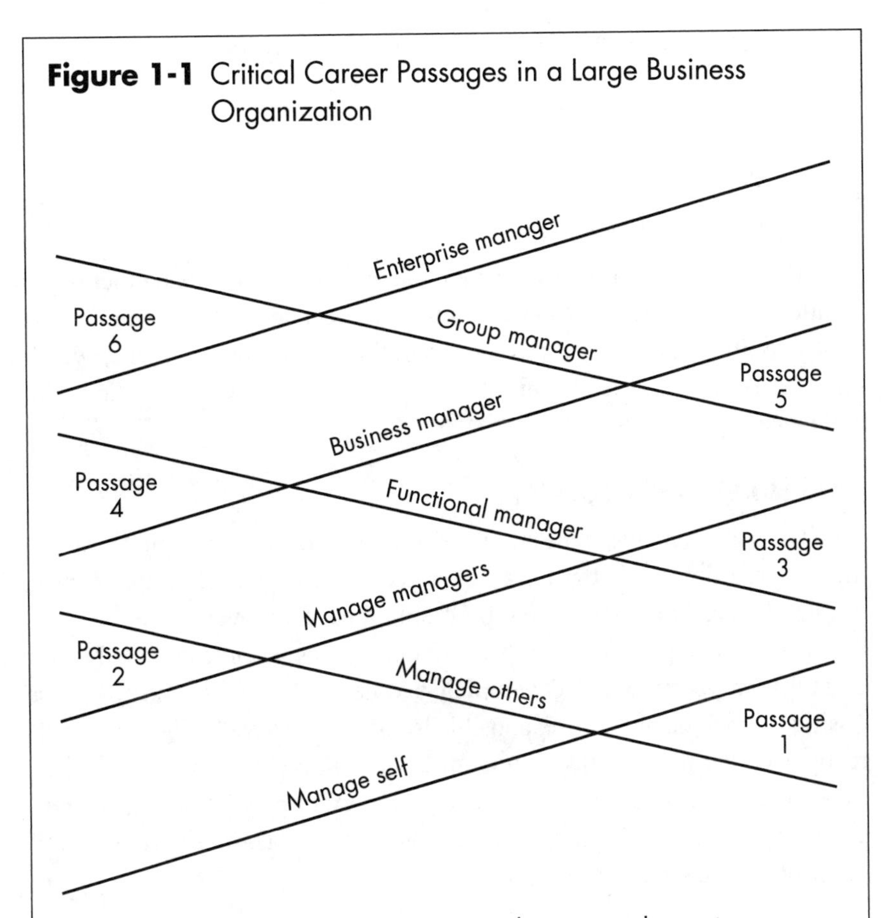

Note: Each passage represents a major change in job requirements that translates to new skill requirements, new time horizons and applications, and new work values.
Source: Based on work done by Walter Mahler called "Critical Career Crossroads." See Walter Mahler and Stephen J. Drotter, *The Succession Planning Handbook for the Chief Executive* (Midland, NJ: Mahler Publishing, 1986).

Case Study—General Electric

General Electric (GE), formerly under the leadership of chief executive officer Jack Welch, created a very successful leadership succession planning process called "Session C."[6] Session C was designed to evaluate each individual's readiness to make a career or leadership turn as well as to provide training programs at the famed Crotonville facility to help individuals learn business, leadership, and cross-cultural skills.

At GE, the management levels are labeled as follows:

- New manager
- Functional leader
- General manager
- Officer (multiple groups or businesses)

GE may not have a smarter or more talented workforce than other organizations, but it has proven better at making a real and lasting commitment to developing great leaders at every level of the organization. At GE, everyone understands that leadership is all about the mastery of specific skills and values.

Case Study—Citigroup

Like GE, Citigroup has done an outstanding job of succession planning for more than a decade. Citigroup has created and successfully implemented internal leadership development programs focused at every level of management. As a large global company, Citigroup has become especially successful at supporting and developing people as they transition to senior positions in which they are responsible for profit and loss.[7] Citigroup is well recognized for the significant amount of coaching the company provides, especially for new chief country managers and for many other critical leadership positions. At Citigroup, coaching is not optional—it is part of the job description and considered essential to success!

Summary

In this first chapter, we have discussed the new performance-based buying and selling environment, leadership as the key to business success, things leaders of buying and selling organizations should know and do (using the CMSEAT findings), and the importance of creating a leadership pipeline to fill the large gap between knowing what to do and doing it that exists in buying and selling organizations worldwide. This chapter has set the stage for the rest of the book, which is focused on leadership competencies and the skills needed to build high-performance buying and selling teams.

Questions to Consider

1. Is (are) the person(s) responsible for your buying or selling organization a highly effective business leader(s)?

2. Does your buying or selling team have a well-established leadership development program?
3. Does your buying or selling organization effectively practice succession planning, and does it have a recognized leadership pipeline?

---

[1] Shawn Zeller, "The Faces of Leadership," *Government Executive,* April 15, 2005, 60.

[2] Gregory A. Garrett and Rene G. Rendon, *Contract Management Organizational Assessment Tools* (McLean, VA: National Contract Management Association, 2005).

[3] Ibid.

[4] Ram Charan, Stephen Drotter, and James Noel, *The Leadership Pipeline: How to Build the Leadership Powered Company* (New York: Jossey-Bass, 2001).

[5] Ibid.

[6] Jack Welch and Suzy Welch, *Winning* (New York: HarperCollins, 2005).

[7] Charan, Drotter, and Noel, op. cit.

Chapter 2

Leadership Competencies: Building High-Performance Buying and Selling Teams

"Leadership is the art of accomplishing more than the science of management says is possible."

—Colin Powell

Introduction

Make no mistake—outsourcing is here to stay, and leadership is the key to business success. It is indeed that simple! However, it is not enough to have highly successful leaders only at the top of your organization. To achieve long-lasting success, as General Electric, Wal-Mart, Southwest Airlines, Dell, IBM, Proctor & Gamble, and others have done, your organization must focus on building leaders at every level, especially in the buying and selling segments.

Leadership at all levels is required in our new performance-based supply environment. Our new economy has created a workplace revolution. No sensible person expects to spend a lifetime working for a single employer anymore. As the famous author and consultant Tom Peters states, today, we are at "the Beginning of Renewed Individual Responsibility. An extraordinary opportunity to take charge of our own lives."[1] Thus, we must each become more aware of our knowledge and skills and how they can add value to our families, friends, companies and organizations, and society.

Leadership is a highly valued skill, especially in the buying and selling business communities, which are struggling to keep pace with increasing product and services demands and the aging business workforce. Thus, understanding the leadership levels within organizations and learning to master for each level the appropriate leadership competencies—composed of numerous specialized skill areas—are critical to long-term employability and professional success. Remember, without true leaders, there can be no organizational, corporate, or team success! Leadership is the driving force for the building of high-performance teams.

The Buying and Selling Leadership Levels and Competencies Model

To guide your thinking, we have created a visual tool, the Buying and Selling Leadership Levels and Competencies Model **(Figure 2-1),** to illustrate the following:

- The seven levels of organizational leadership mastery:
  1. Lead self
  2. Lead others (small, single-function team: buying and purchasing, sales and business development, etc.)
  3. Lead managers (several managers, each at level 2)
  4. Functional leader (responsible for a functional department or area: purchasing, sales, finance, etc.)
  5. Business leader (responsible for several functional departments and areas)
  6. Group leader (responsible for two or more business areas)
  7. Senior executive leader (a top organizational officer and leader)
- The five leadership specialized skill areas (SSAs)
  1. Decision-making
  2. Communications (verbal and nonverbal)
  3. Integrity
  4. Buying and selling business acumen
  5. Interpersonal relations

It is possible for someone to be considered a successful leader at a specific level of an organization without truly mastering all the leadership competencies. However, extensive research and experience show that most people who attain real leadership success have typically mastered at least four of the five SSAs required to become a successful buying or selling team leader.

Figure 2-1 The Buying and Selling Leadership Levels and Competencies Model

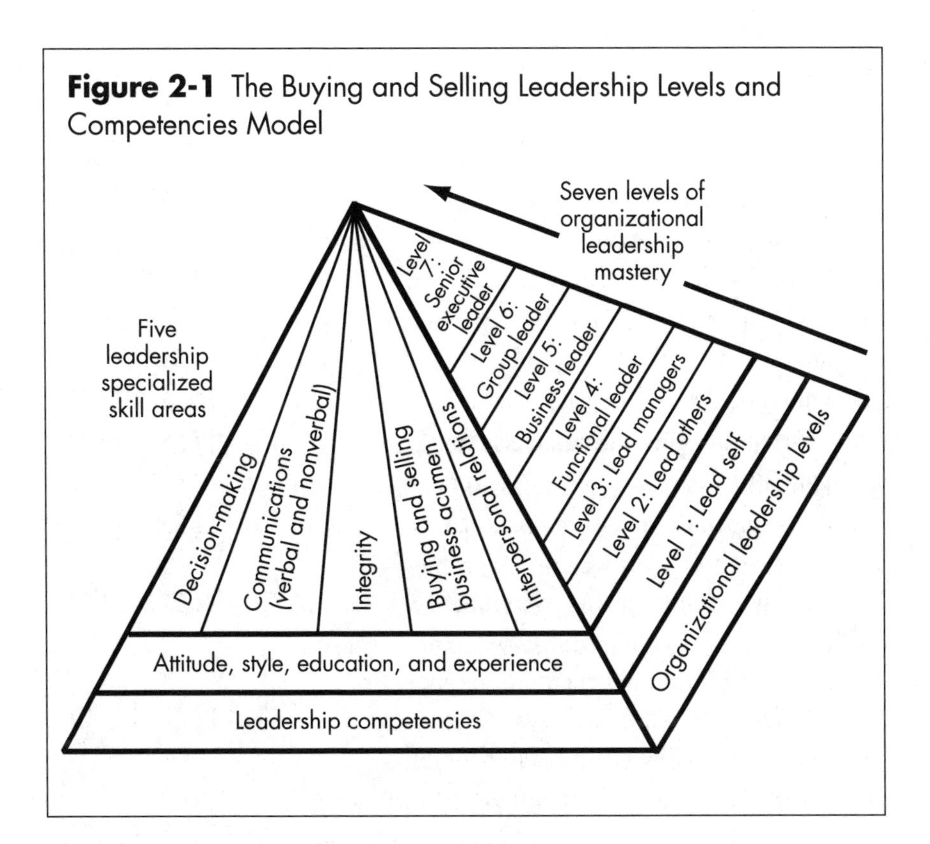

The Buying and Selling Skills to Lead: Self-Assessment Survey

Fill out the self-assessment survey **(Form 2-1)** to evaluate your buying and selling leadership skills. Your answers will help you determine whether you have the skills required and identify the areas in which you may need improvement. Check the number that best reflects where you fall on the scale (1 = Low to 5 = High). The higher the number, the more skill you possess. When you have completed the survey, add the numbers on the following worksheet **(Form 2-2)** and put the total in the space provided. Then assess your score using the Self-Assessment Survey Scoring form **(Form 2-3)**.

Form 2-1 The Buying and Selling Skills to Lead: Self-Assessment Survey

1. I am an excellent buying or selling team leader .... ❐1 ❐2 ❐3 ❐4 ❐5
2. I confront business issues, not people, in a problem-solving environment .... ❐1 ❐2 ❐3 ❐4 ❐5
3. My written buying or selling communications are professional, timely, and appropriate .... ❐1 ❐2 ❐3 ❐4 ❐5
4. I am a person of integrity .... ❐1 ❐2 ❐3 ❐4 ❐5
5. I verbally communicate clearly and concisely .... ❐1 ❐2 ❐3 ❐4 ❐5
6. I am able to make calm, rational business decisions under pressure .... ❐1 ❐2 ❐3 ❐4 ❐5
7. I enjoy solving large complex problems in a buying or selling team environment .... ❐1 ❐2 ❐3 ❐4 ❐5
8. I am willing to compromise when necessary to solve organizational customer or supplier problems .... ❐1 ❐2 ❐3 ❐4 ❐5
9. I am able to consistently achieve high-performance buying or selling results in my organization .... ❐1 ❐2 ❐3 ❐4 ❐5
10. I have extensive education, experience, and training in leadership .... ❐1 ❐2 ❐3 ❐4 ❐5
11. I have extensive education, experience, and training in purchasing, sales and marketing, and supply-chain management .... ❐1 ❐2 ❐3 ❐4 ❐5
12. I have extensive education, experience, and training in my organization's products, services, and business processes .... ❐1 ❐2 ❐3 ❐4 ❐5
13. I am considered an expert in contract management .... ❐1 ❐2 ❐3 ❐4 ❐5
14. I get along well with all of my team members, business partners, and customers .... ❐1 ❐2 ❐3 ❐4 ❐5

Form 2-1 The Buying and Selling Skills to Lead: Self-Assessment Survey, continued

15. I enjoy being responsible for making the tough business decisions (hiring, firing, source selection, and termination).................................. ❐1 ❐2 ❐3 ❐4 ❐5
16. I am highly skilled at using nonverbal communications to achieve business results....... ❐1 ❐2 ❐3 ❐4 ❐5
17. I enjoy coaching others to help them build their leadership skills.. ❐1 ❐2 ❐3 ❐4 ❐5
18. I have extensive education, experience, and training inbusiness administration or law .... ❐1 ❐2 ❐3 ❐4 ❐5
19. I believe in honoring my buying or selling commitments... ❐1 ❐2 ❐3 ❐4 ❐5
20. I treat everyone with respect.............................. ❐1 ❐2 ❐3 ❐4 ❐5

Form 2-2 The Buying and Selling Skills to Lead: Self-Assessment Survey Worksheet

Question number	Self-assessment score (1–5)	Question number	Self-assessment score (1–5)
1		11	
2		12	
3		13	
4		14	
5		15	
6		16	
7		17	
8		18	
9		19	
10		20	
		Total score:	

Form 2-3 The Buying and Selling Skills to Lead: Self-Assessment Survey Scoring	
90+:	You have the knowledge and skills of a successful buying or selling team leader.
80–90:	You have the potential to become a successful buying or selling team leader, after reviewing the specialized skill areas and determining in which areas you need to improve your skills.
65–79:	You have the basic understanding of what it takes to become a successful buying or selling team leader. You need to improve numerous skills to reach a higher level of mastery of leadership.
0–64:	You have taken the first step to becoming a successful buying or selling team leader. You have a lot of specialized skills that you need to improve. With time, dedication, and support (education, experience, and training) you can become a successful buying or selling team leader.

Buying and Selling Leadership Competencies

Traditionally, when people think about what it takes to become a buying and selling team leader, they focus on who you need to know and impress to get promoted. Instead, let us focus on the five SSAs to truly improve leadership performance and team results

- Decision-making
- Communications (verbal and nonverbal)
- Integrity
- Buying and selling business acumen
- Interpersonal relations

Through extensive research and experience we have concluded that these five SSAs are key to becoming a successful buying or selling team leader. For each SSA, we provide a brief summary and a list of the top 10 critical knowledge and skill areas (KSAs) required to become a truly successful buying or selling team leader.

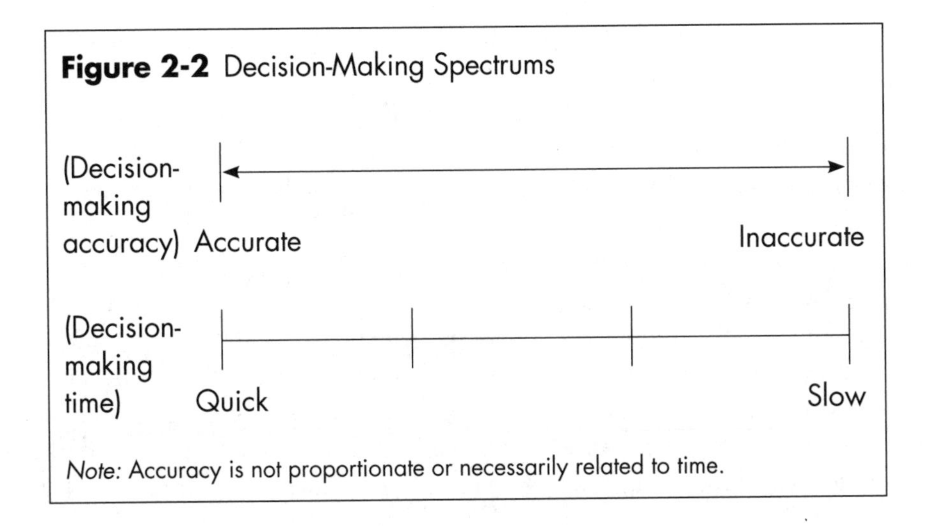

Figure 2-2 Decision-Making Spectrums

Note: Accuracy is not proportionate or necessarily related to time.

Decision-Making Skills

When one is leading a team of business professionals involved in buying or selling—especially complex integrated solutions composed of multiple products or services—the ability to make a timely and accurate business decision is essential to success. Some buying and selling managers serve in leadership positions, yet possess or implement little leadership skill. Many buying and selling business team leaders choose to delegate the tough decision to others. Some of these "master delegators" often blame others for team failures and take full credit for any team success when in reality they provided no real value. We often refer to these poor excuses for team leaders as "Teflon® managers," because nothing sticks to them.

We have all known and worked with people who operate at the extremes of the decision-making spectrum **(Figure 2-2).** Some people are very quick to make decisions, often without effectively gathering data or researching the issue or challenge and without seeking appropriate guidance from others (e.g., legal, finance, information technology, and technical experts). At the other end of the decision-making spectrum, we have all experienced those people who have an extremely difficult time making any decision, a condition commonly referred to as "analysis paralysis." Fortunately, most people operate somewhere between the two extremes. However, many people struggle with the blend of art and science required to consistently make good decisions when faced with multiple choices and no clear best choice.

It is important to note that decision-making time and the accuracy of decisions have consistently proven to have little relationship. Said differently, it is possible to make an accurate decision very quickly. Likewise, it is entirely possible to make a very bad decision either very quickly or after slow, thoughtful deliberation. Clearly, decision-making is a blend of art and science where experience, education, style, judgment, confidence, courage, and risk-taking all come together. Our simple advice is to make the best, most informed decision you can, quickly, on the basis of what your head, heart, and gut tell you is right to do!

Decision-making in business is not about taking a poll as to what is popular or what others want you to do; it is about doing what is right at the right time for the right business reasons. True buying and selling business team leaders will make some bad decisions, but not many. They will learn from their mistakes and grow in confidence, thus making better business decisions in the future. **Table 2-1** summarizes the critical KSAs required to master decision-making in a buying or selling business environment.

Communication (Verbal and Nonverbal) Skills

One of the most important skills one must master to achieve consistent success when leading the buying and selling of products and services is how to communicate **(Table 2-2).** For a buying or selling team leader, all aspects of communications are vital to success. According to numerous studies on adult education, most adults retain more of what they see than what they hear. Likewise, most adults value more how you communicate than what

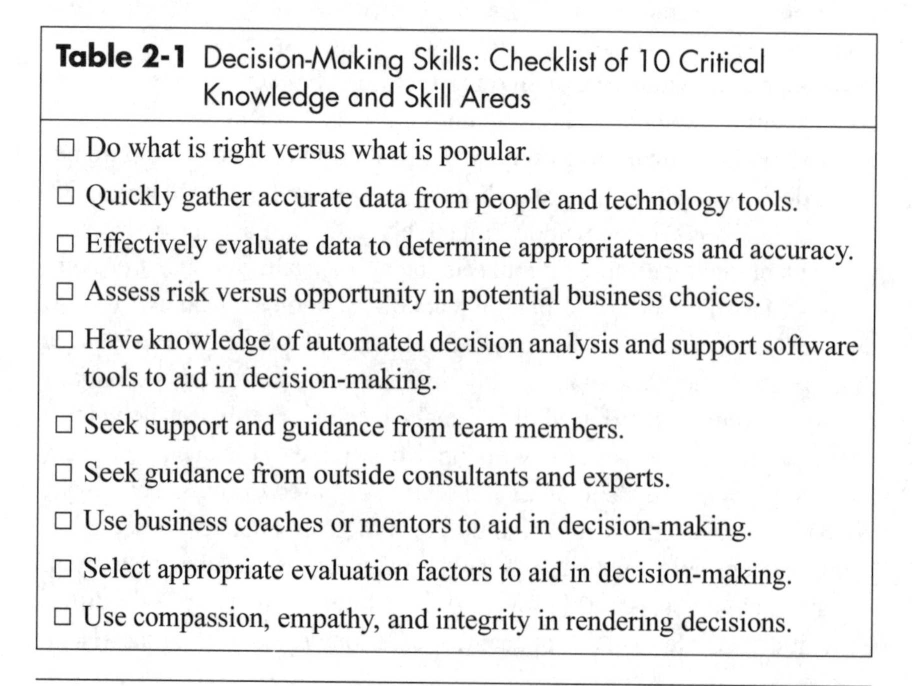

Table 2-1 Decision-Making Skills: Checklist of 10 Critical Knowledge and Skill Areas

- ☐ Do what is right versus what is popular.
- ☐ Quickly gather accurate data from people and technology tools.
- ☐ Effectively evaluate data to determine appropriateness and accuracy.
- ☐ Assess risk versus opportunity in potential business choices.
- ☐ Have knowledge of automated decision analysis and support software tools to aid in decision-making.
- ☐ Seek support and guidance from team members.
- ☐ Seek guidance from outside consultants and experts.
- ☐ Use business coaches or mentors to aid in decision-making.
- ☐ Select appropriate evaluation factors to aid in decision-making.
- ☐ Use compassion, empathy, and integrity in rendering decisions.

you communicate. Further, everyone communicates more through nonverbal means than through the spoken word. Finally, to become a buying or selling team leader, one must think before communicating, especially during contract negotiations, because everything one says, doesn't say, writes, doesn't write, does, and doesn't do will be evaluated by the other side.

Table 2-2 Communication (Verbal and Nonverbal) Skills: 12 Best Practices

1. **Be accurate.** Is your presentation error-free? Many presentations that are sound in all other respects fall by the wayside in this regard. Inaccuracy is usually due to limited time constraints when preparing the presentation.
2. **Be complete but concise.** How much is enough is a mental hurdle that often leads people to load presentations with all sorts of irrelevant information. People often ask, "Is anything missing?" when preparing a proposal, but the counter question, "Is this overkill?" is often ignored. Sheer volume can spell the death knell for presentations far faster than a slim presentation that is loaded with convincing arguments.
3. **Make it persuasive.** Someone has to be convinced about something to make any presentation a winner. So support what you propose with sound reasoning and, if possible, provide solid examples. In short, prove that you can produce what you are proposing.
4. **Don't make fancy promises.** Fight the tendency to offer more than is necessary to be successful. Doing so can lead to promises that the reviewer knows cannot be fulfilled.
5. **Skip the fluff.** All too often, there's an attempt to cover up an inadequacy by padding the presentation with fluff that has no relationship to what is being proposed. For instance, a company that has a renowned scientist in its employ will include that person's credentials in every presentation. But doing so creates skepticism when the subject matter of the proposal has no relationship to the individual's area of expertise. Reviewers wonder if it is being done to beef up an otherwise weak proposal.
6. **Don't ignore problems.** Many presentations accentuate the positive—which is good—but ignore the negative aspects that must be overcome for the project to be a success.

Table 2-2 Communication (Verbal and Nonverbal) Skills: 12 Best Practices, continued

7. **Solve the right problems.** Many presentations try to succeed by covering all of the bases in any ballpark, when the game is being played on only one field. The presentation sounds like, "Here's what you want, but if it isn't, we'll do it your way." This tactic seldom succeeds since it shows a lack of conviction, as well as doubt about what is actually being proposed.
8. **Be creative.** Although you shouldn't wander too far afield, simply laying out a response that minimally complies with what is being sought will not go very far. After all, most proposals will offer something similar. The one that wins will have used some real creativity in demonstrating how to build a better solution.
9. **Watch your numbers.** Long lists of numbers should be placed together in a separate section to provide both better organization and ease of analysis. And don't forget to spend some time thinking about how you will format your data. For example, if you're indicating only a general trend, a graph can be more effective than a lengthy list of numbers.
10. **Combine substance with style.** As any consumer goods manufacturer can tell you, packaging helps sell the product. Therefore, take pains to make your oral or written presentation look good. A proposal strong in substance may overcome the handicap of a sloppy appearance, but you run the risk of a reviewer thinking that a shabby looking proposal may indicate lousy results down the road.
11. **Remember your reader or listener.** It's easy to overlook the potential audience of an oral or written presentation or proposal. Doing so leads to proposals that are targeted toward one person or one group, without considering that the actual decision-maker is someone else. Technical proposals in particular are often prepared with the assumption that they will be evaluated only by those who understand the technical terminology. However, proposals are often reviewed by people who do not understand technical terms and the jargon of the trade. Therefore, it is prudent to prepare proposals that avoid jargon, that do not confuse readers or listeners, and that are not vague.
12. **Don't waste your efforts.** Preparing both oral presentations and written proposals can be expensive—in both time and money. Therefore, it is important to concentrate your resources on those proposals with the highest possible payoff.

Figure 2-3 The Art of Nonverbal Communication

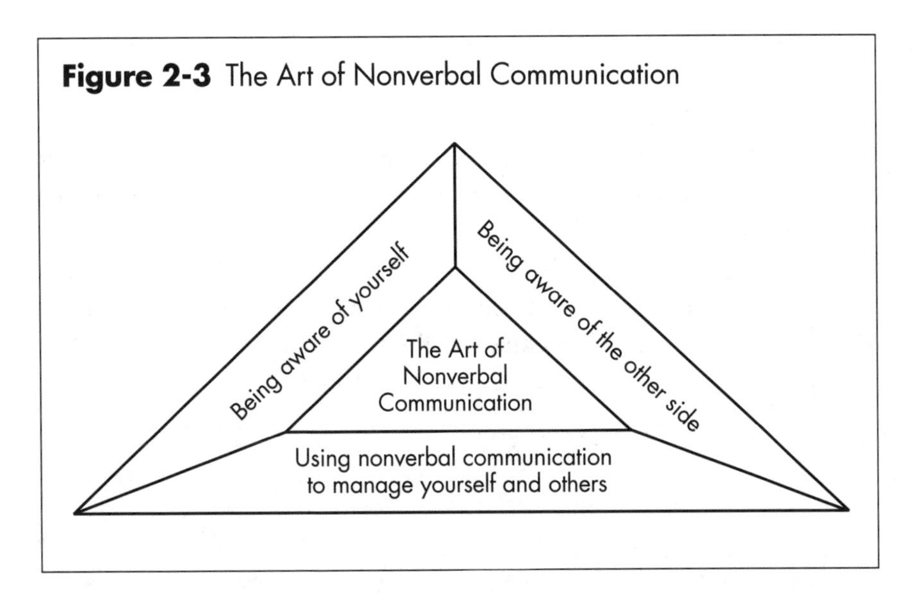

Years of extensive research in communication suggests that nearly 90 percent of the meaning transmitted between two or more people in face-to-face communications is through nonverbal channels. Said differently, only about 10 percent of your message is transmitted by your spoken words. Most people focus on the words they say, not on how they say it, but statistics indicate the importance of nonverbal contract negotiations skills.

Some communication experts have stated that in a typical 30 minute face-to-face contract negotiation meeting, two people can send more than 800 different nonverbal messages. It is not surprising that people often do not understand why the other party does not agree with them. Their words may say one thing, while their nonverbal actions communicate something else. In the book *Nonverbal Selling Power,* Gerhard Gschwandtner discusses the power of recognizing nonverbal communication signals—in yourself and in the other parties.[2]

There are three key aspects of nonverbal communication **(Figure 2-3):**

1. Being aware of yourself
2. Being aware of the other side
3. Using nonverbal communication to manage yourself and others

Often the question arises, how accurate are nonverbal communications when compared with verbal ones? After analyzing videotapes of conversations, D. A. Humphries, a British researcher, found that groupings of nonverbal gestures proved to be more accurate, truthful representations of participants' feelings than their words were.

Interpreting nonverbal communication can prove challenging. However, if you study your own nonverbal behavior and that of others daily, you will begin to understand the gesture grouping process. Nonverbal communication skills can be very valuable in mastering contract negotiations because they allow you to know when people are saying one thing and meaning another.

To make sure you are catching and understanding the nonverbal signals your counterpart is sending, Gschwandtner suggests conducting a body scan **(Table 2-3).** A good formula to follow is to divide the body into five categories: face and head, body, arms, hands, and legs.

<table>
<tr><th colspan="2">Table 2-3 The Language of Nonverbal Communication</th></tr>
<tr><td>Dominance and Power
▪ Placing feet on desk
▪ Making piercing eye contact
▪ Putting hands behind head or neck
▪ Placing hands on hips
▪ Giving a palm-down handshake
▪ Standing while counterpart is seated
▪ Steepling (fingertips touching)</td><td>Submission and Nervousness
▪ Fidgeting
▪ Making minimum eye contact
▪ Touching hands to face, hair, and so on
▪ Using briefcase to guard body
▪ Giving a palm-up handshake
▪ Clearing throat</td></tr>
<tr><td>Disagreement, Anger, and Skepticism
▪ Getting red in the face
▪ Pointing a finger
▪ Squinting
▪ Frowning
▪ Turning body away
▪ Crossing arms or legs</td><td>Boredom and Lack of Interest
▪ Failing to make eye contact
▪ Playing with objects on desk
▪ Staring blankly
▪ Drumming on table
▪ Picking at clothes
▪ Looking at watch, door, and so on</td></tr>
<tr><td>Uncertainty and Indecision
▪ Cleaning glasses
▪ Looking puzzled
▪ Putting fingers to mouth
▪ Biting lip
▪ Pacing back and forth
▪ Tilting head</td><td>Suspicion and Dishonesty
▪ Touching nose while speaking
▪ Covering mouth
▪ Avoiding eye contact
▪ Using incongruous gestures
▪ Crossing arms and legs
▪ Moving body away</td></tr>
<tr><td>Evaluation
▪ Nodding
▪ Squinting
▪ Maintaining good eye contact
▪ Tilting head slightly
▪ Stroking chin
▪ Touching index finger to lips
▪ Placing hands on chest</td><td>Confidence, Cooperation, and Honesty
▪ Leaning forward in seat
▪ Keeping arms and palms open
▪ Maintaining great eye contact
▪ Placing feet flat on floor
▪ Sitting with legs uncrossed
▪ Moving with counterpart's rhythm
▪ Smiling</td></tr>
<tr><td colspan="2">Source: Gerhard Gschwandtner, Nonverbal Selling Power (Englewood Cliffs, NJ: Prentice Hall, 1987).</td></tr>
</table>

Table 2-4 provides a summary of 10 of the critical verbal and nonverbal communications KSAs a buying or selling team leader needs to become successful.

Table 2-4 Communication (Verbal and Nonverbal) Skills: Checklist of 10 Critical Knowledge and Skill Areas
□ Be able to apply the 12 best practices of communications.
□ Be comfortable when communicating to others.
□ Understand the language of nonverbal communication.
□ Know the five categories of the body so that you can identify and group gestures to determine meanings.
□ Be able to orally deliver clear, concise, and compelling communications.
□ Be able to prepare effective written proposals.
□ Be able to ask questions effectively during contract negotiations to gain information.
□ Be able to effectively use audio and visual aids to support oral and written presentations.
□ Practice active listening.
□ Look the part—dress for success.

A Personal Story: Doing What Is Right!

by Gregory A. Garrett

Many years ago, as a captain in the U.S. Air Force, I served as the youngest warranted U.S. government procuring contract officer (PCO) for a major weapon system. I was the PCO for $15 billion of advanced aircraft development and production contracts. I was assigned to the Aeronautical Systems Division at Wright-Patterson Air Force Base, Ohio. Numerous contract managers (buyers)—mostly civilians, some military—supported me, as well as more than 300 technical personnel, including engineers, manufacturing managers, quality assurance specialists, and government property managers. To say the least, it was an incredibly challenging job with intense public and audit oversight. I managed two of the largest contracts in the world, involving thousands of suppliers and hundreds of contract modifications.

Situation. During this period, as the PCO for these advanced aircraft contracts, I was asked one day to have a private meeting with the two-star general who served as the program director for the advanced aircraft program. The general invited me to his office to discuss possible acquisition strategy. He informed me that he wanted to build a new test facility for the advanced aircraft at one of our U.S. Air Force Bases in California. He stated that we needed to get this done very quickly and that we did not have time to conduct a full competition because of the very long procurement acquisition lead time. So, the general requested that I lead the effort to solicit a contract modification to add the design and construction of a new test facility under our current advanced aircraft development and production contracts.

Challenge. At this point, I felt that what the general requested was what he considered best for the program, his career, and possibly the nation. However, I knew what the general asked me to do was in clear violation of the Competition in Contracting Act of 1986, which I had sworn to uphold. I also knew that the general's request to design and build a test facility was well beyond the scope of the contracts. Further, I knew that if I told the general what he wanted to hear I would have a much better chance at rapid promotion.

Choice. So, if you were faced with this challenge what would you do?

My Decision. I informed the general that I clearly understood the program challenge he faced and I would do everything possible to rapidly put out for competition and award a new contract to design and construct a new test facility. I reminded the general that my Contracting Officer's Warrant, which I had sworn as an officer and a gentleman to uphold, prohibited me from violating any U.S. government contracting laws, rules, and regulations. Further, I advised the general that if we did as he suggested, the added work would most likely be terminated as a result of subsequent audits and we would both be subject to significant penalties. The general told me that he would consider my advice, and then he dismissed me. As I returned to my office, I was concerned about my future in the Air Force but was confident that I demonstrated the courage to do what was right—under extreme pressure!

Integrity Skills

Said simply, an individual of integrity is an individual who has principles and lives by them. Said differently, an individual of integrity is an individual who builds trust by managing expectations and honoring commitments on a consistent basis. One of the biggest challenges in creating and maintaining a successful long-term business partnership is building trust through integrity. Trust is like quality; it is difficult to accurately describe, but you know it when it's there.

A reputation for integrity is typically earned by doing what you say you are going to do on a repeated basis; in other words, by honoring commitments. A company can also instill trust when it comes to the rescue of another organization in a time of urgent business needs. Building trust through integrity in business partnerships can take years to accomplish but sometimes can be lost very quickly.

One of the key ways companies can build integrity and trust is by managing the expectations of their business partners. Expectations are assumptions or beliefs about future events. They are usually hopeful and optimistic. Sometimes expectations are pessimistic plans for the worst.

In our current dynamic, high-speed world of e-business, expectations are incredibly high. Too often, people expect the impossible to be achieved without knowing all the facts or details. Of course, sometimes organizations can create virtual miracles, but in many cases, they fall well short of their customers' unrealistic expectations.

No one in business can avoid setting expectations. Everything buying or selling teams say or do—or don't say or do—sets some form of expectation in the minds of others. Most selling teams try to set expectations through their advertising and marketing. However, a buyer's real expectations are typically set by the seller's actual performance in comparison with its promises—commonly referred to by results-oriented business leaders as the "hype-to-results index." The real key to successfully managing expectations and honoring commitments is understanding the process.

The process of managing expectations is primarily a communication process. **Figure 2-4** depicts a variety of simple ways to describe the essential elements. Understanding the process of managing expectations is good; applying it is even better. Unfortunately, because of the speed of business today, organizations frequently react to partial information on the basis of inaccurate assumptions, rather than truly listening and understanding their customers' needs and desires. Often, sellers do not properly distinguish the real difference between a buyer's needs and a buyer's desires.

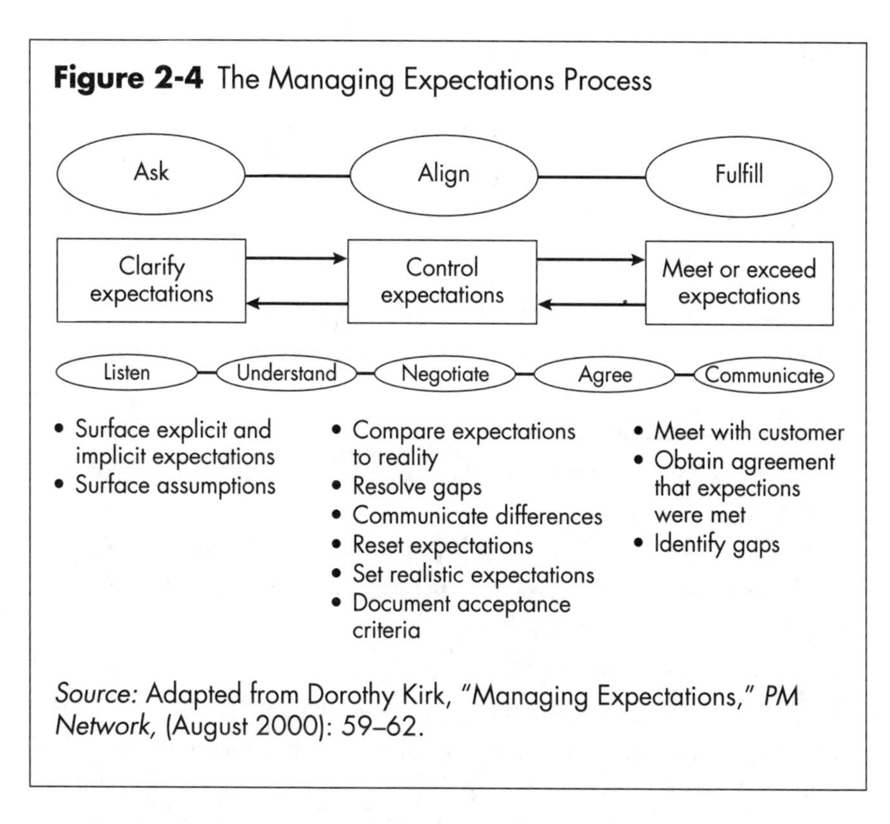

Figure 2-4 The Managing Expectations Process

Source: Adapted from Dorothy Kirk, "Managing Expectations," *PM Network,* (August 2000): 59–62.

Aligning expectations with reality is a critical step in the managing expectations process. Aligning expectations does not mean reducing objectives or requirements to the lowest level. Aligning expectations is about setting a challenging but achievable set of objectives for all parties, based on the realities of the situation (i.e., technology maturity, schedule, budget, scope of work, mutual priorities, and resource availability).

To meet or exceed a buyer's expectations, a seller must first agree with the buyer on what is required, preferably in writing. These requirements, often referred to as "acceptance criteria," include price, schedule, quality, and quantity. It is clearly in the best interest of both parties to ensure that the agreed-on products, services, or solutions will meet or exceed the documented acceptance criteria.

Frequent, open, and honest communication is vital to building successful partnerships between organizations **(Table 2-5).** When meeting with customers to provide status reports on the business partnership, whether on a contract or a program basis, business professionals must learn to deliver the truth, both good and bad. No business partnership goes perfectly, but communicating the good, the bad, and at times the ugly goes a long way to building integrity. What an organization does to overcome business obstacles and successfully communicate those actions with customers can be vital to building integrity even when the final results are not the best.

Table 2-5 Integrity Skills: Checklist of 10 Critical Knowledge and Skill Areas
☐ Listen to team members, customers, and suppliers.
☐ Return phone calls, voice-mail messages, and e-mail in a timely manner.
☐ Treat everyone with respect.
☐ Provide regular communication on contract, program, and partnership status.
☐ Develop a project plan for every deal (scope of work, integrated schedule, work breakdown structure, responsibility assignment matrix, and acceptance criteria).
☐ Develop a risk management plan.
☐ Disclose problems early and mitigate negative impacts.
☐ Back up all verbal agreements and conversations with written documentation.
☐ Be prepared to deliver both good and bad news at multiple levels, both internally and with customers.
☐ Demonstrate passion in honoring commitments.

Buying and Selling Business Acumen Skills

So what does it take to become a true buying and selling business professional? It takes business acumen. Said simply, business acumen is the combination of business education, experience, on-the-job training, and expert mentoring across a diverse range of business topics, including

- Marketing and sales
- Accounting and finance
- Strategic planning and economic forecasting
- Purchasing and supply-chain management
- Operations and project management
- Business law and contract management

Some people believe that if you have good leadership skills you can lead anything. Well, there is some truth in that statement. However, the best leaders know a great deal about the people they are leading. True leaders know what the people do, how they do it, and what challenges they face. As we like to say, "The best leaders have been there, done that, and gotten the t-shirt!" When it comes to real business acumen, education is good, but proven successful experience is best **(Table 2-6).**

Table 2-6 Buying and Selling Business Acumen Skills: Checklist of 10 Critical Knowledge and Skill Areas
☐ Be able to read people—know who to trust.
☐ Know how to market and sell products, services, and integrated solutions.
☐ Be able to develop effective business cases to evaluate risk versus opportunity, both financial and technically.
☐ Be able to assess the financial aspects (revenue, profitability, etc.) of a business project.
☐ Understand strategic business planning, including staffing, training, and professional development.
☐ Be able to execute basic purchasing functions.
☐ Understand how to leverage supply-chain partners to accelerate delivery, reduce costs, and improve performance results.
☐ Be able to plan and successfully execute multiple projects under pressure.
☐ Know the fundamentals of business law.
☐ Understand the entire contract management process and how it works in the organization.

Interpersonal Relations Skills

It has been said that people learn everything they need to know in preschool or kindergarten. That statement is not entirely true; however, we appreciate the importance of learning how to get along with others, especially how to deal with difficult people. As related to leading buying and selling teams, interpersonal skills are extremely important, including building trust, forming partnerships, and resolving conflicts. Interpersonal skills are vital to success both within your organization and with your customers and suppliers.

Developing teamwork that is based on trust and mutual respect with your team members, suppliers, and customers is critical to successful contract negotiations. The greater the level of confidence that your team members and other parties have in your honesty, integrity, and reliability, the easier it will be to create win-win deals. Conversely, without a professional relationship, obtaining even minor concessions is very challenging.

Peter B. Stark and Jane S. Flaherty, consultants and coauthors, offer these 15 building blocks for establishing professional relationships based on trust and mutual respect:[3]

1. Demonstrate your competence.
2. Make sure the nonverbal signals you are sending match the words you are saying.
3. Maintain a professional appearance.
4. Communicate your good intentions.
5. Do what you say you are going to do.
6. Go beyond the conventional relationship.
7. Listen.
8. Overcommunicate.
9. Discuss the undiscussables.
10. Provide accurate information, without any hidden agenda.
11. Be honest, even when it costs you something.
12. Be patient.
13. Safeguard for fairness.
14. Negotiate for abundance, not scarcity.
15. Take calculated risks.

Forming partnerships is vital to successful buying and selling. Partnerships must be formed first within the contract negotiation team and then with the other parties—customers and suppliers. Unfortunately, it can be very challenging to build partnerships with individuals who do not want to build relations. Some people care only about winning the immediate deal.

Dealing with conflicts and untrustworthy parties is a fact of life. Unfortunately, nearly every organization has a few untrustworthy individuals. Some organizations clearly have more than others, and most of us have to find a professional and ethical way to work with them. Conflict is natural, even when dealing with people who are honest and of high integrity. Conflicts often arise out of differences in opinion, viewpoint, organizational goals, personal agendas, and so forth. The key to conflict management is to treat the conflict as a mutual problem that must be jointly solved by addressing the issue, not the person or the position **(Table 2-7).**

Summary

In this chapter, we have provided a brief review of the skills needed to become a successful buying or selling team leader. Using the Buying and Selling Leadership Levels and Competencies Model, we discussed the five SSAs:

- Decision-making
- Communications (verbal and nonverbal)
- Integrity
- Buying and selling business acumen
- Interpersonal relations

Table 2-7 Interpersonal Relations Skills: Checklist of 10 Critical Knowledge and Skill Areas
☐ Work well with others.
☐ Be honest.
☐ Deal with untrustworthy individuals.
☐ Build strong professional business relationships.
☐ Use joint problem solving.
☐ Practice active listening.
☐ Be respectful to everyone.
☐ Practice patience.
☐ Honor your commitments.
☐ Hold people accountable.

We have summarized 10 critical knowledge and skill areas for each SSA. Very few people have truly mastered all five SSAs to the highest of the seven levels of organizational leadership mastery, but many have mastered at least three or four of them. We suggest you go back and complete each of the checklists for the five SSAs and see how well you rate your skills: 9–10 = excellent, 7–8 = good, 4–6 = satisfactory, and 0–3 = poor.

Questions to Consider

1. How important are decision-making skills when leading a buying or selling team of business professionals?
2. Do you have all of the business acumen skills you need to effectively lead your buying and selling team?
3. Which communication skills have you mastered?
4. Is it necessary to have unimpeachable integrity when buying or selling large, expensive, and complex products services and integrated solutions?
5. How effectively do you work with others?

---

[1] Tom Peters, *Talent* (London: Dorling Kindersley, 2005), 5.

[2] Gerhard Gschwandtner, *Nonverbal Selling Power* (Englewood Cliffs, NJ: Prentice Hall, 1987).

[3] Peter B. Stark and Jane Flaherty, *The Only Negotiating Guide You'll Ever Need* (New York: Broadway Books, 2003), 53-56.

Chapter 3

The Six Steps to Success: A Leadership Process to Improve Buying and Selling

"A leader's job is to look into the future and see the organization not as it is, but as it can become!"

—Norman Vincent Peale

Introduction

In this chapter, we provide a simple yet proven effective path to achieving long-lasting success through leadership. We call this path the Six Steps to Success (S3), a leadership process to improve buying and selling. The S3 can be applied to any aspect of business or personal life. But the focus of this book is to help business professionals who are involved in buying or selling complex and expensive products, services, and integrated solutions to build high-performance teams through the power of real leadership. We are 100 percent confident that the S3 leadership process works because we have been there, done that, and gotten the t-shirts!

The S3 Leadership Process

Figure 3-1 illustrates the simple, yet proven, highly effective S3 leadership process.

Step 1: Think the Talk

Years ago, our fathers, who are patient and wise men, told us to think before we talked. Some of you may be thinking, "Surely you jest!" ("No, we are not jesting, and don't call us Shirley!") But we have learned over the years that many business people have not mastered the skill of thinking before

Figure 3-1 The Six Steps to Success (S3) Leadership Process

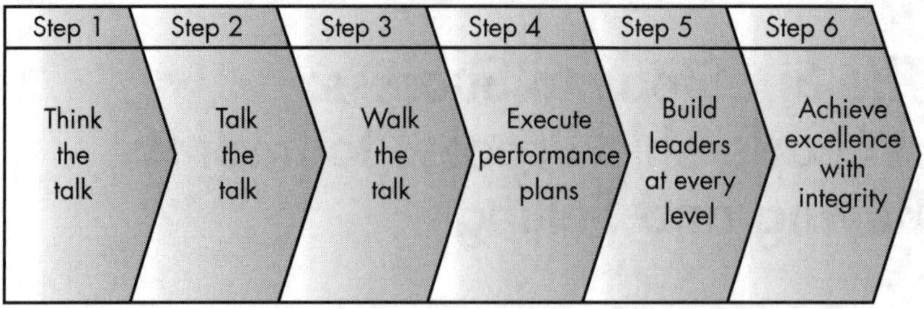

Step 1	Step 2	Step 3	Step 4	Step 5	Step 6
Think the talk	Talk the talk	Walk the talk	Execute performance plans	Build leaders at every level	Achieve excellence with integrity

talking. In fact, today many people are not only talking before they think but also calling, e-mailing, and instant messaging before they think.

On a more serious note, we have learned the following:

- Your *thoughts* guide your *words.*
- Your *words* guide your *actions.*
- Your *actions* guide your *habits.*
- Your *habits* guide your *character.*
- Your *character* guides your *life!*

In the words of the famous consultant Dr. Stephen Covey, author of the best-selling book *The Seven Habits of Highly Effective People,* "Begin with the end in mind!"[1] Your thoughts are your guide to success. Thus, you must learn to focus your thinking, choose whom to spend your time with, realize your attitude affects your altitude, and select the right mentors to guide your thinking.

Many people believe life is an accidental journey, because they do not really accept accountability for the many thoughts, words, actions, habits, and resulting decisions they have made throughout their life. Instead, we view our lives as a journey in which we have achieved nearly everything we have set our minds to achieve. We have become successful by focusing our thoughts, words, and actions to guide our habits and build our character. Some people say we have just been lucky. We do not disagree, but we believe we have created our luck by beginning with the end in mind—starting with the talk before we ever talk the talk. Just food for thought. We discuss this first step in the S3 leadership process in more detail in Chapter 4.

A Personal Story: The Fearless Leader

by Gregory A. Garrett

I remember a gentleman in one of my former offices walking around one day with a t-shirt on that read "I am a Fearless Leader." I inquired where he obtained this thought-provoking t-shirt, and he said he had received it as a gift for completing a week-long leadership seminar. I asked him if he felt the leadership training had empowered him to become a more effective team leader. He quickly responded, "Yes, I am convinced I am now and will be a fearless leader." I recall observing his improved leadership performance for several months after this training.

I met this same gentleman again several years later and unfortunately he had lost his positive leadership drive. He was no longer thinking positive thoughts or taking positive actions; instead he had become very negative, overly critical of others, and was not getting the job done. Though still on the job, he had essentially retired—which several months later, with the guidance of others, he decided to do!

Perhaps you have known someone like the gentleman I just described. Unfortunately, many people are unable to sustain a high level of leadership because they lack the drive to become a successful business leader. Leadership training can be a very effective tool to help stimulate positive thoughts, energy, and actions; however, without additional training, coaching, or mentoring most people do not achieve lasting or consistent high-performance leadership. A t-shirt does not make you a leader, but it may help boost your confidence. Confidence in your knowledge and skills is vital to your success as a leader!

Step 2: Talk the Talk

To successfully talk the talk, a leader must (1) deliver the message, (2) look like a leader, and (3) know what to say.

1. **Deliver the message.** To improve communications skills, a leader should

- Learn to be a proactive listener.
- Deliver messages in person or by telephone. Do so with passion, commitment, and a positive, "can do" attitude; people usually can spot a fake.
- Use tone, pauses, loudness, pitch, and inflection to communicate what is important.
- Use body language to reinforce verbal communication. Body language includes eye contact, hand motions and gestures, and facial expressions.
- Practice, develop, and refine communication skills daily.

2. **Look like a leader.** Some people foolishly believe that saying the right things makes appearance unimportant. Wrong! Appearance always matters, because it communicates so much. Although physical attractiveness helps in some instances, how one chooses to dress, stand, sit, and use other nonverbal physical communication methods and techniques has a dramatic effect on how effectively one's message is delivered **(Table 3-1).**
3. **Know what to say.** To effectively talk the talk, a person also must know what to say. Communicating customer needs and desires, as well as the status of the marketplace, to team members is vital. The organization's vision and goals need to be communicated precisely and repeatedly, hence ensuring that everyone knows his or her role, responsibilities, and performance metrics in achieving those goals. In addition, the organization's business challenges in terms of budget, expenses, profitability, and loss should be regularly explained. Finally, effective leaders communicate the importance of creating a performance-based business—and reward results. Chapter 5 presents a more detailed and compelling discussion of the need to talk the talk.

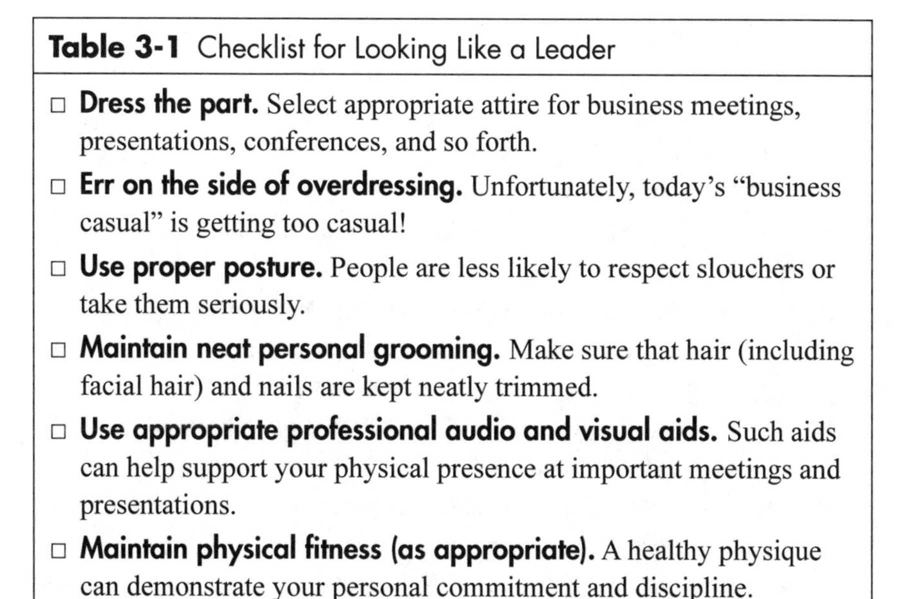
Table 3-1 Checklist for Looking Like a Leader

- ☐ **Dress the part.** Select appropriate attire for business meetings, presentations, conferences, and so forth.
- ☐ **Err on the side of overdressing.** Unfortunately, today's "business casual" is getting too casual!
- ☐ **Use proper posture.** People are less likely to respect slouchers or take them seriously.
- ☐ **Maintain neat personal grooming.** Make sure that hair (including facial hair) and nails are kept neatly trimmed.
- ☐ **Use appropriate professional audio and visual aids.** Such aids can help support your physical presence at important meetings and presentations.
- ☐ **Maintain physical fitness (as appropriate).** A healthy physique can demonstrate your personal commitment and discipline.

Step 3: Walk the Talk

Learning to practice real leadership is challenging. Leadership is not about micro management; it is about becoming a force-multiplier. Novice team leaders often make the mistake of doing the work their team members are responsible for doing instead of holding them accountable, providing appropriate coaching and support, or changing personnel when needed. Novice business leaders frequently fail to quickly recognize team members' strengths and weaknesses, resulting in additional problems and potential business failures. Novice team leaders are hesitant to remove poor performers or disruptive individuals from their team; instead they allow the ineffective worker to negatively affect team and business performance for an extended period of time. The following proven best practices can help ensure the motivation of others to accomplish your desired results:

1. Listen to customers and team members and understand their needs and desires.
2. Take proactive, appropriate actions to help customers and team members achieve their needs and desires.
3. Teach employees and customers about leadership by honoring commitments.

4. Hold people accountable for their actions or inaction and ensure team members have well-defined and mutually agreed-on roles and responsibilities.
5. Conduct frequent team meetings with all team members either in person or through teleconferencing or the Internet.
6. Display a positive, "can do" attitude with a blend of realism and practicality.
7. Conduct frequent customer and supplier meetings with key decision-makers to assess relationship and project performance results against goals, using agreed-on performance metrics.
8. Develop and live by a code of conduct that includes honesty, integrity, and mutual respect.
9. Develop, document, and distribute the organization's vision statement, goals, and performance metrics and results. Distribute these items using e-mail, posters, Web site ads or articles, company newsletters, and CD-ROMs. When distributing performance metrics and results, include information about customer satisfaction, product and service quality, employee satisfaction, delivery times, cycle times, revenue, and expenses.
10. Recognize and reward individuals and contract negotiation teams for outstanding performance. Tie pay to performance if possible.

Chapter 6 will provide a more detailed discussion of the importance of learning Step 3.

Step 4: Execute Performance Plans

As in Step 3, Walk the Talk, for Step 4 it is essential that all team members, customers, and suppliers have well-defined and mutually agreed-on roles, responsibilities, and performance metrics. To achieve consistent high performance in buying or selling products, services, and integrated solutions, you must ensure that everyone involved plays a part in executing the overall performance plan. Said differently, achieving success in business, especially buying or selling complex integrated solutions, requires everyone involved—buyer, seller, subcontractors, every person from each functional area—to know and do the right actions at the right times.

Creating, communicating, aligning, and executing project and contract performance plans indeed require a blend of art and science. Although strategy and planning are essential to business, the most valuable skills in today's increasingly complex business environment are the execution of the performance plan and the ability to overcome obstacles. In Chapter 7, we discuss this topic in much greater detail, focusing on tools, techniques, and best practices to ensure successful contract and project execution.

Step 5: Build Leaders at Every Level

In his book, *Jack: Straight from the Gut,* former General Electric chairman and chief executive officer Jack Welch states how important it is for business leaders to provide frequent feedback to all their team members at every level of the organization, to help them grow and develop their skills.[2] Welch expresses the need for business leaders to fairly evaluate all team members and rate them as A-, B-, or C-level individuals. While every team member is valued, those individuals evaluated as A-level (top performers) must be highly cherished, rewarded, trained, and mentored to ensure that the organization retains top talent.

To build buying or selling leaders at every level of an organization, senior executives should ensure that every buying or selling team leader has a multi-year professional development plan designed to achieve the following:

- **Undergraduate-level education.** Desired formal educational programs (i.e., bachelor's degree in business specializing in accounting, finance, marketing, management, purchasing, supply-chain management, or other appropriate area)
- **Buying or selling experience.** Appropriate number of years of experience in buying or selling a diverse range of products and services of increasing value and complexity
- **Multifunctional business experience.** Appropriate number of years of experience in diverse functional areas (sales, bid and proposal management, contract management, engineering, manufacturing, quality, purchasing and supply-chain management, accounting, etc.)
- **Professional continuing education.** Completion of appropriate business management and professional development courses, covering marketing and sales, purchasing, risk management, contract management, and project management
- **Professional certification.** Designation as a certified purchasing manager (CPM), certified professional contracts manager (CPCM), certified federal contracts manager (CFCM), certified commercial contracts manager (CCCM), or project management professional (PMP)

- **Graduate-level education.** Completion of an M.B.A., M.S. in systems management, M.S. in project management, or other appropriate degree
- **Portfolio of successful business results.** This portfolio should include

    1. Number of customers, projects, and contracts led
    2. Total value of sales contracts and projects led
    3. Win rate of bids and proposals submitted
    4. Percentage of products or services delivered on time
    5. Percentage of contracts or projects completed on budget
    6. Team member feedback
    7. Customer feedback
    8. Supplier feedback

This list is just a beginning. Chapter 8 provides a more detailed discussion of the art and science of building buying and selling team leaders at every level of an organization.

Step 6: Achieve Excellence with Integrity

So how do you measure excellence, especially in the world of buying and selling? Said simply, buying and selling is all about trust! We discuss this topic in detail in Chapter 9.

To further demonstrate the practical application of the Six Steps to Success Leadership process, we have conducted numerous interviews of buying and selling business professionals from both the U.S. government and industry to share their real-life experiences. The following selected interview is just one of the 14 selected interviews within this book.

Selected Interview

Name: Lenn Vincent, RADM, USN (Ret.)

Job Title: Industry Chair

Organization: Defense Acquisition University (DAU)

Location: Fort Belvoir, Virginia

Key Responsibilities: Liaison with industry to establish "pipeline" of industry students available to attend DAU courses and reach out to industry leaders for their participation as speakers in the executive courses.

Brief Resume: Lenn Vincent is the Industry Chair at the Defense Acquisition University. He uses his defense and industry experience, expertise, and perspective to advise the DAU management team, the Office of the Secretary of Defense, and the uniformed services on matters relevant to contracting and program management issues.

As a former vice president at both CACI International and American Management Systems, Mr. Vincent was responsible for working with senior Department of Defense and industry leaders to build long-term business relationships and help identify solutions to acquisition, logistics, and financial management challenges. He has more than 30 years of broad-based and in-depth leadership and management experience in acquisition, supply-chain management, logistics, and financial management.

When he retired from the U.S. Navy on August 1, 1999, at the rank of rear admiral, he was the commandant of the Defense Systems Management College (DSMC). Before leading DSMC, Mr. Vincent served as the logistics, ordnance, and fleet supply officer for the commander-in-chief of the Pacific Fleet, where he established policy and coordinated logistics requirements to support supply-chain operations in the Pacific Fleet and Indian Ocean. Mr. Vincent was the commander of the Defense Contracts Management Agency and also served as the senior acquisition executive responsible for procurement policy within the Defense Logistics Agency. He holds a master's degree in business administration from George Washington University. He is president of the National Contract Management Association and serves on its Board of Directors.

Questions and Answers

Question: What personal leadership characteristics are most important for building successful buying or selling teams?

Answer: Integrity, ability to foster collaboration, ability to communicate a vision with clarity and enthusiasm, competence, commitment, and confidence.

Question: What are the core competencies of a successful buying or selling team leader?

Answer: Establishing a clear vision and goals to achieve, knowing the requirements, focusing unwaveringly on customer satisfaction, being willing to trust and empower, exercising good communication skills, fostering collaboration, knowing when and how to recognize people, and knowing oneself.

Question: What are the most significant challenges you must overcome to be a successful buying or selling team leader?

Answer: Knowing and understanding the requirements and ensuring that they match customer and stakeholder expectations, resisting and eliminating "me win, you lose" scenarios and attitudes, understanding the intrinsic motivation of the team, and ensuring that the goals and metrics established drive the right behavior.

Question: In regard to the S3 leadership process, which step do you believe is the most important? Why?

Answer: I think all six steps are extremely important; however, I believe that Step 3, Walking the Talk, is the most important. It seems to me that if you indeed walk the talk, you will have focused on all the success criteria for leadership excellence.

Question: Please provide a brief personal experience that you believe best illustrates leadership in buying or selling.

Answer: I have had many personal experiences on the buy side but thought it might be interesting to illustrate an experience on the sell side.

While I was at American Management System (AMS), we came up with the concept of developing an automated contract management system that industry could use to manage its proposals and its resulting contracts, integrate internal stakeholders, secure data integrity, and connect with customers 24/7.

To execute the concept, I had to convince AMS leaders that the concept was a good business idea and that they should make the investment required to ascertain the requirements, to develop software, and to market. Not a small challenge! We built an integrated team of subject matter experts, technicians (software designers and developers), and industry partners. Over a two-year developmental period, I had to continually remind the team and AMS leadership what the end game was and convince them the effort would be worth the investment. My communication and leadership skills were put to the test during this time as we were looking for our first customer.

After a competitive process, we won our first customer—a very demanding one. After an initial testing period, our customer's representatives did not like what they saw of the software design and the prospective usability in their environment. The morale of our technical folks was dashed by the comments of our new customer, but over a short period of intense "leveling" meetings—both within the AMS team and with the customer—the team became stronger and our relationship with the customer became very positive. Throughout this development effort, we were able to recognize the achievements of not only the team but also individuals who were making significant contributions.

As we began to deploy and implement the automated system across our customer's enterprise, it was a challenge to get our "techies" out of their comfort zones (cubicles) to join our deployment teams in the customer's spaces, to help ensure that the users understood the system and were satisfied with the new tool. The deployment team leaders aligned their teams and executed their roles and responsibilities like the pros they had become. This high-performance state did not happen overnight. It was nurtured with trust, empowerment, a vision of what could be, and continuous communication up, down, and horizontally, both inside and outside AMS—and with commitment to achieving the vision by all the stakeholders.

Summary

Building a high-performance buying or selling team is difficult, and maintaining a high performance level for an extended period of time is a tremendous challenge, but observing the work and results of a high-performance team is a real pleasure. In this chapter, we have introduced the S3 leadership process and provided a brief insight into some of the many key actions one must take when following the S3 leadership process. We have focused on what business professionals involved in buying and selling complex products, services, and integrated solutions must know and do to achieve excellence with integrity.

In the following six chapters, we discuss each of the steps of the S3 leadership process in more detail. Chapters 4 through 9 include checklists of best practices, case studies (from both the public and the private sectors), personal stories, and selected interviews (similar to the one you just read) with current business professionals facing real-world leadership challenges in buying and selling complex products, services, and solutions. The individuals selected for interviews represent both government and commercial business sectors, both buyers and sellers, and leaders at all seven organizational levels of leadership.

Questions to Consider

1. Do you consistently practice the S3 leadership process?
2. Which step or steps of the S3 leadership process do you sometimes struggle to do?
3. Which steps of the S3 leadership process do you do well?
4. Which steps of the S3 leadership process is most important?

---

[1] Stephen R. Covey, *The Seven Habits of Highly Effective People* (New York: Free Press, 1989).

[2] Jack Welch, *Jack: Straight from the Gut* (New York: Warner, 2001).

Chapter 4

Leadership Step 1: Think the Talk

"Begin with the end in mind."
—Stephen Covey

Introduction

Most athletes are taught to visualize themselves performing a sport, especially a difficult movement or series of actions, before actually doing it. Likewise, we have learned it is best to think through an important oral presentations and then verbally practice in private before ever giving it in public. The more you think the talk before giving the talk, the better the talk will be. However, it is not enough just to think about what you are going to say before you say it.

This chapter discusses the numerous proactive actions that you can take to better focus your thoughts before you speak. Since effective and compelling communication is a vital competency of leadership, the ability to think clearly and focus positive thoughts before talking is essential to success. In this chapter, we discuss the following 10 actions to improve your ability to think the talk:

1. Focus on positive thoughts.
2. Read, watch, and listen to uplifting materials.
3. Practice active listening.
4. Associate with positive people (those who inspire you to a higher level of performance).
5. Select two coaches or mentors.

(Workbook p27)

6. Understand your team members (their goals and objectives).
7. Understand your customers (their needs, goals, and budget).
8. Picture yourself as you want others to see you.
9. Think about the effect of your words on others before you say them.
10. Think about your nonverbal messages.

On the basis of experience and research, we are confident that if you apply some or all of the 10 proactive actions discussed in this chapter, you will improve your ability to talk the talk, by first learning to think the talk—thus improving your leadership and team performance.

Focus on Positive Thoughts

We all carry with us what is often called "mental baggage"—negative thoughts based on past mistakes, failures, self-doubt, received criticism, and perceived shortcomings. Mental baggage can serve as a self-motivator to do better, to learn from past mistakes, and to strive to a higher level of performance, or it can contribute to failure through lack of confidence, self second-guessing, analysis paralysis, or a "can't do" attitude. It has often been said that attitude determines altitude. We believe there is a lot of truth in this realization: a positive, "can do" attitude does contribute to success.

A positive, "can do" attitude alone is not enough to achieve success. However, people who possess such an attitude convey a positive energy to others, which may help the team overcome challenges and achieve success. In the world of buying and selling, no one likes or wants to work with a person who is constantly negative. Negative people are usually focused on why what needs to be done cannot be done for the budget or in the time frame permitted. People want to work with buying and selling professionals who know the rules of the game and know how to ethically and appropriately overcome challenges to achieve success. A buyer who constantly says "no" does not add significant value to the organization, unless every proposed deal is a really bad deal. Likewise, a salesperson who bids on everything and says "yes" to every customer request usually costs the organization more than the revenue and profit that person contributes.

Focusing your thoughts on the positive side of the business equation allows you to think creatively and potentially develop innovative, breakthrough solutions to business problems. We all get upset and frustrated by setbacks. Everyone makes mistakes; the key to success is how you deal with these challenges and how quickly you bounce back from failures. The greatest success stories come from the ability to take a failure and find a way to achieve success. In life, in business, and especially in buying and selling, a positive attitude goes a long way toward helping you and stimulating others to achieve success.

Selected Interview

Name: Kenneth L. Dixon, CPCM

Job Title: Director, Contracts

Organization: BAE Systems

Location: Austin, Texas

Key Responsibilities: Responsible for leadership and oversight of a 22-person Contracts and Export Compliance Department for a large global aerospace and defense contractor.

Brief Resume: Twenty-four years' experience in contract administration and management—10 years with General Dynamics' Fort Worth Division and 14 years with BAE Systems in Austin, Texas. Primary duties include reviewing, approving, and signing export license applications, technical assistance agreements, and manufacturing license agreements for submission to the U.S. Department of State. Advise company officials and employees regarding exportability issues and Department of Commerce regulations.

Negotiate and manage contracts, subcontracts, and other agreements between the company and its government and nongovernment customers and suppliers, both domestic and international. Draft, coordinate, negotiate, and execute proprietary information agreements, teaming agreements, license agreements, international representative agreements, and strategic alliances with other companies. Actively participate in the development, review, and sign-off of major proposals.

University of Dallas, Irving, Texas: Master of Business Administration, August 1987, with concentration in acquisition and contract management

University of Maryland, Heidelberg, Germany: Bachelor of Science, May 1981, with concentration in business management and political science

Questions and Answers

Question: In regard to the Six Steps to Success (S3) leadership process, which step do you believe is the most important? Why?

Answer: They are all important, but the first step, Think the Talk, is the foundation for the rest of the process. I firmly believe that having a healthy state of mind is absolutely critical to achieving optimum personal performance and influencing others to achieve their maximum potential. It is more than just thinking before talking. Our thought process, as well as the ability we have to use it to shape our view of the world, is a very powerful thing. The extent to which we succeed in this first step sets the stage for success or failure in the other steps in the process.

Question: What are the core competencies of a successful buying or selling team leader?

Answer: One key competency is the ability to connect with the people on the team on a personal level. Nobody wakes up and thinks, "I really want to be a mediocre employee today." People want to do something meaningful, to make a difference, to feel like they are contributing to something important. It's the leader's job to connect with that part of every person on the team, to help that person find the power within himself or herself to succeed.

Question: Please provide a brief personal experience that you believe best illustrates leadership in buying or selling.

Answer: Our company is currently undergoing a tremendous amount of change through mergers, acquisitions, divestitures, and reorganizations. Our specific business unit is being merged into a larger part of the company, and there is a great deal of fear and anxiety on the part of the employees. At first, our team fell into the trap of negative thinking, which resulted in low morale and even lower performance. Once I realized that my own state of mind had a significant effect on the ability of my team to deal with all of the changes, things started turning around. There are still days when I have to force myself to stay on track, but it has been worthwhile. The team is more resilient today and focused on being a significant part of a larger, high-performance group.

Read, Watch, and Listen to Uplifting Materials

People's thought are often based on their environment. If a person focuses on negative aspects of life and business; chooses to read, watch, and listen to negative materials; and associates with people who display negative thinking, then achieving success is going to be a significant challenge.

Conversely, you can choose to create a positive environment. People who focus on reading, watching, and listening to uplifting materials and who carefully select the people they associate with tend to display a more positive "can do" attitude and are much more likely to find a path to success. Many of the old sayings are true:

- Success does often breed success.
- People with higher expectations do achieve more.
- People who are surrounded by a positive environment do tend to have greater self-confidence.

So, the key is to be selective in what you choose to spend your time reading, watching, and listening to, both on the job and in your free time. Do not allow yourself to become an accidental victim of a negative environment, which constantly makes you feel upset, frustrated, powerless, or depressed. Actively choose to create a positive mental environment for yourself. Here are five things you can do to create positive energy through what you read, watch, and listen:

1. Read books you find interesting and motivating.
2. Read professional business magazines and journals that feature best practices and success stories (*Harvard Business Review,* Harvard Business School's *Negotiation* newsletter, *Contract Management* magazine, *Journal of Contract Management, PM Network,* International Association for Contract and Commercial Management

(IACCM) electronic newsletters, Center for Advanced Purchasing Studies (CAPS) benchmarking reports, etc.).

3. Watch positive, uplifting movies and television (everybody has their own favorites).
4. Listen to positive, uplifting music and books on tape.
5. Spend your time as much as possible with positive people, both at work and at home.

So our challenge to you is to take charge of your environment, as much as possible, and to create an environment that fosters positive thinking!

Practice Active Listening

Like many people in our Western culture, we love to talk. However, we have learned over the years that the more and better we listen, the more compelling will be our communication. In the words of the best-selling consultant, Dr. Stephen Covey, in his book *The Seven Habits of Highly Effective People,* "Seek to understand, then to be understood."[1] Most people in business—especially those working in buying and selling—are way too busy talking to be bothered with actively listening to their customers and suppliers. **Table 4-1** provides a summary of seven best practices for active listening.

Table 4-1 Seven Best Practices for Active Listening
1. **Take time.** If you feel that someone is troubled or needs to talk, listen with attention. Listening is not a waste of time. If you can help that person clear his or her mind, you will also clarify later communication between the two of you.
2. **Be understanding.** If the speaker becomes extremely emotional, let the emotion pass until it is exhausted. Show you understand and that you feel the subject is important. Remember, the judo expert does not oppose force but steps aside and lets it pass.
3. **Limit your verbal reactions.** While the speaker continues to talk, confine yourself to what has been called a series of "eloquent and encouraging grunts:" "Hmmm," "Oh," or "I see." If the speaker pauses, say nothing. A nod or other nonverbal form of feedback may encourage him or her to continue.
4. **Do not attempt to evaluate what has been said.** Remember, there are no absolutes, especially in an emotional situation.
5. **Do not give guidance, even if asked to do so.** The speaker is searching for his or her own creative solution.
6. **In retrospect, analyze the information you have received in different ways.** Shift levels vertically (different positions) and horizontally (different points of view) to see how it might apply to your own problems and growth. And remember, you can learn as much, if not more, from "losers" as from "winners." These terms are meaningless to a good listener.
7. **Be silent.** Silence is the listener's strength and skill.

Associate with Positive People

It may sound somewhat corny, but you often become like the people you associate with, so choose your friends and associates carefully. Of course, in business you cannot always choose who you work with or have to do business with. What you can do is control how you act and react to the people you engage with professionally and personally. Further, through your words and actions, you can inform others that you prefer and enjoy working with people who treat others with respect and display a proactive, positive, and "can do" attitude.

A Personal Story: Working with a Bully
by Gregory A. Garrett

Unfortunately, the real world is full of difficult and challenging people. Some people can evolve from the negative or dark side to the positive side of the force.

Situation. Years ago, I was required to work with a very challenging customer. This customer was the chief executive officer (CEO) of a major corporation. He enjoyed being difficult. In fact, he used his highly emotional nature and intimidating size, voice, and confrontational style to get what he wanted. Further, this challenging customer enjoyed making others uncomfortable by using foul and unprofessional language. Several of the top executives of my firm tolerated this CEO's terrible behavior, saying "the customer is always right," "don't take it personally," or "he treats everyone that way."

Challenge. If you were faced with a customer CEO who was a bully, who treated everyone in your supplier organization terribly, what would you do?

My decision. I arranged a closed-door, face-to-face meeting with the customer CEO. I informed him that as a former officer of the U.S. Air Force, as a gentleman, and as a leader of my firm, I did not appreciate his rude, disrespectful, and unprofessional behavior to myself or any members of my firm. Further, I stated that if he continued his use of foul and unprofessional language, I would walk out, and our firm would no longer do business with his organization.

Customer-bully reaction. The CEO bully thought I was bluffing. He resumed his terrible behavior. I walked out of his office. I refused to answer his calls for three days. Of course, I had previously coordinated this plan of action with my partners, and they agreed the plan was necessary and appropriate. Eventually, the CEO bully, who needed our firm's services, apologized to me, never again yelled at me or our team members, and never again used foul language toward anyone in our firm.

Summary. You cannot always pick your customers, but you can control how you deal with them. Sometimes tough love works and sometimes it doesn't, but no one deserves to be treated disrespectfully. Either way, my team learned a powerful lesson about my conviction that everyone be treated with respect. Our teamwork soared after we achieved a respectful and professional business environment.

Select Two Coaches or Mentors

It is critical that you select two coaches or mentors to help you guide your thinking, planning, words, and actions both in the short term and in the long term. We suggest you select two people senior to you (by 10 or more years) who have been there, done that, and gotten the t-shirt. Our experience and research shows that most people benefit from having one mentor from within their current organization (at least two levels above them) who knows them, the organizational structure, and the office politics. Likewise, it is very valuable to find an outside expert—if possible someone you admire and would like to emulate—and ask that person for periodic guidance and career advice.

Remember to pick your mentors carefully. Select people who will provide clear, candid, and concise advice as to what you should consider doing to further develop your talent as a buying or selling professional and as a business leader. Try to find mentors who will help motivate or stimulate you to achieve more than you thought or considered was possible. If the mentors you selected do not provide the level of feedback you need—whether too much or too little—then work with them to adjust the coaching or find yourself another mentor.

Understand Your Team Members

To build a high-performance team, you must understand your team members' goals and objectives, both professionally and personally. The better you know your team members, in an appropriate and ethical manner, the more likely you are to be able to motivate them to achieve higher levels of performance. The best way to get to know your team members is to spend time with them in face-to-face meetings, conferences, training sessions, teleconferences, and net-meetings and in communications such as e-mails.

Remember to keep your meetings professional and ethical. Avoid any appearance of favoritism.

A Personal Story: A New Officer's Leadership Lessons

by William C. Pursch

As a brand new second lieutenant fresh from Fort Benning Infantry Officers Orientation Course, I was assigned as a platoon leader. The platoon was stationed in Aschaffenburg, Germany, but was on maneuvers at the Hohenfels Training Facility in Bavaria. It was December 1960, and there was plenty of snow all around when I joined my platoon in the field.

As I approached my platoon to meet my platoon sergeant for the very first time, I noticed that half the platoon was wearing German uniforms and the other half was wearing World War II American uniforms. My platoon sergeant greeted me, "Nice to meet you, sir! Sir, they want me to wear a German uniform, and those b____ds shot me, and I ain't going to put on that uniform." The words "What are your actions and orders at this time?" rang through my head. This was the standard question at the Infantry School after you had been presented with a difficult situation in the Leadership Reaction Course.

Although many different principles of leadership had been taught to me at the Infantry School (yes, basic leadership can be taught), three immediately came to mind:

- Know your men and look out for their welfare.
- Do not ask someone to do something you would not be willing to do.
- Set the example.

After a long silence, during which I was scrambling to buy time to come up with my answer, and during which half the platoon had heard the platoon sergeant's comment, I responded, "All right, platoon sergeant, why don't you take charge of the men in American uniforms, and I will wear the German uniform and take charge of that group of men." He grinned from ear to ear, stepped back, gave me the best salute I can remember, and said, "Yes, sir! Welcome to *your* platoon, sir!"

If you were to watch the movie *Armored Command,* starring Howard Keel and Tina Louise, you would see a grinning, grizzled sergeant prodding a group of German prisoners up a hill, with his bayonet fixed to his rifle. I am in the middle of the group of prisoners with my hands on my head in surrender. The good news was that we got to see the movie for free after release because we "starred" in it. The bad news was that Tina Louise did all her filming at a studio in Nuremberg and never came to the set at Hohenfels, much to the chagrin of the participants.

For the rest of my managerial career, I always tried to remember and follow those three principles of leadership I learned so long ago.

Understand Your Customers

What is it that your customers value most? Customer service, on-time delivery, and lowest price are usually at the top of the list for most customers, but it does vary with the customers' needs and market conditions. Most companies do not just sell products and services; they provide delivered solutions. In nearly every industry, sellers are improving their supply chain to offer greater value to their customers, including next-day delivery, customized handling, and specialized marking and labeling, but most sellers do not truly know the cost.

Because of the shortcomings of conventional accounting methods and average-cost assumptions, most companies do not typically know their real costs from deal to deal or at a project level. Unfortunately, overzealous sales forces will often give away some or all profitability in order to get the business, often motivated more by their own sales compensation plan than what is best for their company.

A Supply Chain Executive Board analysis of 750,000 order records from three companies in the consumer products, process, and electronics industries found that firms that provide uncontrolled supply-chain services sacrifice substantial profits—up to 20 percent—for just a 3 to 4 percent improvement in revenue growth. What's more, separate analyses of customer and product profitability revealed that 40 percent of unprofitable orders are placed by the perceived "best" customers, or those who are ranked among the top 20 percent of the most profitable. Further, the study showed that 55 percent of the unprofitable orders placed by large customers are for products that are, on average, considered profitable.[2]

To truly understand its customers, an organization needs to deal with facts about what its customers need; what delivering products, services, and solutions to meet those needs costs; and what the customers' level of loyalty is. **Figure 4-1,** The Loyalty Ladder, depicts how business customers display loyalty in a predictable sequence as they move up the loyalty ladder. You can determine which rungs your customers stand on by analyzing sales records, talking to sales teams, and conducting customer surveys and focus groups.

Picture Yourself as You Want Others to See You

It is important for a business professional to periodically perform a self-examination. Said differently, you should take some time to assess your personal strengths and areas of improvement. Further, it is wise to conduct a 360° survey of your performance by gathering data, either formally or informally, from your supervisors, peers, employees, customers, and suppliers. Once you gather these data, perform a personal analysis. Then ask your supervisors and mentors to help you create action plans to improve your leadership and team performance. Creating an accurate mental picture of yourself can help you relate to others more effectively and allow you to focus on areas for improvement.

Think About the Effect of Your Words on Others

It is very important to think ahead, so that you do not say one thing when you mean another. Too often people do not take the time to stop and think before they speak. Unfortunately, people sometimes allow their emotions to overcome their intelligence. Emotional outbursts can cause people to say things that may not be accurate but may result in others doing just the opposite of what was originally intended.

In business, the ability to control your emotions is very important. In the world of buying and selling complex products, services, and integrated solutions, controlling your emotions is essential to success. Displaying emotions can be both appropriate and effective in the buying and selling process, such as showing excitement about new products or services your sales team is offering or demonstrating a passion for delivering quality

Figure 4-1 The Loyalty Ladder

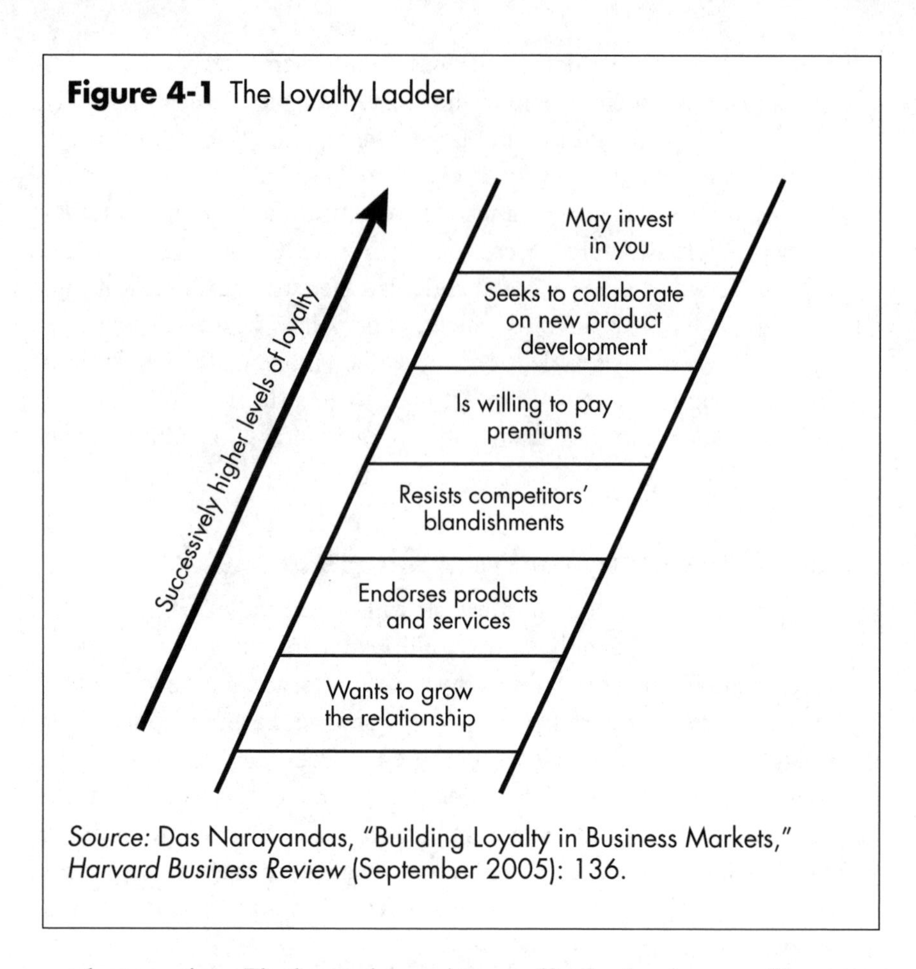

Source: Das Narayandas, "Building Loyalty in Business Markets," *Harvard Business Review* (September 2005): 136.

products on time. The key to becoming an effective buying or selling team leader is to think about your words and your use of emotions before you speak or display your feelings.

Selected Interview

Name: Linda F. Riviera

Job Title: Contracting Officer

Organization: National Aeronautics and Space Administration (NASA)

Key Responsibilities: Contract negotiation and administration, purchasing, contact pricing, subcontract management, and business management within the procurement organization.

Brief Resume: Linda Riviera began her career in procurement at NASA in 1991, as a contract specialist. She has served in progressively more responsible positions, including contracting officer in the Mission Operations Directorate Business Management Office, the International Space Station Procurement Office, and most recently the Institutional Procurement Office. Ms. Riviera has participated in several process improvement teams at NASA and has received several awards and commendations. Most recently, she received the Center Director Commendation, for "outstanding efforts in supporting professional development and training within the Office of Procurement." Ms. Riviera began her contracting career working for the International Business Machines Corporation in Arlington, Virginia.

Ms. Riviera earned a Bachelor of Business Administration in 1978 from New Mexico State University. She is the president of the Space City Houston chapter of the National Contract Management Association (NCMA).

Questions and Answers

Question: What are the core competencies of a successful buying or selling team leader?

Answer: There are many other core competencies identified by various leadership models. NASA's leadership model identifies six core competency areas: practicing personal effectiveness; managing information and knowledge; working internationally; using business acumen; leading and managing others; and demonstrating discipline competency. Personal effectiveness identifies those skills I believe to be of utmost important to a successful buying or selling team leader. Those competencies include establishing mutual respect with the members of the team, listening to and understanding others, facilitating open communications, and maintaining a high level of integrity and honesty.

Question: What are the most significant challenges you must overcome to be a successful buying or selling team leader?

Answer: I think the most significant challenge for me to overcome is to learn to delegate work to others. I have positioned myself in the past to take on additional work that could be delegated to a team member. Although my intentions were to help the team meet deadlines or milestones, as an effective team leader I could be using my leadership skills to mentor or coach a team member who could have performed the task.

Question: In regard to the S3 leadership process, which step do you believe is the most important? Why?

Answer: I consider Step 1, Think the Talk, the most important step. I believe that an individual's success is limited only by what they believe they can or cannot do. Starting the talk is key. I believe that we all have qualities that can make us effective leaders. Thus, taking the proactive steps to positive thinking, to believing and visualizing ourselves as leaders, will make the journey a reality.

Question: Please provide a brief personal experience that you believe best illustrates leadership in buying or selling?

Answer: Several years ago I was selected to work as a contracting officer supporting the source evaluation boards for the International Space Station Program Office at NASA Johnson Space Center. What made this experience unique was that the program was planning on awarding several major contracts and conducting simultaneous source-selection evaluation boards. To accomplish this effort, a team of contracting officers, led by the procurement manager, was selected. Over the next several years, the procurement team worked closely with the technical team to help develop the contract strategies, met with industry to solicit comments on the strategies, developed Web sites to keep potential offerors updated on all aspects of the procurement process, and worked collectively through the entire source-selection evaluation board process.

The result was the award of four major contracts with no protests. Upon award, the team solicited industry comment again, through a survey, on aspects of the procurement process that were positive and areas that could have been improved. The overwhelming positive responses from industry and the cutting-edge procurement processes that were developed and used redefined the source-selection evaluation process at Johnson Space Center. In my opinion, the effective leadership of the program as well as the technical and procurement teams made this endeavor successful.

Think About Your Nonverbal Messages

As discussed in Chapter 2, the effective use of nonverbal communications is vital to success as a team leader. Because more information is communicated nonverbally than verbally, it is not enough to just think before you speak. You must also think before you write, use facial expressions, use hand and arm gestures, and so forth. Many people have learned to control their word choice. Some people are skilled liars. However, most people have not learned to effectively control their full range of nonverbal cues, especially those people who say one thing and mean another. Understanding the power of nonverbal communication, taking the time to read others' nonverbal cues, and thinking about how you will use nonverbal messages to help achieve your goals is essential to success. Remember, communication skills are vital to business, especially buying and selling products, services, and solutions.

Selected Interview

Name: Rene G. Rendon

Job Title: Lecturer

Organization: United States Naval Postgraduate School

Location: Monterey, California

Key Responsibilities: Teach graduate acquisition, contracting, and program management courses as part of the school's master of business administration (MBA) programs.

Brief Resume: Dr. Rene G. Rendon is on the faculty of the U.S. Naval Postgraduate School, where he teaches acquisition and contract management courses in the MBA and master of science programs. Before his appointment at the Naval Postgraduate School, he served for more than 22 years as an acquisition and contracting officer in the U.S. Air Force, retiring at the rank of lieutenant colonel. His Air Force career included assignments as a warranted contracting officer for the Peacekeeper intercontinental ballistic missile and the F-22 programs, a contracting squadron commander for an Air Force pilot training base, and the director of contracting for the Air Force's space surveillance satellite and space launch rocket programs.

Dr. Rendon has earned bachelor's, master's, and doctoral degrees in business administration and has taught contract management courses for the government contracts program at the University of California–Los Angeles. He was also a senior faculty member for the Keller Graduate School of Management, where he taught MBA courses in project management and contract management.

He is a certified professional contracts manager with NCMA, a certified purchasing manager with the Institute for Supply Management, and a certified project management professional with the Project Management Institute. He has received the prestigious Fellow Award from NCMA, and he was recognized with the U.S. Air Force Outstanding Officer in Contracting Award.

Questions and Answers

Question: In regard to the S3 leadership process, which step do you believe is the most important? Why?

Answer: I believe the most important step of the S3 leadership process is the first step—Think the Talk. This step reflects what I consider to be the most significant aspect of any real personal change, and that is that real change must first be internalized and purpose driven—that is, real change begins on the inside and then permeates to the outside. Thus, real change happens from the inside out. A leader cannot begin with to Talk, Walk, Execute, Build, or Achieve, if the leader has not first internalized the change. Think the Talk is part of that first step. To become a successful leader, one must first change from the inside, in terms of attitudes, beliefs, values, morals, and so forth. Only when the leader has changed from the inside can the leader expect the outside (words, actions, habits, character) to change. Integrity, the most important leadership characteristic, is when an individual's inside (attitudes, beliefs, values, and morals) is integrated and aligned with the individual's outside (words, actions, habits, character).

Question: Please provide a brief personal experience that you believe best illustrates leadership in buying or selling.

Answer: My most common experiences that best illustrate leadership in buying involve situations that require breaking down the contracting functional silo in order to take on a more strategic perspective of the project. In one situation, in order for me to meet my customer's needs, I was forced to look beyond the restrictions of the contracting regulations to find a solution to my customer's supply problem. Being careful not to violate any statutory requirements, I was able to craft a contracting solution that met all parties' needs. This solution involved identifying a potential contractor in a sole-source environment by using "other than normal" market research techniques and successfully persuading the contractor to do business with the government. In the end, the contract was completed successfully, and both parties were satisfied.

Another situation involved contracting for the recovery effort after a natural disaster had severely affected our military installation. With more than three feet of water on the flightline and no electricity, potable water, or natural gas, the military installation, as well as the surrounding area, was declared a natural disaster area by the president. Only through teamwork with our base operations support contractor and our other base agencies were we able to provide a successful quick response to the base recovery efforts. Keeping focused on the military mission and knowing our base infrastructure and commercial market were critical to the team's success. Our previously developed contingency plans definitely played a part in our successful recovery. (See Mark R. Floyd, Gary L. Wendon, and Rene G. Wendon, "Emergency Contracting: Responding to Natural Disaster," *Contract Management,* February 1999, 8–11).

Summary

In this chapter, we have discussed the first step—Think the Talk—of the S3 leadership process. We have examined 10 actions that you can take to improve your leadership skills and your team's buying or selling performance. Many people believe leadership begins with their words. We submit that leadership begins with your thoughts. Your ability to focus your thinking definitely contributes to your success or failure as a team leader. In the next chapter, we discuss the second step—Talk the Talk.

Questions to Consider

1. How well do you think before you talk?
2. How many of the 10 actions discussed in this chapter do you regularly perform to focus your thinking?
3. Have you selected two mentors to help guide your thinking?
4. Which of the 10 actions discussed in this chapter are most important to help people achieve leadership success?

---

[1] Stephen R. Covey, *The Seven Habits of Highly Effective People* (New York: Free Press, 1989).

[2] Supply Chain Executive Board. Institute of Supply Management, Benchmarking Study, 2003–2004, Center of Advance Purchasing Studies, Scottsdale, AZ, 2005.

Chapter 5

Leadership Step 2: Talk the Talk

"A true leader has the confidence to stand alone, the courage to make tough decisions, and the compassion to listen to the needs of others."

—Unknown

Introduction

It is important to verbally communicate the organization's vision, performance goals, key metrics, and code of conduct to everyone repeatedly. Doing so helps the buying and selling teams stay focused on what is important to achieve. All too commonly, managers lack consistency in their words and actions. Many senior managers, directors, and executives seem to float on a wave of indecision, with only a plan *du jour,* lacking a consistent focus. If a buying or selling team loses focus, it typically will not achieve high performance. If the buying or selling team leaders do not verbally give clear and compelling guidance, the team will often get caught up in the managerial indecision. Managerial indecision causes team members to become confused. Confusion causes a loss of productivity throughout the organization. Thus, effective buying and selling team leaders know the value of and the need to regularly talk the talk to the team.

Many people believe actions speak louder than words. We agree. However, speaking the words and then following up with consistent actions speaks the loudest. In fact, those individuals who learn to think the talk, talk the talk, and then walk the talk usually are viewed as highly effective leaders!

However, merely saying something is not enough. In this chapter, we focus on knowing what to say, learning how to deliver the message, looking like a leader, knowing when to listen, understanding how to observe others, practicing the talk, realizing the power of being nice, applying the power of technology tools, and using the power of questions. As a leader of a buying or selling team, the art of verbal communication is key to your success.

Know the Top 10 Topics to Talk About

From research and experience we have developed a simple list of the top 10 topics that business leaders should talk about to buying and selling teams **(Table 5-1).**

The most important topic that buying and selling business leaders should regularly discuss with their teams is the organization's code of conduct. Integrity, respect, and ethical business behavior are fundamental and imperative to achieving long-term success in buying and selling. Some people dismiss the need to talk about integrity. However, if people are not frequently reminded of the importance of ethics and integrity, they may lose focus. Later, under pressure to achieve revenue targets or to quickly procure products and services, they may make unethical business decisions. Making unethical business decisions has certainly happened many times worldwide, in numerous buying and selling organizations. So remember to keep your buying or selling team focused on the theme, "Integrity, respect, and ethical behavior is job number one."

Table 5-1 Top 10 Topics to Talk About
1. Organization's code of conduct—"Integrity, respect, and ethical behavior is job number one"
2. Organization's vision, goals, metrics, results, and challenges
3. Customer's needs, goals, budget, and challenges
4. Team's performance goals, metrics, results, and challenges
5. Team's roles, responsibilities, and performance schedule
6. Subcontractors' performance goals, metrics, results, and challenges (tied to team and organization)
7. Individual performance goals, metrics, results, and challenges (tied to team and organization)
8. Individual leadership development
9. Individual strengths and best practices
10. Individual weaknesses and performance improvement plan

Some would argue that talking about your customer should come first or second, but we disagree. We believe that integrity, respect, and ethical behavior are most important. Next, we believe that your organization's vision, goals, metrics, results, and challenges should be clearly communicated to everyone. It is possible to achieve customer satisfaction but to lose money and go out of business.

Talking about your customers and their needs, goals, budgets, and challenges is essential to buying and selling success. Team members should be provided information about their customers on a regular basis. Likewise, team members should be required to spend a certain portion of their time talking or meeting with customers.

If you want your team members to achieve high performance, you must regularly inform them of their team performance goals, metrics, and current and past results. We suggest a monthly meeting to assess performance and stimulate performance actions.

It is vital that all buying and selling team leaders clarify roles, responsibilities, and performance schedules so that everyone knows the game plan. Specifically, you want everyone to know who is accountable for what, when, where, why, how, and how much.

Given the importance of subcontractors in the buying and selling process it is very important that all buying and selling team leaders effectively communicate to all appropriate parties the subcontractors' performance goals, metrics, results, and challenges.

Every buying and selling team leader should regularly discuss with his or her team members their individual performance goals, metrics, results, and challenges. These discussions should be done in face-to-face meetings, if possible, or in private telephone discussions.

Every buying and selling team leader should regularly discuss with all directly reporting team members their respective individual leadership development plans. Specifically, the supervisor should discuss with each team member that individual's steps taken, next steps, and future leadership challenges.

To reinforce positive behavior, buying and selling team leaders should routinely inform team members of their skill strengths and demonstrated best practices.

All buying and selling team leaders should regularly provide constructive feedback to their team members regarding respective skill weaknesses. The team leader should work with each team member to develop a customized performance improvement plan. No one is perfect—we can all find ways to further improve our performance.

Selected Interview

Name: Paul R. Rosengrant

Job Title: Director of Contracts

Organization: EPS Corporation

Location: Tinton Falls, New Jersey

Key Responsibilities: Contract management, subcontract management, and proposal development.

Brief Resume: More than 20 years of experience in government contracting. Extensive knowledge of Federal Acquisition Regulations, Joint Travel Regulations, and other associated government acquisition regulations. More then 12 years of managerial experience. Army Materiel Command Procurement Intern Program graduate.

B.A., Business Administration, Gettysburg College, Gettysburg, Pennsylvania. 1984.

Active officer in the NCMA Fort Monmouth Chapter; vice president of programs (2003/2004 program year), president (2004/2005, and 2005/2006 program years).

Questions and Answers

Question: What personal leadership characteristics are most important for building successful buying or selling teams?

Answer: I have always found that being a good listener and allowing for team input and ideas is very helpful in building a successful team. A team that feels appreciated and part of the whole process will perform better in the long run.

Question: What are the core competencies of a successful buying or selling team leader?

Answer: Strong communication skills, both verbal and written, diverse experience, and a proven track record.

Question: What are the most significant challenges you must overcome to be a successful buying or selling team leader?

Answer: Delegating authority and giving responsibilities to others is my most difficult challenge. When I do that, my job becomes easier and more successful.

Learn How to Deliver the Message (Talk)

There is no one best way to talk the talk. Style, personality, and situations vary. Yet there are 12 best practices **(Table 5-2)** that many leaders follow to ensure that their communication is effective.

Table 5-2 Deliver the Message: 12 Best Practices

1. Keep your message (talk) clear and concise.
2. Use active-voice words.
3. Demonstrate by your word choice, tone, pitch, and volume your commitment and passion.
4. Adapt your style and approach to the audience.
5. Be sincere.
6. Use powerful examples and case studies.
7. Be compelling.
8. Use nonverbal cues to reinforce your words.
9. Use audiovisual aids.
10. Use humor as appropriate.
11. Relate to your audience through similar background or personal stories.
12. Practice, practice, practice.

Some people love to talk the talk, especially in public. However, many people dread public speaking for a wide variety of reasons. To be an effective buying or selling team leader, one must become an effective oral communicator. Generally, the more experience or practice you have delivering the message (talk), the better speaker you will become.

Another best practice for improving your ability to effectively deliver the message is to record one of your presentations. Then listen and carefully observe your presentation on the audio- or videotape and take notes on what you did well and on what you need to improve. Obtaining feedback from others who have carefully viewed your presentation can also help you improve your performance in the future. So be receptive to feedback from others. Take time to understand what you can do better when verbally communicating with others so that you can improve how you deliver the message.

Look Like a Leader

No, you do not have to look like a movie star or super model (though, of course, that does help) to be an effective team leader. However, appearance does count! People do judge others by their appearance. Looking like a leader is key, because how you choose to dress and your overall physical appearance communicates volumes about you to others. It is important to maintain physical fitness for your health and energy to lead others.

Demonstrating leadership can be both mentally and physically challenging, thus staying in good overall health helps you become a more effective team leader. **Table 5-3** shows 10 best practices to look like a leader.

Table 5-3 Look Like a Leader: 10 Best Practices

1. Select appropriate style and color of clothes.
2. Dress the part (appropriate for the situation).
3. Maintain personal grooming (hair, face, teeth, hands, and nails).
4. Err on the side of overdressing (never be too casual when doing business).
5. Be aware of your physical presence (height and weight).
6. Use appropriate nonverbal cues (facial gestures, eye contact, arm movements, and hand gestures).
7. Do not slouch, lean, or hunch your shoulders—stand tall.
8. Do not stand still or stiff—move to engage others.
9. Wear appropriate jewelry (classy, but not too much bling).
10. Shine your shoes—look good from head to toe.

It is regrettable that people often judge others largely by their appearance. But given that appearance matters, it is vital to look like a leader so people will listen to what you have to say. You may be able to talk the talk, but if people do not respect the way you look, they often will not respect what you say. So take the time to look like a leader so that others will value what you have to say.

Know When and How to Listen and Observe Others

As we stated in Chapter 4, it is critical to think before you talk. A key action to take before you talk is to listen to others. It is essential that you understand your customers, suppliers, team members, peers, and supervisors before you talk. Practicing active listening is key to successfully delivering the message.

A valuable skill to master is to listen and observe others before, during, and after you speak. Some people believe you must practice active listening before you speak. Some people believe you must carefully observe people's actions and physical reactions (nonverbal messages) while you are speaking. Still others believe you must actively listen after you speak to gather feedback. In reality, all these statements are correct. **Table 5-4** provides a simple yet effective list of listening best practices.

Table 5-4 Listening: Five Best Practices
1. Don't talk. This best practice is obvious but a hard one to do. Don't interrupt, keep listening. Don't react, keep listening.
2. Act interested. Pretty soon, you will be. Take notes. Ask questions. Clarify and confirm.
3. Use attentive body language. Send listening signals. Make eye contact. Lean in. Nod (nodding encourages the talker to talk and tell you more). Think.
4. Eliminate distractions. Create your own listening confessional. Don't let your eyes wander. Get rid of noise. Reduce diversions. Remember what it feels like to be ignored.
5. Let listening be a solution. Sometimes the other side just wants to be heard. Never stop listening (keep learning).
Source: Ronald M. Shapiro and Mark A. Jankowski, *The Power of Nice: How to Negotiate So Everyone Wins* (New York: Wiley, 1998), 85.

The ability to read the nonverbal gestures of others can help you to real-time tailor your message. The ability to tailor your message will help you ensure that others value, understand, and support your verbal communication.

Practice the Talk

Practice leads to better performance, especially when it comes to public speaking. Whether you are addressing one person, several people, or a large audience, it is essential to practice the talk before you deliver the talk. We offer seven best practices to help you more effectively practice the talk **(Table 5-5).**

Table 5-5 Practice the Talk: Seven Best Practices
1. Think the talk.
2. Talk the talk—aloud.
3. Practice the talk in front of a mirror.
4. Practice your nonverbal gestures too.
5. Practice in front of others.
6. Practice the talk with audio and visual aids.
7. Record the talk.

Understand the Power of Nice

Never make another person feel small or unimportant. Take the time to be polite and kind to others. Be aware of your word choice and nonverbal messages. Be understanding and show mercy to others through your words. Politeness generally wins people over; being rude and disrespectful upsets people. Said simply, if you are respectful of others through your words and actions, they will be more respectful of you.

Learn to take the time to thank your team members. Never treat others as second-class people. Do not abuse your authority or power; treat everyone with respect. Be kind. Be grateful to others. A true leader treats everyone with respect and shows sensitivity and kindness to others through words and actions. Being a jerk, abusing power, and being rude to others are not a recipe for success. In fact, bad behavior may be effective for the short term, but in most cases it results in long-term failure. Remember, most people respond much better to politeness than rudeness, so be pleasant and kind to others!

The power of nice is the best way for you, as a buyer or seller, to get what you want. The power of nice is all about helping the other parties also get what they want. The power of nice is focused on using politeness, sincerity, and sensitivity as leverage to understand your customers or suppliers better. Through the power of nice, you will come to value and appreciate your customers' and suppliers' needs, allowing you to create a win-win situation. You can be a nice person and still get what you are after; just do not be naive. Use the verbal power of nice as a tool through your words and subsequent actions **(Table 5-6).**

Table 5-6 Power of Nice: Seven Best Practices
1. Find something nice to say to everyone.
2. Don't be afraid to say thank you.
3. Practice politeness—say "Please," "Excuse me," and so forth.
4. Use positive reinforcement words—say "We value your support," "I appreciate your work," "I agree," "You are correct," "What can I do to help?," "Excellent job," "Nicely done," "Great job," "Outstanding," and so forth.
5. Pat people on the back or shake their hand, as appropriate.
6. Look people in the eye and say "Well done!"
7. Write and send thank you notes.

Apply Technology Tools to Improve Communications

Increasingly, people are separated by geography, time, and—as your organization goes global—language and culture. Information technology tools will help you address these separations and allow you to create a seamless virtual corporate environment that supports the pursuit of new business. Organizations that can create this seamless virtual business environment are the ones that will succeed. Knowing how to leverage resources globally provides a tremendous advantage over competitors. The key to creating this environment is understanding the depth and breadth of information technology tools available and picking the right ones for yourself and your organization.

Vendors and applications are constantly changing and evolving to bring more capabilities to the desktop. The intent of this discussion is to focus on the types of tools available, with illustrative examples. Although numerous specific vendors and applications are cited throughout this discussion, no endorsement or recommendation is made of any particular vendor or application.

Technology has made it possible to plan and conduct business meetings in a wide variety of media that are constantly evolving. Though not exhaustive, the following list covers the fundamental types of tools available for meetings, along with the advantages, disadvantages, and best applications for each. For many business meetings, it is likely you will have a mix of media, allowing for maximum engagement of all participants. All of the tools mentioned can be used by organizations of all sizes; however, there are security considerations to keep in mind if you use them over the Internet or public phone network.

When considering tools for buying and selling meetings, one also needs to take into account communication needs in terms of communication flow. As shown in **Figure 5-1,** communication flow falls into three basic types: broadcast (i.e., one-way send), exchange (i.e., send and receive), and collection (i.e., one-way receive).

Figure 5-1 Communication Flow Process

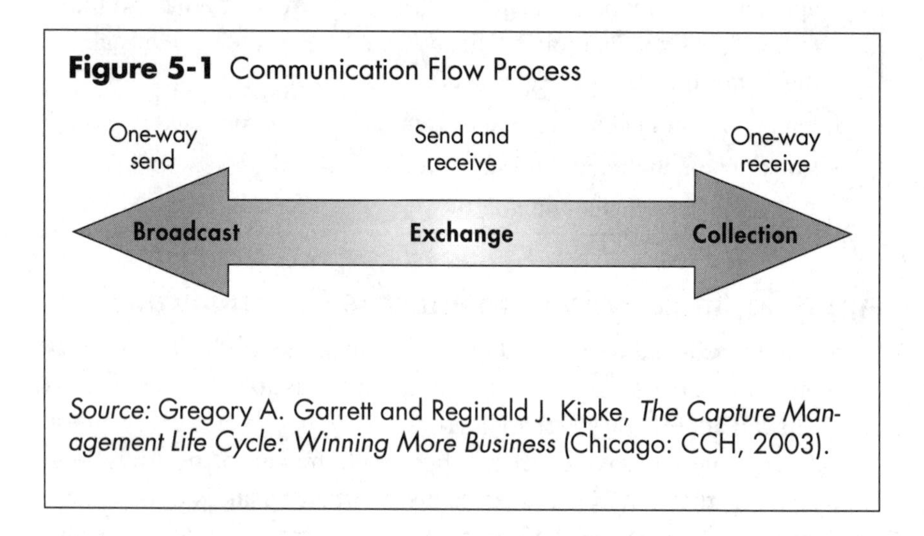

Source: Gregory A. Garrett and Reginald J. Kipke, *The Capture Management Life Cycle: Winning More Business* (Chicago: CCH, 2003).

Face-to-Face Meetings

With advances in technology and a continued competitive focus on reducing expenses, face-to-face meetings are often overlooked as a critical tool in buying and selling. As you invest in information technology tools, don't naively believe you will (or more importantly should) eliminate face-to-face meetings. Face-to-face meetings are essential to building relationships and developing trust and are an irreplaceable tool for customer meetings, contract negotiations, and discussions with suppliers or partners. Don't be "penny wise and pound foolish" when it comes to investing in technology tools to the exclusion of face-to-face meetings.

Conference Bridges

Voice conference bridges have become the primary alternative to face-to-face meetings. Voice conference calls have the advantages of being easy to use and of allowing participation from remote locations, thus saving travel expenses and time. Conference bridges are very effective for disseminating information to a large audience, exchanging information between a small number of speakers, or holding short meetings. They have the disadvantage of providing only voice interaction. However, with a little planning, presentation materials can be distributed in advance to participants, which significantly increases the effectiveness of such interaction.

Because of their ease of use and relative affordability, conference bridges are also frequently misused, wasting countless hours of participants' potentially productive time. Conference calls should always have a specific purpose, agenda, and limit. Avoid endless "marathon" or open-ended calls with a large group, in favor of multiple shorter calls with fewer participants. Shorter calls not only save the time of participants but also are more focused and productive because you will not lose the attention of participants.

Conference bridges have become so commonplace that many fail to take appropriate precautions to ensure against eavesdropping by unwelcome participants. Always use a conference bridge that provides audible tones when someone joins or leaves the call or that screens participants by name or with an access code, and always take roll. Many conference bridges now offer two access codes: one for participants and one for the host. Such bridges not only provide additional security but also protect against unwanted use of the bridge by someone other than the host. Finally, be sure to change bridge numbers and access codes regularly and publish them only to the participants needed for the call.

Collaboration Software

Recent developments have created a number of software collaboration tools, such as Microsoft® NetMeeting®, Intel® ProShare®, and Sun™ ShowMe™. These tools allow for the real-time exchange of visual information using personal computers (PCs). Not only can all users see the information being shown (e.g., a presentation, spreadsheet, or document) on their PC screens; if permitted by the host, they can be given control to make changes to the information. These tools are ideal for contract negotiation planning meetings in which you want to exchange and edit information, such as strategy sessions, terms and conditions development sessions, or practice or mock contract negotiations. They can also be used effectively for a wide variety of business meetings.

Most collaboration software tools also permit simultaneous voice on the same data connection, although the voice quality can be very poor. If you find this to be the case, you can use a collaboration software tool in conjunction with a voice conference bridge. Although this setup requires separate voice and data connections, it provides the best of both worlds: high-quality voice along with interactive sharing of visual information using PCs.

If you have a private data network protected by a fire wall, you have some built-in security against eavesdropping by unwelcome participants. Most collaboration software tools either include or can be used in conjunction with other software applications to provide as much as 128-bit security encryption. Although such setups do make it more difficult for others to eavesdrop, no method is fail-safe, so do not share highly proprietary or sensitive information using such tools over public networks or the Internet.

Video Web Conferencing

Until recently, video conferences required expensive equipment and network infrastructure, thus limiting their widespread use. With the introduction of inexpensive PC Web cameras, it is now possible to have a video conference as easily as making a telephone call. Video Web conferencing can be done by using many of the collaboration software tools mentioned previously or by using standalone packages. Although the quality of such video conferences often leaves something to be desired, they can be useful for one-on-one meetings—especially in a broadcast mode to give remote participants a greater sense of connection for something like a kick-off meeting. Video conferencing raises the same security considerations as software collaboration tools.

Interactive Chat

The last tool that can be used for meetings is interactive chat software, such Microsoft® Windows® Messenger, Netscape® AOL® Instant Messenger™, and Yahoo!® Messenger. Interactive chat allows you to establish a connection between one or more parties and to exchange text or graphics on a virtual bulletin board. Although this tool is very useful for short, frequent communication between a small number of parties, it can also be used quite effectively as a coaching tool by managers with employees at other locations. On conference calls, you can establish an instant messaging connection with a new employee on the same call and use this connection to provide tips or even answer questions. This real-time feedback is invaluable in helping the new employee learn faster, handle problems better, and establish credibility quicker with others.

E-mail

E-mail has become the most common tool for exchanging documents and collecting information. With your e-mail service, you can establish a team e-mail or broadcast list that team members can use to easily share information with everyone. If your e-mail travels over a public network or the Internet, be aware that of security issues. Be wise about what to send by e-mail, and caution all team members to be wise also.

Extremely easy to use and nearly universally accessible, e-mail is also one of the most frequently abused tools for sharing documents. Don't constantly broadcast e-mail messages to your team. Take the time to write concise, clear, and articulate e-mails. If you are using e-mail to exchange documents, be aware of the size of the files and how long it may take team members to download them. Compress large files using applications such as WinZip®, PKZIP®, or StuffIt®, and try to limit the number of times documents are sent and re-sent by the team.

War Room

A business planning workroom, traditionally referred to as a "war room," has tremendous value for companies with a geographic concentration of employees. The term "war room" is a reference to a command center in the military where information on a battle is collected and displayed to support decisions by the battle commander and staff. A war room gives the team a secure (i.e., lockable), dedicated workspace where information can be collected and posted for use by the team, promoting team building and creating continuity on large complex deals or those that span long periods of time. The use of war rooms to support the capture of large deals continues to be the norm at successful government contractors such as Lockheed Martin, General Dynamics, Boeing, Raytheon, and SAIC.

With new technology, war rooms are being replaced with "virtual war rooms." One common way to build a virtual war room is by using a server on your company network to establish a file-sharing point accessible to the team. There is a wide range of sharing point applications, from the simple to the sophisticated, including such applications as Microsoft® SharePoint™, Open Text® Livelink®, and IBM® Lotus® QuickPlace®.

One of the major considerations in the type of file-sharing point you create is who has access to view documents and who has access to edit and add documents. You should make documents readily available to the team; however, you generally do not want them to be changed or overwritten. Most applications allow you to limit some users to "read-only" access to prevent them from overwriting documents.

There are also considerations of access to information within the buying or selling team and between teams, so you need to consider how information can be partitioned. For example, not everyone on the team needs access to pricing information, and even fewer should have access to the internal business case information. Most applications allow access permissions to be established for each folder of files, and many permit limiting access on a file-by-file basis. Be sure to wisely balance the need for security with the costs—if you establish file-level permissions, someone will have to establish and monitor them as files are created and new team members join the project.

Intranet Web Site

You can also establish a file-sharing point by creating an intranet Web site to post documents for the team, using applications such as Microsoft® FrontPage® or hypertext markup language (HTML). One of the inherent benefits of an intranet site is that only the intranet administrator can add or edit documents. There are a variety of ways to limit access.

Use the Power of Questions

The skillful use of questions can be a powerful way to gather information, demonstrate concern, and effectively communicate with others. Unfortunately, outside of law schools, questioning skills are seldom taught. There are two main types of questions: closed-ended and open-ended.

Closed-ended questions can be used to direct a conversation to a desired area or to gain commitment to a certain position. For example, "If we meet your requirement, you will award the contract to us, correct?" Likewise, closed-ended questions can be helpful for buyers and sellers when you are trying to achieve a concession or close a deal. For example, "If we include an extended warranty and one year of technical support at no additional charge, would you be willing to pay full price for the computer equipment?" The purpose of closed-ended questioning is to start a conversation, confirm a deal, or gain a concession from another without extended discussions.

Open-ended questions yield much more information than closed-ended questions do. Open-ended questions often begin with one of the five w's (who, what, where, when, or why) or how. Open-ended questions are more effective to gain information because they do not lead the respondent in any specific direction or certain position. For example, "What would it take to make you happy with this deal?" or "What kind of feedback have you received about this software?"

So what are the advantages of asking questions? See **Table 5-7**.

Table 5-7 12 Reasons People Ask Questions

1. Engage others in thinking.	**7.** Check level of interest.
2. Gain information.	**8.** Reach agreement.
3. Clarify information.	**9.** Determine behavioral style.
4. Refocus attention.	**10.** Gain participation.
5. Verify information.	**11.** Give information.
6. Check understanding.	**12.** Reduce tension.

The manner and timing of a question is as important or more important than its content. Structure your questions carefully. Consider the timing of your questions. The following are a few key points to help you maximize the power of questions:

1. Have a goal for each question.
2. Know the other party.
3. Begin with broad questions, and then move to more specific questions.
4. Know when to ask each question.
5. Know whom to ask each question.
6. Build on previous statements.
7. Seek permission to ask a question.
8. After you ask a question, stop talking.
9. Listen to others' responses.
10. Take good notes or minutes, and document items requiring action.

A Personal Story: The Grand Inquisitor and the Apprentice

by Gregory A. Garrett

Years ago, I made a big transition from serving as an active-duty U.S. Air Force (USAF) military officer who was assigned as an acquisition action officer at USAF headquarters in the Pentagon, to working in a small business. The founder and president of the small business was my boss. I joined the small business because of the great opportunities and challenges it offered. Plus, I had great respect for the founder and president, who offered to coach me as his apprentice. The small business had fewer than 15 full-time employees, fewer than 20 independent consultants, and less than $5 million in annual revenue. I often referred to the founder and president of this small business (with deep affection) as "The Grand Inquisitor." He often referred to me as his young apprentice.

The founder and president of the small business was extremely skilled at three things:

1. He was willing to take risks.
2. He attracted great talent to his firm.
3. He was able to gather and analyze vast amounts of information quickly through his outstanding questioning skills.

During the four years that I served with the firm, I learned a great deal from "The Grand Inquisitor," especially about using the power of questions. In 1997, we sold the firm. At the time of sale, the firm had more than 150 full-time employees, more than 300 independent consultants, a Who's Who list of multinational Fortune 100 companies as clients, and annual revenues expected to exceed $100 million. Spending four years in this small business prepared me to become a business leader in one of the largest, most successful companies in the world. Serving as an apprentice to a highly successful business leader can be a valuable experience, especially if that leader can help you grow your skills and prepare you for future success.

So how well do you ask questions? Do you take the time to consider your questions before the conversation begins? Do you ask clarifying questions? How willing are you to take business risks? Just food for thought.

Summary

In this chapter, we have discussed the second step of the Six Steps to Success (S3) leadership process. Specifically, we have examined numerous aspects of effectively communicating with others in a buying or selling business environment. We have provided numerous best practices proven effective in communication, ranging from the top 10 topics to talk about, to how to deliver the message, how to look like a leader, how to listen and observe, the power of nice, how to apply technology tools, and the power of questions. Further, we have provided valuable buying and selling insights through the personal story and interview to help you improve how you talk the talk.

In the next chapter, we discuss Step 3, Walk the Talk. Talk is good, but cheap. In life and in business, it is performance and results that count. Remember, our focus is on business excellence with integrity; talk is just one step in the process.

Questions to Consider

1. How effectively and frequently do your organization's key business leaders communicate with you?
2. How effectively does your supervisor talk the talk?
3. How well do you deliver a message?
4. How effectively do you use the power of nice?
5. How well do you use the power of questions?

Chapter 6

Leadership Step 3: Walk the Talk

"The way to gain a good reputation is to endeavor to be what you desire to appear."
—Socrates

A Personal Perspective: *Honor Your Commitments*
by Gregory A. Garrett

The U.S. military tradition runs deep in my family. For more than three generations, members of my family have served in the U.S. Marines and U.S. Army, and I served as an officer in the U.S. Air Force. In the U.S. military, you are taught the importance of sacrifice and the need to serve a larger purpose than yourself. You are taught to live your life by a code—duty, honor, country. You are taught that your word is your bond. For most U.S. military officers, the code is how we choose to live our lives; serving our country is considered an honor.

Often today, I work in an environment in which many people I encounter do not choose to live their personal or professional life by a code of honor, ethics, and integrity. Unfortunately, during the past 30 years, many people have come to view such things as outdated, old school, not highly relevant. As a result, we live in an age when many people lie, cheat, steal, deceive, and blame others on a daily basis for nearly everything. Today, criminals are often celebrated, sometimes elected to public office, and some are even given their own television shows to tell others how to do business.

It may sound corny, but I believe in the old school approach—honor your commitments, respect others, and choose to be a person of excellence. As a chief compliance officer, it is my job to help others achieve business excellence with integrity, which is easy to say but hard to do. I find that most of my time is spent implementing education, training, and awareness programs to help people know what is right so that they can choose to do what is right. Ultimately, if a person was not raised in an environment that taught him or her to care about being a person of excellence—a person of honor, ethics, and integrity—then it is very hard for any organization to prevent that person from exercising bad judgment and committing ethical violations.

I have learned that honor, ethics, and integrity all start at home with the family and then are either supported or not supported by friends, the community, and the workplace. At the workplace, ethical behavior really begins with the tone at the top of the organization. Whether you are in the public or the private business sector, it is how and what the senior organizational leaders say, do, and don't do that determines whether your organization is able to achieve excellence with integrity. While talk is always important, it is how you choose to walk the talk that counts. So remember the old school approach: honor your commitments, respect others, and strive to become a person of excellence who makes a positive difference in the lives of others.

Introduction

In this chapter, we focus on the importance for buying and selling leaders of mastering the ability to walk the talk or, in other words, honoring their commitments. Specifically, we address the 10 key actions listed in **Table 6-1.**

Table 6-1 Walk the Talk: 10 Key Actions for Buyers and Sellers
1. Communicate the organization's vision, goals, metrics, and results.
2. Listen to your team members.
3. Listen to your customers.
4. Leverage your suppliers.
5. Hold people accountable.
6. Conduct appropriate team meetings.
7. Display a positive, "can do" attitude.
8. Provide appropriate supplier evaluation.
9. Recognize and reward individual and team performance.
10. Facilitate knowledge transfer and management.

Communicate the Organization's Vision, Goals, Metrics, and Results

An effective buying or selling team leader regularly communicates to team members the organization's vision, goals, performance metrics, and results. Communicating the organization's vision is very important to helping all team members develop a shared understanding or common bond regarding where you want the organization to be in the future. Sharing the organization's goals with all team members and appropriate business partners is vital to success. Everyone needs to know, understand, and support the organization's goals.

To make the organization's vision and goals become reality, you must develop and communicate appropriate performance metrics to regularly assess the organization's progress toward the desired goals. In addition, successful team leaders have learned it is a proven best practice to regularly inform all team members about the status of business results. Everyone needs to know what is happening within the organization. The team needs real-time, accurate information so that team members can appropriately evaluate performance and determine what is working and what is not working. When you are communicating your organization's vision, goals, performance metrics, and results, it is best to use a multimedia approach **(Table 6-2).**

Remember, most adults need to see, hear, read, and discuss information multiple times before they can commit the information to memory. Further, if the information is not reinforced regularly, then it usually will not be valued and could be lost or erased from memory.

Table 6-2 Communications Through a Multimedia Approach
▪ Face-to-face meetings
▪ Teleconferences
▪ Web site
▪ E-mails
▪ Net meetings
▪ Video conferences
▪ Personal notes and letters
▪ Posters
▪ Stickers and mementos

Listen to Your Team Members

As a buying or selling team leader, your primary job is to serve as a force multiplier. Said differently, as a team leader, your job is to help motivate others to achieve a higher level of performance than they would achieve if left alone. To become a force multiplier it is essential to understand what helps motivate your team members (e.g., a challenging job, more coaching, a mentor, an opportunity for training, an opportunity for travel, flexible hours, more money, increased respect, an opportunity to feel needed, an opportunity to help others, an opportunity to relocate, positive feedback from others, a new job or growth opportunity, a promotion, a new office, more vacation time).

The best way to find out what motivates your team members is to ask. We suggest that you first ask all of your team members individually what you can do to help them improve their performance. Listen and take notes. Later, have a face-to-face meeting or private teleconference with each team member to discuss what you can do and plan to do to help him or her achieve those goals and the organization's goals. Listening is the key to unlocking the potential for higher team performance. As previously discussed, it is important to practice proactive listening, engaging your eyes, ears, and mind at the same time.

Listen to Your Customers

It is equally critical to listen to your customers—to seek to understand their problems, needs, desires, budgets, and time lines. Few things are as important to buying and selling team leaders as spending quality time with their customers—seeking to improve mutual understanding, building a strong professional relationship, and developing a sense of trust and mutual respect.

Regrettably, customers are not always right. Sometimes customers are wrong. Sometimes they have unrealistic expectations. A professional buying or selling team leader will teach both customers and team members what is fair and reasonable for all parties concerned.

Taking the time to listen to your customers does not imply that you must or should always agree with them; however, you should always know what the customer wants, when the customer wants it, why the customer wants it, and what the customer is willing to pay to get it!

In addition, it is very important to work with customers to develop customized or tailored solutions (products and services) that meet their current needs and, if possible, can be scaled to meet their future needs. We have also learned that it is vital to mutually create performance-based requirements, joint performance-based metrics, and contract incentives to properly motivate business success. Remember, real business success can occur only if you take time to listen to your customers.

There are numerous proven, effective means to listen to your customers, including the following:

- **Telephone surveys.** Phone surveys are excellent methods if time is of the essence, the questions are not intrusive, and the survey is not too long. Great care must be taken to verify accuracy. Phone surveys are excellent listening tools, but they have limitations, because there are no visual aids and because people often will not participate for long periods of time.
- **E-mail surveys.** E-mail surveys can be slightly longer than telephone surveys because respondents fill out the questionnaires at their own pace. Well-crafted questionnaires help eliminate potential interviewer bias. E-mail surveys allow companies to gather a greater quantity of information than telephone surveys. Respondents also have more opportunity to think about their answers and provide more detailed information. Additionally, e-mail surveys allow respondents to answer questions anonymously, while providing a way to present the

business opportunity to customers in a high-quality, standardized manner. E-mail surveys also have limitations. First, the response rate is generally lower than with other survey tools. Second, the surveys may get lost among other e-mails. Third, respondents may not complete the entire survey.

- **Customer visits and interviews.** One of the best ways to gather customer information and assess customer satisfaction is to go to the customer's location and ask the customer's representatives what they like and do not like about your company and its products or services and what they perceive as your company's strengths and weaknesses. A major advantage of customer visits and personal interviews is that the interviewer can gather information from verbal and nonverbal responses to questions. Customer visits are very expensive, especially if customers are spread over a wide geographic area. **Table 6-3** provides tips for sellers conducting customer interviews.
- **Customer focus groups.** These groups consist of customer representatives brought together to participate in discussions of topics, questions, products, or services. Customer focus groups are sometimes referred to as user groups and can be very effective when dealing with improvements to existing products, product features, and customer support services. Limitations to customer focus groups include (1) a dominant individual who overly influences discussions, (2) an ineffective moderator who allows discussions to diverge from the topic, and (3) time constraints.
- **Front-line customer contact.** Perhaps the most valuable customer feedback is found in the day-to-day personal discussions, e-mails, telephone calls, conference calls, and actual work that employees share with the customer.

Table 6-3 Tips for Sellers Conducting Customer Interviews

- The interviewer must have a professional appearance.
- The interviewer must have a thorough knowledge of the specific characteristics and requirements of the customers' projects.
- The interviewer should clarify the roles and responsibilities of the **seller's** key personnel who interface with the customer.
- The interviewer should seek to understand what the customer perceives as the **seller's** strengths and areas for improvement.
- The interviewer should understand the customer's key performance areas and metrics.

Leverage Your Suppliers

According to the *2005 Cross-Industry Benchmarking Survey of Outsourcing*, conducted by the *Center for Advanced Purchasing Studies*, more than 45 percent of the revenue that a typical company earns is spent outsourcing (purchasing products and services from other companies).[1] For the past four years, the use of outsourcing has been increasing at an average rate of 5 percent each year. Thus, it is clear that outsourcing, in both the public and the private business sectors, is increasing and is vital to business success. **Table 6-4** provides a summary of 12 best practices of supply-chain management that have proven effective when outsourcing.

Table 6-4 Supply-Chain Management: 12 Best Practices

1. Retain only core work (products, services, and solutions).
2. Outsource the rest of the work (to vendors or subcontractors).
3. Reduce the number of suppliers.
4. Improve demand forecast accuracy.
5. Increase inventory turns.
6. Decrease outsourcing costs per unit by leveraging major vendors and subcontractors for lower prices.
7. Increase standardization of products, as much as possible and as appropriate.
8. Increase global sourcing, especially in geographic areas of lower labor costs.
9. Maximize economies of scale.
10. Seek global demand for products and services.
11. Increase automation and database integration between business partners using enterprise resource planning software tools and Web-based trade exchanges.
12. Use technology tools to increase speed to market, reduce costs, and obtain real-time accurate information.

However, more and more companies in this e-business age have realized that supply-chain management as a procurement concept is good, but not good enough. To create a truly integrated supply chain, a new global hub or trade exchange for each industry must be created that will allow all players to connect their internal systems to the internal systems of other companies through the Web. Real integration means providing enterprise resource planning (ERP) between buyers, sellers, and subcontractors as appropriate.

Buyers can achieve an integrated supply chain only if they develop trusted partnerships with suppliers, who, in turn, serve as value-added business service providers. Today, large vertical trade exchanges, built cooperatively by industry participants, are changing the nature of competition. Many winning companies have decided that because the Web is so accessible and efficient, competing on the basis of connectivity throughout the supply chain is no longer good business. As a result, many competitors are cooperating to build efficient Web connections and then competing to use these new capabilities to achieve greater customer satisfaction.

E-business is forcing businesses worldwide to re-examine how they do business. Today, the questions that chief executive officers (CEOs) have to answer are more like "How do I design, manufacture, or outsource and distribute products, services, and solutions to meet or exceed my customer's needs?" than "What quantity of my off-the-shelf products do I have to sell in order to make my quarterly or annual revenue target?" Winning companies realize that they must help customers reduce their internal direct and indirect procurement costs. The following case studies describe a few recent best practices.

Case Study: Cisco Systems

By employing its own Internet strategy and solutions, Cisco Systems has successfully maintained its agility, culture of empowerment, and competitive advantage. All of Cisco's business operations, including finance, supply-chain management, and employee communications, are Internet based. Today, Cisco transacts nearly 90 percent of orders and 82 percent of customer support inquiries over the Web. Using outsourcing and the Internet has allowed Cisco to create a virtual manufacturing system that seamlessly manages 37 global plants as one. Cisco's Internet technology and global, real-time, project-level accounting allow the company to virtually close their financial books each fiscal quarter within 24 hours.

Case Study: Hormel Foods

Hormel Foods recently completed installation of Oracle Internet Procurement at all of its 50 locations. Employees at these sites can now create purchasing requisitions for non-production items and have them automatically routed for approval, as well as track and access information in real time. Self-guiding online catalogs allow workers to search for goods and services from approved suppliers. Most of the savings associated with the implementation of Oracle® Internet Procurement result from Hormel's procurement personnel no longer spending considerable time on routine purchases. Additional savings will be realized through the elimination of non contract purchases. Hormel also values the fact that its procurement personnel now have more time to devote to the professional tasks of creating, managing, and leveraging partnerships with its suppliers.

Case Study: The Limited

The Limited is regarded as one of the world's most successful retailers of apparel. Although all of its retail outlets are located inside the United States, it has successfully established global sourcing practices. The process from product design to shipment of garments to stores takes fewer than 60 days, a dramatically lower cycle time than its competitors require. In addition, superior global supply-chain management allows The Limited to have garments designed by numerous companies throughout Europe, produced by local manufacturers in Asia and elsewhere, and shipped using global logistics networks to Columbus, Ohio, where the garments are distributed to the thousands of retail outlets of The Limited, Express, Victoria's Secret, Abercrombie and Fitch, Lerner, Henri Bendel, and others.

Case Study: The Ford Motor Company

The Ford Motor Company Customer Service Division, supplying more than 500,000 service parts to more than 10,000 dealerships around the world, faced delivery variables for any given part ranging from 30 percent per time period to 400 percent. Yet the division required virtually on-demand availability for each service or repair. The Ford division partnered with a team from Cap Gemini Ernst & Young to improve legacy systems integration using distribution resource planning tools that improved forecasting and inventory visibility throughout the supply chain. Tools were developed to measure volatility and to streamline inventory lead time, thereby shortening supply-chain lead times. Customer fill rates improved from 93 percent to 98 percent in the United States and from 93.6 percent to 96.8 percent in Europe.

Hold People Accountable

To be held accountable, people must know their roles and responsibilities. Team members contribute to the accomplishment of project and customer goals by fulfilling roles and responsibilities. Contributions can include both formal and informal service to the team. Formal contributions typically include the expected roles and responsibilities of a specific functional discipline. Informal contributions often vary depending on each team member's personal strengths, including computer skills, negotiating skills, writing skills, planning skills, analytical and technical skills, and communication skills.

Every buying or selling team must create its own member roles and responsibilities on the basis of project requirements and the talents of the team members. Team members' roles and responsibilities must evolve as the environment changes. Likewise, members must be comfortable in a frequently changing environment. Many organizations spend a great deal of time and money developing standard "role and responsibility" documents for employees. While having such standard documents is good, being able to alter and adapt them quickly and cost-effectively is not only better but also critical in today's ever-changing business environment.

Team member roles and responsibilities should include

- A clear and concise statement of each individual's objectives and expected results
- An understanding of each individual's scope of work and level of accountability
- An understanding of each individual's span of resources control, including people, funds, facilities, and equipment

The following are several proven tools and techniques for building, sustaining, and improving accountability and teamwork in a complex, outsourced project environment. The key to successfully implementing these tools and techniques is knowing when to use them and how to tailor them to a specific situation.

Project Charter

A key action to gain recognition and support for a new project and its team is to formally charter the project, program, or program management office. The charter should perform several functions:

- Identify the project or program and its importance to the organization.
- Appoint a project leader.
- Acknowledge the members of the integrated (multifunctional) project team (customer, supplier, and supply-chain partners).
- Establish top-level responsibilities and authority.
- Establish the resource commitment (people, funds, facilities, etc.).
- Confirm the project or program executive sponsor or champion.
- State overall customer-focused project goals.

Form 6-1 provides a project charter outline to help teams develop effective formal project charters for their major projects or programs.

Form 6-1 Project Charter Outline

1. Project name or title: ____________________ **2.** Date: __________

3. Importance of project: ______________________________

____

____

4. Overall scope of project: ______________________________

____

____

5. Name of project leader: ______________________________

6. Project team members and roles: ______________________________

____

____

7. Authority and responsibilities of project leader: __________

____

____

8. Customer-focused project goals: ______________________________

____

____

9. Resources commitment: ______________________________

____

____

10. Project executive sponsor and champion: __________

____

____

Code of Conduct

Table 6-5 provides a sample code of conduct successfully used by several senior program management directors and vice presidents at Lucent Technologies to simply and concisely convey the importance of mutual respect in building teamwork and achieving project status.

Most organizations and companies have detailed guidelines for professional and ethical business practices to ensure their employees are good corporate citizens and obey all appropriate federal, state, and local laws, regulations, and business guidelines. Today, more than ever, professional business conduct is imperative to achieve short-term and long-term success. For integrated project teams with customers, sellers, and supply-chain partners working closely together, professional and ethical behavior by all is mandatory. **Figure 6-1** illustrates some of the common legal conduct issues that must be addressed to ensure proper employee business conduct.

Table 6-5 Project Team: Code of Conduct (sample)

- **R** = Be Respectful of others' time, opinions, ideas, and contributions
- **E** = Empower people to make decisions and do their jobs
- **S** = Support the Lucent "Team" and individual team members
- **P** = Practice Professional behavior at all times
- **E** = Escalate and handle problems Early before they become a crisis
- **C** = Have a "Can Do" attitude
- **T** = Trust others to listen and do the right thing

Source: Gregory A. Garrett

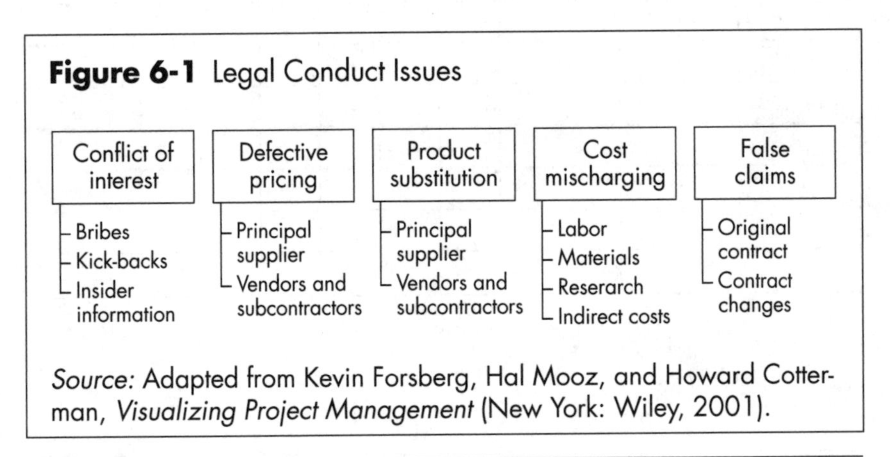

Figure 6-1 Legal Conduct Issues

Source: Adapted from Kevin Forsberg, Hal Mooz, and Howard Cotterman, *Visualizing Project Management* (New York: Wiley, 2001).

Responsibility Assignment Matrix

One of the easiest yet most effective ways to communicate team members' project duties is through the use of a responsibility assignment matrix (RAM). **Form 6-2** provides a basic RAM that can be tailored for any project.

Form 6-2 Responsibility Assignment Matrix

Team member/ role/name/ phone/ e-mail	Concept phase			Design phase			Implementation phase			Operations and maintenance phase		
	Task	Task	Task	Task	Task	Task	Task	Task	Task	Task	Task	Task

Form 6-3 provides another example of how a RAM can be simply developed to ensure that roles and responsibilities are clearly understood by all team members.

Form 6-3 Responsibility Assignment Matrix

Role	Responsibilities
Project Leader	Creates capture plan, working with team members, including identification of deliverables, work tasks, resources and time line
	Ensures information is communicated throughout team and between subteams
	Monitors work tasks to ensure overall time line is met
	Manages stakeholder approval session and ensures company approvals are secured
	Oversees Alert-Jeopardy-Escalation Plan and ensures timely resolution of issues
	Oversees change control plan and ensures approved changes are communicated to team
	Develops risk mitigation plan working with team leaders
Proposal Manager	Acts as single point of contact regarding development of customer deliverables
	Collects inputs, edits, formats, and produces finished deliverables
	Runs pink team and red team reviews
	Oversees production, packaging and shipment of customer deliverables
Sales Manager	Acts as the single point of contact to address all customer matters
	Develops win themes and strategies
	Leads completion of competitive assessment
	Translates customer business needs into technical and delivery requirements
	Serves as a surrogate for the customer to answer questions, provide assumptions and/or direction regarding missing or unclear information
	Writes executive summary

Form 6-3 Responsibility Assignment Matrix, continued

Role	Responsibilities
Technical Manager	Acts as the single point of contact to address all technical matters
	Identifies, organizes, and directs technical personnel to complete technical response
	Identifies, organizes, and directs technical support to design the solution
	Translates customer business needs into technical requirements for the solution
	Certifies that all components of the solution are properly reflected in the pricing
	Supports assessment of competitors solution technical strengths and weaknesses
	Identifies and recommends strategies to mitigate technical risks
Project (Delivery) Manager	Acts as the single point of contact to address all delivery matters
	Identifies, organizes, and directs program management, order and billing, engineering, installation, documentation, training, and OA&M personnel to complete delivery response
	Identifies, organizes, and directs support resources to create a delivery plan
	Translates customer business needs into delivery requirements for the solution
	Certifies that all components of the delivery plan are properly reflected in the pricing
	Supports assessment of competitors solution delivery strengths and weaknesses
	Identifies and recommends strategies to mitigate delivery risks

Form 6-3 Responsibility Assignment Matrix, continued

Role	Responsibilities
Pricing Manager	Acts as single point of contact to address all pricing matters
	Identifies, organizes, and directs pricing personnel to complete pricing response
	Supports business manager in development of business case
	Ensures appropriate approvals have been secured for pricing included in response
	Certifies pricing is complete and accurate
	Supports assessment of competitors solution pricing and creation of price targets
	Identifies and recommends strategies to mitigate pricing risks
Contractual Manager	Acts as single point of contact to address all contractual matters
	Identifies, organizes, and directs contracts, legal and purchasing personnel to complete contractual response
	Certifies that all terms and conditions are consistent with company polices and that all contractual language has been properly approved
	Supports assessment of competitors solution contractual strengths and weaknesses
	Identifies and recommends strategies to mitigate contractual risk

Source: Adapted from Gregory A. Garrett and Reginald J. Kipke, *The Capture Management Life Cycle* (Chicago: CCH, 2003).

Multiparty Participation Matrix

It is vital for everyone—the customer, a principal supplier, and vendors or supply-chain partners—to understand who does what and who is the leader in specific project activities throughout the project life cycle. **Form 6-4** is a multiparty participation matrix designed to help clarify each party's role throughout the typical integrated project management process.

Form 6-4 Multiparty Participation Matrix

	Buyer	Seller	Vendors or supply-chain partners		
Integrated project management process element			**Vendor A**	**Vendor B**	**Vendor C**
1.0 Concept					
1.1 Describe project and determine project management need					
1.1.1 Create opportunity overview					
1.1.2 Determine need for project management services					
1.1.3 Assign project manager and provide funding					
1.1.4 Determine project and project management level					
1.2 Conduct project risk assessment					
1.2.1 Conduct business case and technical design reviews					
1.2.2 Write project qualification report					

Legend: I = Information only P = Participate in process
L = Lead process

Form 6-4 Multiparty Participation Matrix, continued

	Buyer	Seller	Vendors or supply-chain partners		
Integrated project management process element			**Vendor A**	**Vendor B**	**Vendor C**
1.2.3 Review project qualification report					
1.3 Obtain decision to proceed					
2.0 Pre-award planning					
2.1 Identify planning resources					
2.2 Assess levels of participation					
2.3 Convene planning team					
2.4 Develop preliminary project plan					
2.4.1 Review and understand customer requirements					
2.4.2 Revise preliminary scope statement					
2.4.3 Develop preliminary work breakdown structure					
2.4.4 Develop preliminary project schedule					
2.4.5 Develop preliminary staffing plan					

Legend: I = Information only P = Participate in process
L = Lead process

Form 6-4 Multiparty Participation Matrix, continued

	Buyer	Seller	Vendors or supply-chain partners		
Integrated project management process element			**Vendor A**	**Vendor B**	**Vendor C**
2.4.6 Develop preliminary project budget					
2.4.7 Develop preliminary test and acceptance plan					
2.4.8 Develop preliminary risk management plan					
2.4.9 Develop proposal baseline configuration					
2.5 Support proposal and contract negotiation process					
2.5.1 Develop preferred and mandatory terms and conditions					
2.5.2 Finalize bid–no bid decision					
2.5.3 Submit proposal					
2.5.4 Assist in contract negotiations					
2.5.5 Revise risk management plan					
2.5.6 Document lessons learned					

Legend: I = Information only P = Participate in process L = Lead process

Form 6-4 Multiparty Participation Matrix, continued

	Buyer	Seller	Vendors or supply-chain partners		
Integrated project management process element			**Vendor A**	**Vendor B**	**Vendor C**
3.0 Post-award planning					
3.1 Review and summarize contract					
3.1.1 Validate customer requirements through internal requirements analysis					
3.1.2 Review contract requirements and prepare contract tracking summary					
3.1.3 Prepare functional baseline					
3.1.4 Attend post-award orientation with customer					
3.2 Reissue project charter and build project team					
3.2.1 Determine project team structure					
3.2.2 Reissue project charter					
3.2.3 Develop resource responsibility matrix					
3.2.4 Finalize staffing plan					

Legend: I = Information only P = Participate in process
L = Lead process

Form 6-4 Multiparty Participation Matrix, continued

	Buyer	Seller	Vendors or supply-chain partners		
Integrated project management process element			**Vendor A**	**Vendor B**	**Vendor C**
3.2.5 Obtain resource commitment					
3.2.6 Obtain logistical support					
3.3 Conduct internal project kick-off meeting					
3.4 Conduct project plan workshop					
3.4.1 Plan workshop and notify team members					
3.4.2 Develop project plan					
3.4.2.1 Create baseline work breakdown structure at work package level					
3.4.2.2 Create baseline project budget					
3.4.2.3 Create baseline project schedule					
3.4.2.4 Develop supporting project plan elements					
3.4.3 Prepare supporting plans					
3.4.3.1 Revise risk management plan					
Legend: I = Information only P = Participate in process L = Lead process					

Form 6-4 Multiparty Participation Matrix, continued

	Buyer	Seller	Vendors or supply-chain partners		
Integrated project management process element			**Vendor A**	**Vendor B**	**Vendor C**
3.4.3.2 Prepare finance plan					
3.4.3.3 Prepare baseline implementation plan					
3.4.3.4 Prepare customer relations plan					
3.4.3.5 Prepare baseline subcontracting plan					
3.4.3.6 Prepare quality assurance plan					
3.4.3.7 Prepare training plan					
3.4.3.8 Prepare safety plan					
3.4.3.9 Prepare product baseline and test and acceptance plan					
3.4.3.10 Prepare transition plan					
3.4.3.11 Prepare life-cycle management plan					
3.4.3.12 Prepare baseline configuration management and change control plan					
3.4.3.13 Prepare project management plan					

Legend: I = Information only P = Participate in process
L = Lead process

Form 6-4 Multiparty Participation Matrix, continued					
	Buyer	**Seller**	**Vendors or supply-chain partners**		
Integrated project management process element			**Vendor A**	**Vendor B**	**Vendor C**
3.4.4 Develop allocated baseline and detailed system design					
3.4.5 Document and distribute kick-off and workshop minutes					
3.5 Develop integrated project plan					
3.5.1 Coordinate supporting plans					
3.5.2 Prepare baseline project plan for customer review					
3.6 Hold customer kick-off meeting					
3.6.1 Develop and distribute the agenda					
3.6.2 Establish roles and responsibilities					
3.6.3 Review baseline project plan					
3.6.4 Review change control process					
3.7 Finalize baseline project plan					
Legend: I = Information only P = Participate in process L = Lead process					

Form 6-4 Multiparty Participation Matrix, continued

	Buyer	Seller	Vendors or supply-chain partners		
Integrated project management process element			**Vendor A**	**Vendor B**	**Vendor C**
4.0 Implementation					
4.1 Establish and maintain project management information system					
4.1.1 Organize and coordinate project information flow					
4.1.2 Receive and review project status reports					
4.2 Monitor and control project					
4.2.1 Audit project performance					
4.2.2 Issue regular project status reports					
4.2.3 Hold regular project status meetings					
4.3 Manage cost, schedule, and resource variance					
4.3.1 Manage cost variance					
4.3.2 Manage schedule variance					
4.3.3 Manage resource use					

Legend: I = Information only P = Participate in process L = Lead process

Form 6-4 Multiparty Participation Matrix, continued

Integrated project management process element	Buyer	Seller	Vendors or supply-chain partners		
			Vendor A	Vendor B	Vendor C
4.4 Control changes to project					
4.4.1 Identify and communicate change					
4.4.2 Evaluate effect on budget, schedule, and architectural baseline					
4.4.3 Execute contract change					
4.4.4 Implement change					
4.5 Manage technical progress					
4.5.1 Review technical progress					
4.5.2 Conduct quality reviews					
4.6 Manage contract with customer					
4.6.1 Review customer contract compliance					
4.6.2 Document and control contract changes					
4.6.3 Monitor customer billing and payment					
4.7 Manage suppliers					
4.7.1 Review supplier performance					

Legend: I = Information only P = Participate in process L = Lead process

Form 6-4 Multiparty Participation Matrix, continued

	Buyer	Seller	Vendors or supply-chain partners		
Integrated project management process element			**Vendor A**	**Vendor B**	**Vendor C**
4.7.2 Manage subcontract changes					
4.7.3 Review supplier billing and monitor payments					
4.8 Manage risk					
4.8.1 Review status of high-risk events					
4.8.2 Reassess risk based on environmental and project changes					
4.9 Manage test and acceptance					
4.9.1 Perform predelivery or milestone test and acceptance					
4.9.2 Perform final system test and acceptance					
4.10 Obtain customer sign-off					
5.0 Close-out					
5.1 Transition to operations and support					
5.1.1 Hold customer satisfaction review					
5.1.2 Hold transition meeting					

Legend: I = Information only P = Participate in process
L = Lead process

Form 6-4 Multiparty Participation Matrix, continued

	Buyer	Seller	Vendors or supply-chain partners		
Integrated project management process element			**Vendor A**	**Vendor B**	**Vendor C**
5.1.3 Establish customer follow-up and monitoring process					
5.2 Close out project internally					
5.2.1 Prepare and review final schedule and cost reports					
5.2.2 Verify final project billing					
5.2.3 Finalize historical project documentation					
5.3 Hold final project team critique and review					
5.3.1 Review all plans to ensure project completion					
5.3.2 Provide team and individual recognition					
5.3.3 Disperse project team					

Legend: I = Information only P = Participate in process
L = Lead process

Conduct Appropriate Team Meetings

To successfully walk the talk, you must conduct frequent team meetings to keep all team members well informed. The frequency (daily, weekly, biweekly, monthly) will vary with the situation. The communication media or mode (face to face, teleconference, net meeting, e-mail, video conference) will vary as well, depending on numerous factors. The key is to practice good business judgment and seek feedback from team members on the value of the meetings, their frequency, and the delivery mode. Some simple rules to remember when planning and conducting team meetings:

- Always have a purpose for the meeting.
- Do not conduct the meeting if the right people are not available.
- Always prepare and distribute an agenda for the meeting.
- Be prepared for the meeting.
- Take good notes.
- Assign action items to people in the meeting.
- Ask questions.
- Seek advice.
- Prepare and distribute meeting minutes and action items.
- Follow up after the meeting.

Selected Interview

Name: Steve Hill

Job Title: Chief Executive Officer

Organization: The AEgis Technologies Group, Inc.

Location: Huntsville, Alabama

Key Responsibilities: Provide a strategic vision and lead strategic planning. Lead, coordinate, and direct all business development efforts. Provide leadership and direction to the senior management team, including vice presidents of the services and products divisions, technology group directors, and directors of operations. Establish and maintain the corporate legal counsel, banking, and outside accounting relationships and representation. Plan for and secure adequate financial working capital. Establish, direct, revise, and oversee the tracking and reporting of all annual budgets and subbudgets for each corporate fiscal year. Recruit, hire, and retain a talented workforce. Mentor and provide guidance to directors for their professional development and training.

Brief Resume: Mr. Hill is cofounder of AEgis Technologies and serves as chief executive officer. As CEO, Mr. Hill provides ongoing executive direction of the AEgis Technologies Group, Inc. and its subsidiary organizations, divisions, sites, infrastructure, and operations. Direct reports include the vice presidents of the services and products divisions and elements of the indirect administrative infrastructure (facilities and administrative, general and administrative, and site operations).

Mr. Hill received a B.S. in electrical engineering from the University of Alabama in Huntsville and has spent most of his 20-year professional career developing, applying, and managing modeling and simulation technologies.

Questions and Answers

Question: What are the most significant challenges you must overcome to be a successful buying or selling team leader?

Answer: Navigating the constant change in the industry and marketplace. Building solid, trusting relationships with employees and customers. Continually finding ways to motivate and empower people to achieve. Staying ahead of the technology curve in products and services. Acknowledging the need to let go and delegate important activities to subordinate roles. Setting and systematically adjusting goals and priorities.

Question: In regard to the Six Steps to Success (S3) leadership process, which step do you believe is the most important? Why?

Answer: They are all important. One could argue that without all six a leader will not be successful or, at least, his or her effectiveness will be suboptimal. The most important step to me personally is Walk the Talk. A leader must have a recognized code of ethics that clearly demonstrates commitment to honesty and integrity. Leaders must listen to their customers and employees to shape their vision and set appropriate goals. They must communicate that vision and hold people accountable to achieving performance-based objectives. And, of course, they must recognize and reward outstanding contributions to the success of the team and organization. All these factors contribute to the leader's credibility with employees and customers. Without credibility, a leader will fail, because he or she cannot motivate and influence people.

Question: Please provide a brief personal experience that you believe best illustrates leadership in buying or selling.

Answer: Leadership is seldom tested during prosperity, but generally through adversity. Over the past couple of years, my leadership was tested when I had to make some hard decisions related to a new software product. The company had invested a significant amount of resources into the development, marketing, and launch of the product. Key employees had a tremendous amount of seat equity and pride in the product, I and other executive managers had plenty of ego involved in trying to make the product successful, and we had a relatively large sunk investment. The product was losing money and our best-laid plans for marketing and selling the product were not working. I made several difficult decisions to cut costs, reorganize the division, and restructure our approaches. I took full responsibility for past poor decisions, communicated clearly the necessity for change, and laid out a new vision for the future. It was not easy, it was not popular with some people, but it needed to be done. The product is now on the road to recovery and profitability. Leadership requires commitment, communication, and the ability to influence and motivate people.

Display a Positive, "Can Do" Attitude

It has been said that your attitude often determines your altitude—in life and in business. No one likes to work with a person who whines, complains, and is negative—it is upsetting and depressing. In comparison, most people enjoy working with someone who has a positive, "can do" attitude and is always up for a challenge. In both buying and selling, your attitude can and often does affect your performance results. People who set higher goals typically achieve more than those who set lesser goals.

Provide Appropriate Supplier Evaluation

Numerous software companies have developed a wide array of database management enterprise resource planning (ERP) tools to facilitate communication in supplier relationship management (SRM). In addition to the numerous SRM software applications available, there are a number of simple, cost-effective tools to help manage supply-chain partners:

- **Principal supplier key actions matrix. Form 6-5** (pages 126–127) provides a useful matrix of key actions that principal suppliers (prime contractors) should perform to successfully manage outsourced projects involving customers and supply-chain partners or subcontractors or vendors.
- **Subcontractor evaluation form. Form 6-6** (pages 128–129) provides a simple, but effective means of evaluating important aspects of a potential supply-chain partner's capabilities.
- **Subcontracting plan outline. Form 6-7** (pages 130–131) is an outline that can be used to prepare a comprehensive subcontracting plan.

Form 6-5 Principal Supplier Key Actions Matrix

	Type of plan											
Plan element	**Risk mgmt.**	**Finance**	**Project mgmt.**	**Marketing and sales**	**Vendor mgmt.**	**Quality assurance**	**Training**	**Safety**	**Test and acceptance**	**Transition**	**Life-cycle mgmt.**	**Config. mgmt.**
Customer relationship management			X	X						X	X	
Customer responsibilities during implementation			X	X								
Customer responsibilities for acceptance review			X	X					X			
Customer responsibilities for change management			X	X								X
Customer responsibilities over project life cycle			X	X							X	
Deliverables requirements and testing			X			X			X			
Design and management of project for a smooth transition			X	X	X					X	X	
Inclusion of risk management strategies in appropriate plans	X	X	X	X	X	X	X	X	X	X	X	X

Form 6-5 Principal Supplier Key Actions Matrix, continued

Plan element	Type of plan											
	Risk mgmt.	Finance	Project mgmt.	Marketing and sales	Vendor mgmt.	Quality assurance	Training	Safety	Test and acceptance	Transition	Life-cycle mgmt.	Config. mgmt.
Project implementation and management training	X		X				X	X	X	X		X
Provision for customer billings		X		X					X			
Provision for principal supplier payment		X		X								
Quality of vendors					X	X						
Provision for vendor payment		X			X							
Quality training requirements				X		X	X					
Vendor responsibilities during implementation			X		X	X						

Form 6-6 Subcontractor Evaluation Form

Level	Low 1	2	3	4	High 5	NOT REQ	Description
Access to equipment							Owns or can acquire equipment required for job
Condition of equipment							Equipment in good repair—maintenance ability
Adequate insurance							Adequate insurance, bonded, and so forth
Access to manpower							Ability to staff and manage required workforce
Dependability and reputation							Work record of contractor
Flexibility							Adaptability to work methods
Job knowledge							Knowledge of required work processes
Job knowledge (ability to learn)							Capacity to learn new work processes
Job experience							Experience with similar jobs or technology
Quality assurance process							Documented QA process
Quality performance							Results of QA inspections exist
Safety performance							Safety processes and equipment—reports (if available)
Local-country national							Subcontractor based in or has tie to country or region of worksite
Supervision experience							Experience as work supervisor
Timeliness of billing reports							Process for billing—need for close supervision by project manager

Form 6-6 Subcontractor Evaluation Form, continued

Level	Low ⟵ 1	2	3	4	⟶ High 5	NOT REQ	Description
Willingness to compromise							Adaptability to work with others
Delivery performance							Ability to deliver on time

Note: Rate the subcontractor on each characteristic, from 1 (least desirable) to 5 (most desirable). If a particular characteristic does not apply, mark the "NOT REQ" box (for not required) instead. Use the ratings to compare subcontractors.

Form 6-7 Subcontracting Plan Outline

1.0 Overview

The subcontracting plan explains the overall project approach to using third-party suppliers or supply-chain partners on the project. Third-party suppliers may provide hardware, perform services, or develop and provide software used in the system. The principal supplier's (prime contractor's) responsibility for supplier management is to ensure that all subcontracted elements are fully integrated into the overall system, and that they are managed integrally throughout the project. Explain the project approach to using subcontractors, and generally describe which project elements will be performed by third-party suppliers. Generally describe the process of managing those suppliers.

2.0 Project Elements to be Subcontracted

Use the work breakdown structure (WBS) to identify which elements will be subcontracted. Describe why subcontractors will be performing those elements and why the principal supplier cannot or should not do the work internally. For each element, discuss the specific requirements for the subcontractor. Provide a schedule showing when subcontracts will be awarded for each element.

3.0 Identification and Selection of Subcontractors

Discuss how subcontractors will be selected. If subcontractors will be competitively selected, identify which principal supplier organizations will be responsible for preparing statements of work and other requirements documentation. Typically, they will be the organizations that have responsibility (shown in the responsibility matrix) for the WBS elements being subcontracted. For each WBS element to be subcontracted, identify the third-party supplier that will perform the work. If that supplier is already known, there is usually no need for a formal procurement procedure.

Form 6-7 Subcontracting Plan Outline, Continued

4.0 Subcontract Management

4.1 Discuss the overall process for managing the subcontracts. What principal supplier organizations will provide legal and contracting support? Who will be responsible for administering subcontract changes and modifications? Who will review progress and approve payment of supplier invoices?

4.2 As each subcontract is awarded, establish a subcontract tracking summary in a file for that subcontract. Use the summary to record the progress of the subcontract throughout its life.

4.3 Assign a project team member or organization the responsibility for managing each subcontract. Identify the responsible parties in this section of the subcontracting plan, as well as on each subcontract tracking summary.

5.0 Supplier Participation in Project Management

Discuss the level of supplier participation in the project management process. Some suppliers may be responsible for major portions of the project. If so, there should be representatives from those suppliers on the project steering committee to facilitate project control and communication. Discuss supplier input to the project management information system. Discuss the level of reporting required from suppliers, and ensure that the input and reports are listed as contractual requirements in the subcontracts.

Recognize and Reward Individual and Team Performance

Regardless of the business environment, buying and selling team leaders should appropriately recognize and reward outstanding performance through awards such as

- Team leader of the quarter or year
- Coach of the quarter or year
- Buying or selling team of the quarter or year
- Team member of the quarter or year

Taking the time and making the effort to formally recognize and reward team members for outstanding performance builds stronger teams and reinforces positive behavior. Recognition may include personal letters of recognition or accomplishment, certificates, e-mail, and phone calls. Rewards can and should vary from saying thank you to cards, gifts, plaques, gift certificates, bonds, stocks, stock options, cash, and so forth. Many organizations have developed a formal nomination process for recognizing and rewarding outstanding performance. **Forms 6-8** and **6-9** provide example nomination forms for a recognition and awards program.

Form 6-8 Team Recognition and Rewards Program Nomination Form: Teamwork Award		
Team name:____________________ Nominated by:____________________ Phone number: __________ E-mail:__________		
Part I. Provide a brief description of the team's accomplishments, including the type of support the team members provide to the customer.		
Part II. Provide information on identification of problems and opportunities and describe how these problems and opportunities contributed to project team goals and customer satisfaction.		
Team members		
Name	**Organization and supervisor**	**E-mail, location**
1.		
2.		
3.		
4.		
5.		
6.		
7.		
8.		

Form 6-9 Team Recognition and Rewards Program Nomination Form: Coach of the Quarter Award
The Coach of the Quarter Award is designed to recognize those individuals who devote their time and effort to facilitating, developing, and training their people. This award recognizes their commitment to achieving and maintaining a world-class project team. Name of nominee:________________ Nominated by:________________ Date submitted:________________
Part I. Explain how this individual demonstrates support to the individuals who report to him or her. Include personal performance platform items, such as sets objectives with employees; provides ongoing guidance and feedback, both formal and informal; supports career development activities; and conducts timely and meaningful performance reviews. Provide examples.
Part II. Provide at least three examples of how this individual exhibits the values of the company, motivates others, and fosters teamwork.
Part III. Briefly describe how this individual supports the initiative of a highly skilled workforce by developing human potential or providing training and learning opportunities while contributing to the success of the project and customer goals.

Facilitate Knowledge Transfer and Management

Because the buying and selling business workforce is aging, it is essential to capture and document the lessons learned by and best practices of senior leaders. Likewise, it is important to transfer the valuable knowledge of senior leaders to newer members of the organization. There are numerous means for capturing, documenting, sharing, and transferring knowledge within a buying or selling organization, including the following:

- Use a sales and business development database for knowledge management. It should be a globally accessible, Web-based data repository that is keyword searchable.

- Use a purchasing and supply-chain management database for knowledge management. It should be a globally accessible, Web-based data repository that is keyword searchable.
- Use a current, accurate, and well-documented buying or selling business methodology. The methodology should include processes, forms, tools, and templates.
- Use an enterprise wide information system.
- Have a sales or business development center of excellence. It should consist of a formal or informal team focused on sharing knowledge throughout the organization.
- Have a purchasing or supply-chain management center of excellence.
- Have a contract management center of excellence.
- Hold monthly "lunch and learn" programs that are conducted by recognized internal organization experts.
- Hold quarterly all-hands meetings featuring presentations by top-performing team members sharing best practices.
- Hold senior leaders focus groups.
- Have a buying and selling community of practice (a group of people in the same functional area sharing knowledge with each other).

Selected Interview

Name: Ron Smith

Job Title: Vice President of Contracts

Organization: GovConnections, Inc.

Location: Rockville, Maryland

Key Responsibilities: Chief compliance official, responsible for all compliance and contract management. Manage contracts portfolio, including federal, state, and local education customers. Manage capture team, including contracts, internal support teams, and consultants. Manage negotiation and implementation of new federal and state and local education contracts.

Brief Resume:

Vice President of Contracts—GovConnection, Inc.

Manager, Public Sector Contracts—Hewlett Packard Corporation

Director, Contracts and Bids, North America—Compaq Computer Corporation

Manager, Public Sector Contracts—Compaq Computer Corporation

Strategic Planning Manager, R&D Center—Northrop Grumman

Director, Government Policy—Grumman Corporation, Woodbury, New York

Director, Corporate Contracts and Business Policy—Grumman Corporation

Contracts Manager and Business Manager—Grumman Corporation

Vice President of Operations—Data Monitor Systems Inc.

Education:

B.A. in journalism, University of Oklahoma, 1971. Graduate studies at the University of Oklahoma and University of Houston

Certification:

Certified Professional Contracts Manager (CPCM); Lifetime Certified Purchasing Manager (CPM); Fellow, National Contract Management Association (NCMA); Director-at-Large, NCMA Board of Directors 2005–2008

Questions and Answers

Question: What personal leadership characteristics are most important for building successful buying or selling teams?

Answer: Supporting and coaching. The ability to motivate and coordinate extended teams of professionals who are interacting with partners and customers continuously. Specific attributes include the following:

- Subject matter knowledge
- Planning and organizational skills
- Analytical skills
- Decisive style for tactical decision-making
- Coaching style for developing subordinates
- Supportive management style for working with professional teams, including functional peers in legal, finance, and senior staff
- Disciplined approach to measuring and controlling the business

Question: What are the most significant challenges you must overcome to be a successful buying or selling team leader?

Answer: Benign neglect—from senior staff members who lack detailed understanding of the role of contracts in the business, to key team members, who may develop to a high level of self-direction and autonomy but still require attention and accountability.

Said another way: Management perception above and people below.

Question: In regard to the S3 leadership process, which step do you believe is the most important? Why?

Answer: Walk the Talk, which is the execution step that converts planning and communication into action. It is also the validation step that demonstrates to senior staff and team members that the planning is legitimate, logical, practical, and executable. Without this step, no person or plan can be taken seriously.

Question: Please provide a brief personal experience that you believe best illustrates leadership in buying or selling?

Answer: When I was in the aerospace business, I made a horrific negotiation mistake (basically disclosed our entire negotiating position). I confessed to my boss, and we started to work through the options. I self-consciously suggested, "Maybe I could bluff my way through." He said, "You can't bluff, but you can lay down all your cards and prove to them that you have a winning hand." That's exactly what happened. Later I tried to apologize for my mistake. He just shrugged and said, "You brought me an error of commission; I only punish errors of omission." I never let him down again, ever.

Summary

In this chapter, we discussed the importance to buying and selling leaders of mastering the ability to walk the talk. We began our discussion with a personal perspective concerning the importance of honoring your commitments to team members, customers, and suppliers. Then we addressed 10 key actions to walk the talk, with practical forms, lists of best practices, and case studies to help you to learn by doing.

In the next chapter, we discuss the importance of developing, integrating, and executing performance plans that tie the organization's strategic goals to team and individual performance. Remember, buying and selling is about achieving excellent business results with integrity through leadership.

Questions to Consider

1. How well do your organization's buying or selling team leaders communicate a vision, goals, performance metrics, and business results?
2. How well do your buying or selling team leaders listen to their team members?
3. How well does your organization leverage your suppliers to add value for your customers?
4. Do your organization's buying and selling team leaders hold others accountable?
5. Do you conduct appropriate team meetings?
6. How effectively does your organization provide feedback to your suppliers?
7. How effectively do your buying or selling team leaders facilitate knowledge transfer within your organization?

[1] Center for Advanced Purchasing Studies, "Cross-Industry Benchmarking Survey of Outsourcing," www.ism.ws.

Chapter 7

Leadership Step 4: Execute Performance Plans

"Simplicity is the ultimate sophistication."
—Leonardo da Vinci

Introduction

There is an old saying, "If you don't know where you are going, then any road will get you there." In the business of buying and selling products, services, and solutions—in both the public and the private sectors—it is very important to have a plan. Specifically, it is crucial to develop, integrate, and execute mutually agreed-on performance-based plans and contracts. Said differently, it is good to create performance plans and contracts for the buyer, the seller (prime contractor), the subcontractors, and all team members. It is better to integrate the performance plans between the buyer and the seller with appropriate performance requirements flowing down to the subcontractors. Finally, it is best for everyone involved in buying and selling to execute their roles, responsibilities, individual performance plans, and performance-based contracts.

In this chapter, we focus on three primary performance areas: (1) using performance-based contracts between buyers and sellers and understanding the five critical components of them, (2) using performance or balanced scorecards in buying and selling organizations, and (3) conducting individual performance assessments. Remember, achieving flawless execution is a great goal for any buying or selling organization, but it all begins with a performance plan.

Selected Interview

Name: Philip E. Salmeri, CPCM

Job Title: Consultant

Organization: M&M H Design Inc.

Location: King George, Virginia

Key Responsibilities: Provide program management and contract management training and in-house consulting support for all phases of program life.

Brief Resume: Mr. Salmeri, CPCM, has more than 25 years of government contracting experience with the U.S. Navy and the U. S. Air Force. He has served as a contracts negotiator, contracting officer, branch head, and program manager. He was the national vice president for the Mid Atlantic Region of the National Contract Management Association (NCMA) for the 1999/2000 program year. He is the elected national director for the Mid Atlantic Region for 2004–2006. Mr. Salmeri is an associate professor at the College of Southern Maryland. He is the founder and first president of the Dahlgren Chapter of NCMA. Mr. Salmeri has received the Meritorious Service Award in Scholarly Research from the Southeastern Consortium for Electrical Engineering Education. He represented the assistant secretary of the Navy for acquisition reform for the 1996 industry road shows as the expert on the use of past performance information in source selection. He has written and conducted the approved best-value source selection course for the Federal Aviation Administration's acquisition management system. He is the author of *Negotiations—Strategies, Tactics, and Countermoves.*

Mr. Salmeri is involved with integrated product team education and consulting efforts, where his focus is on building bridges between the project manager and the contracting officer. He is a recognized expert on best-value procurement. He has conducted numerous seminars and workshops on performance-based service contracting using both metric and subjective approaches. His in-house performance-based service contracting approach is to have the project managers work with the contracting officers and potential contractors in a workshop environment that results in the accomplishment of actual work products. He is the president of Salmeri Seminars and M&M H Design Inc., a service-disabled veteran–owned small business.

Questions and Answers

Question: In regard to the Six Steps to Success (S3) leadership process, which step do you believe is the most important? Why?

Answer: Step 4, Execute Performance Plans. I believe that the following sums it up: "Achieving success in business, especially buying or selling complex integrated solutions, requires everyone involved—buyer, seller, subcontractors, every person from each functional area—to know and do the right actions at the right times."

Question: Please provide a brief personal experience that you believe best illustrates leadership in buying or selling.

Answer: As branch head for a research and development contracting shop, I had the luxury of having a diverse workforce at my disposal. I was challenged with this diversity since some of the government contract specialists were highly educated and able to take on the most difficult and challenging tasks, while others were capable only of handling simple, repetitive tasks that would normally bore the pants off the more capable team members. I used this diverse talent pool to the organization's benefit by assigning appropriate contract actions based on individual strengths. I assigned simple, repetitive tasks to those who were in their comfort zone with such actions, while the more challenging or sexy efforts went to those who embraced the challenge of a not so boring task. The *big* challenge was to reward each of these contributors appropriately while not insulting or offending the others.

Using Performance-Based Contracts

Performance-based contracts have been used successfully to buy and sell products, services, and integrated solutions in both the public and the private business sectors for many years. The critical aspect is customer requirements. The buying organization must determine its needs, be able to communicate its needs in terms of performance-based requirements, and be able to create challenging yet realistic performance-based metrics to hold its suppliers accountable. Typically, performance-based contracts contain these five critical components:

1. Performance work statement, also known as performance-based statement of work
2. Quality assurance surveillance plan (QASP)
3. Performance-based metrics
4. Contractual incentives (positive or negative)
5. The right pricing arrangement (type of contract)

The buying organization should develop these critical components in partnership with its suppliers.

First Critical Component: Performance Work Statement

Although a performance-based contract does not direct how the work is to be accomplished, which should be determined by a supplier with specialized business knowledge, the performance work statement should provide a mix of measurable objective and subjective performance requirements.

There are important reasons for spending the time and effort to analyze the work to be performed. This stage is the beginning of the effort to specifically identify needs. As development of the performance work statement and the quality assurance surveillance plan progresses, it becomes evident why participants should include the output desired and why functional area representatives should at this time eliminate vague, confusing, or incomplete requirements. This stage is an excellent opportunity for the functional managers to ask whether particular services are required.

All tasks required of the supplier should be analyzed for clarity and simplicity, to ensure that the seller will understand the requirements. This analysis will improve supplier performance and reduce friction between the buyer and the seller. Sellers generally use higher costs to hedge against perceived contracting risks. If the buyer eliminates questionable or ambiguous requirements, the seller's concern about risks is reduced and so are costs.

After developing a specific list of desired capabilities, the buyer should specify performance requirements for each of the tasks identified as required outputs. A performance work statement can be a powerful tool for informing the seller of the buyer's needs while allowing the seller the flexibility to be innovative, creative, and not bound by detailed product or service specifications.

Second Critical Component: Quality Assurance Surveillance Plan

The QASP establishes the plan that will be followed to ensure that the buyer receives the performance that it is paying for. The information developed through this plan provides objective evidence of acceptable performance and also provides the means through which deductions may properly be taken for unacceptable performance. To accomplish this goal, the QASP should be carefully planned. The makeup and depth of the plan depend on the size and complexity of the contract. Generally, the QASP will contain

- A statement of the plan's purpose
- The name, specific authority, and responsibility of the technical representative or quality assurance evaluator, including alternates
- Instructions on how to use the plan
- A surveillance schedule
- The surveillance methods that will be used
- Appropriate documentation for each method (e.g., schedules, checklists, reports)
- The performance requirements summary
- Sampling guides for each task to be sampled
- Deduction and incentive formulas, as appropriate

Properly written, the QASP can be an excellent communications tool. In fact, it is a good idea to discuss it with the seller so that all surveillance methods are understood. The QASP should be included in the solicitation, to reinforce the buyer's emphasis on the quality assurance aspect of the performance-based contracting process.[1]

The performance work statement and the QASP should be prepared and read together during surveillance. The goal of these documents is to clearly state the buyer's requirements and how the buyer will determine acceptable and unacceptable performance.

Third Critical Component: Performance-Based Metrics

Form 7-1 lists many of the key performance areas and related metrics commonly used in complex contracts to buy or sell products, services, or integrated business solutions. No one performance area or metric is more important than the others. In fact, most buying organizations are developing a balanced scorecard composed of numerous metrics to evaluate their performance and the performance of their suppliers. Every organization should decide which performance areas and related metrics are most appropriate for its business and related contracts.

Form 7-1 Key Performance Areas and Metrics

Buyer and seller key performance areas	Checklist of buyer and seller key performance metrics

Financial	□ Return on investment
	  □ On budget (planned expenses versus actual expenses)
	□ Cost reduction (current costs versus future costs)
	  □ Implementation costs
	  □ Operations costs
	  □ Maintenance costs
	  □ Support costs
	□ Return on assets
	□ Net present value
	□ Cost performance index
	□ Revenue generated (annual and quarterly)
	□ Days of sales outstanding
	□ Revenue or expense to head count
	□ Inventory turns

Form 7-1 Key Performance Areas and Metrics, continued	
Buyer and seller key performance areas	**Checklist of buyer and seller key performance metrics**

Schedule	□ Number of milestones on time
	□ On-time delivery percentage (mutually agreed to date)
	□ Number of days in cycle time (order to delivery)
	□ Earned value method
	  □ Budgeted cost of work schedule
	  □ Budgeted cost of work performance
	□ Schedule performance index

Technical	□ Capacity volume □ Operating time per usage □ Capabilities and features □ Speed □ Number of product failures or outages
Quality	□ Mean time between failure □ Mean time to repair □ Number of complaints □ Number of defects
Source: Gregory A. Garrett, *Managing Complex Outsourced Projects* (Chicago: CCH, 2004), 46.	

Fourth Critical Component: Contractual Incentives

The care with which performance-based contracting is developed and the direct relationship between the performance work statement and the QASP create a vastly improved understanding between the buyer and seller. The contractual incentives selected by the buyer should accomplish the same goal. Incentives can emphasize areas in which superior performance is desired and inadequate performance is particularly undesirable. Consequently, incentives may be positive, negative, or both. Deductions represent the value of tasks not performed satisfactorily.

The mutual understanding of positive and negative performance incentives is established in the solicitation and may be discussed during source selection. Incentives reflect reasonable value to the buyer; they should not be provided to attain the specified minimum requirements of the contract. Incentives to be innovative and perform in a highly satisfactory manner must be built into the entire performance-based contracting process. Discussions with the seller to change values for deductions should be conducted with careful analysis so that incentives are effective for their intended purposes.

Fifth Critical Component: The Right Pricing Arrangement

The pricing arrangement or contract type will affect the performance-based contracting process significantly. When deciding which type of contract to use, the buyer should ask two questions:

1. Can the buyer properly describe the requirements in a performance-based statement of work?
2. Can sellers accurately estimate the cost to perform the contract with the information provided in the solicitation?

Procurement planning is necessary to ensure that sufficient workload data are available to accurately describe tasks in the performance work statement. This task is easier if the contract is replacing a previous contract for the same product or services. If there are enough data to develop an effective performance work statement, a QASP, and appropriate performance metrics, then in most cases a fixed-price contract should be selected. However, many factors must be considered when selecting the right pricing arrangement to ensure that the seller is properly motivated to achieve mission success.

Both buyers and sellers must be aware of the many types of contract pricing arrangements available in order to choose the right type for each situation. Over time, three general pricing arrangements categories have evolved: fixed price, cost reimbursement, and time and materials. These categories and the contract types in each category are described later, along with information on determining contract price and using pricing arrangements to balance the risk between contracting parties. In today's complex business world, a solid understanding of contract pricing options is essential for meeting business objectives.

Assessing Requirements to Determine Costs

Contract cost is determined by the contract requirements, which fall into two main categories: technical and administrative.

Technical Requirements

The performance work statement should contain technical requirements that describe what the buyer wants to buy in terms of desired performance results or outputs that must be rendered by the seller. The seller's costs will be determined by the consumption of resources—labor, capital, and money—necessary to provide products and services that meet these technical requirements.

Administrative Requirements

Contract clauses describe other terms and conditions that require the seller to consume resources, although the terms and conditions relate only indirectly to the technical requirements. The following clause excerpt provides an example:

> **Company-Furnished Property**
>
> ... orders from ABC Company shall be held at the Seller's risk and shall be kept insured by the Seller at the Seller's expense while in Seller's custody and control in an amount equal to the replacement cost thereof, with loss payable to ABC Company.

The insurance requirement will cost money, but it is only indirectly related to the technical requirements of the project. Contracts contain many such administrative requirements.

Pricing Contracts

Contract pricing begins with a determination of the cost of performing the contract. To determine contract cost, a business professional who manages contracts must thoroughly analyze a prospective buyer's solicitation and develop a work breakdown structure from the technical and administrative performance requirements. Next, he or she decides how the work will be implemented—that is, the order in which it will be performed and the methods and procedures that will be used to accomplish it. On the basis of these plans, the business professional estimates the performance costs so that a price can be proposed. After the company has agreed on a contract price, it will be obligated to complete the work at that price unless a different arrangement can be negotiated.

To estimate performance costs, the following questions must be answered: What resources (labor, capital, money) will be needed to do the work? In what quantities will they be needed? When will they be needed? How much will those resources cost in the marketplace?

Estimating techniques do not necessarily require the development of detailed answers to these questions. For instance, parametric estimates, which are used at a very high level, do not involve the type of analysis implied by the four questions. Nevertheless, some level of response to those questions is implicit in every cost estimate.

Uncertainty and Risk in Contract Pricing

The business professional's cost estimate will be a judgment—that is, a prediction about the future, rather than a fact. When the project manager says, "I estimate that the contract will cost US$500,000 to complete," that statement really means, "I *predict* that when I have completed the project according to the specifications, statement of work, and other contract terms and conditions, I will have consumed US$500,000 worth of labor, capital, and money."

The problem with this prediction, as with all predictions, is that no one will know whether it is true until all the events have occurred. Predictions are based largely on history; people assume that cause-and-effect relationships in the future will be similar to those in the past. However, people frequently have an incorrect or incomplete understanding of the past. In addition, they may carry out even the best-laid plans imperfectly because of error or unexpected events. All these factors can cause the future to materialize differently than predicted.

Thus, the business professional's estimate may be incorrect. If it is too high, the company's proposal may not be competitive. If it is too low, the contract price may not be high enough to cover the project costs, and the company will suffer a financial loss.

However sound the cost estimate, the contract price must be negotiated. Every negotiated price is a compromise between the extremes of an optimistic and a pessimistic prediction about future costs. The range between these two extremes is called the "range of possible costs." The compromise results from negotiation between a risk-avoiding buyer and a risk-avoiding seller.

The risk-avoiding buyer wants to minimize the risk of agreeing to a higher price than necessary to cover the seller's costs plus a reasonable profit. Thus, the buyer tends to push the price toward the more optimistic end of the range of possible costs. The risk-avoiding seller wants to avoid the risk of agreeing to a price that may not cover its actual performance costs or allow a reasonable profit. Thus, the seller tends to push the price toward the more pessimistic end of the range of possible costs.

The consequence of uncertainty about the future is risk, or the possibility of injury. A seller who undertakes a contractual obligation to complete a project for a fixed price but has estimated too low will suffer financial loss, unless it can shift the excess costs to the buyer or avoid them altogether. The effort made to avoid the injury will be proportional to its magnitude and related to its cause and direction.

Developing Pricing Arrangements

Over the years some standard pricing arrangements have evolved. These arrangements fall into three categories: fixed price, cost reimbursement, and time and materials contracts (the Project Management Institute designates unit price contracts as a fourth category). These contract categories have developed as practical responses to cost risk, and they have become fairly standard formal arrangements. Incentives can be added to any of the contract types in these three categories; they are discussed in detail later in this chapter. **Table 7-1** lists several common contract types in these categories.

These pricing arrangements are manifested in the specific terms and conditions of contracts—that is, in the contract clauses. No standard clauses for their implementation exist. Therefore, the contracting parties must write clauses that describe their specific agreement.

Table 7-1 Contract Categories and Types

	Fixed price	Cost	Time and materials
Types of contracts	Firm fixed price Fixed price with economic price adjustment Fixed price incentive	Cost reimbursement Cost plus a percentage of cost Cost plus fixed fee Cost plus incentive fee Cost plus award fee	Time and material Unit price

Using Performance or Balanced Scorecards

The balanced scorecard is a method for translating strategic themes into actionable and measurable objectives that are ready for execution at all levels of an organization. More than 50 percent of the Fortune 1,000 and 40 percent of companies in Europe use a form of the balanced scorecard, according to Bain & Co.[2] The balanced scorecard helps organizations build bridges between several dichotomous elements of strategy. Increasingly, organizations are realizing the importance of creating a balanced approach to their diverse strategic objectives, in achieving overall higher levels of performance.

Michael Tracy and Fred Wiersema, authors of the best-selling book, *Discipline of Market Leaders,*[3] list three strategic objectives of market leaders:

1. Operational excellence
2. Product leadership
3. Customer intimacy

The balanced scorecard serves the needs of many organizations worldwide that need to make strategy actionable. The balanced scorecard helps ensure that performance areas, related metrics, and strategic themes are balanced with financial and nonfinancial (customer satisfaction, quality, on-time delivery, etc.) leading and lagging indicators.

A properly developed balanced scorecard has the following characteristics:[4]

- Its methodology is suited for managing business strategy.
- It uses a common language at all levels of the organization.
- It uses a common set of principles to manage day-to-day operations as well as to frame the organization's strategy.
- It is designed to identify and manage business purposes.
- It provides a balance between relatively opposing forces in strategy.
- It aligns strategic goals with objectives, targets, and metrics.
- It cascades to all levels of the organization.

How Can You Create a Balanced Scorecard Program for Your Buying or Selling Team?

Professors Robert Kaplan and David Norton declare that strategy is a set of hypotheses about cause and effect in their book, *Balanced Scorecard.*[5] They identified four perspectives that can guide organizations as they translate strategy into actionable terms.

1. Financial perspective
   - What are the financial targets?
   - What drives these targets?
   - What kind of profit and revenue is to be achieved?
   - In a nonprofit organization, what budget guides you?
2. Customer perspective
   - Who are the customers?
   - How do you delight them?
   - Which segments do you wish to address?
   - What goals do you wish to achieve with partners?
   - What are your goals for the distribution channels?
3. Internal perspective
   - Which processes must we be the best at to win customers?
   - What internal activities do we need to sustain competencies?
4. Learning and growth perspective
   - What must we be great in performing?
   - How do we train our people to improve their performance?
   - What climate and culture nurtures growth?
   - What do we have to do in developing our people to achieve organization objectives?

Figure 7-1 Balanced Scorecard Framework

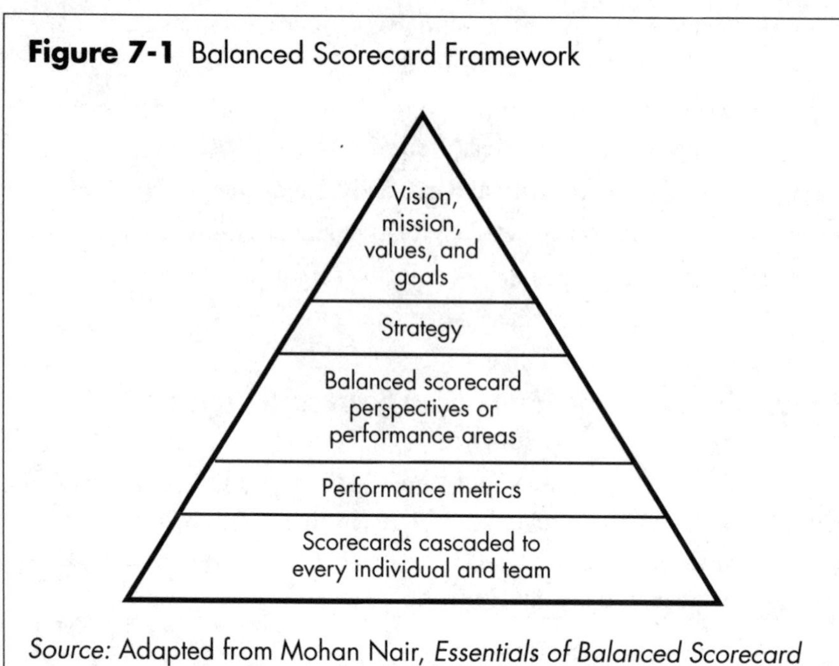

Source: Adapted from Mohan Nair, *Essentials of Balanced Scorecard* (New York: Wiley, 2004).

Simply stated, a balanced scorecard program should integrate an organization's vision, mission, values, and goals with its strategies, performance areas, and metrics for each individual and team in an organization. **Figure 7-1** illustrates how the various components of the balanced scorecard should be linked or mapped.

What Are Some of the Pros and Cons of the Balanced Scorecard Approach to Improve Performance?

There are numerous advantages or pros of using the balanced scorecard approach to improve performance:

- It facilitates communication.
- It helps the organization gain greater self-knowledge.
- It focuses the organization's leaders on what is most important.
- It provides a common communications tool to inform everyone in the organization of the vision, mission, values, goals, strategies, key performance areas, metrics, and performance targets to achieve success.

- It provides a road map with which every individual and team can map their performance responsibilities to the organization's balanced scorecard program.
- It helps translate strategy into action at every level of an organization.

Likewise, there are several disadvantages or cons when developing and implementing the balanced scorecard approach:

- Contested performance metrics
- Contested performance measurements
- Resistance to change
- Charges of seeking a quick and easy solution
- Extent of time required to inform, educate, and train people in the proper use of the program
- Possibility of getting caught up in the process and losing sight of what is most important
- Possibility of assuming that people really get it
- Underestimation of the total cost of implementation of the program, especially if one or more software applications are deployed to facilitate it

Table 7-2 provides a brief summary of a few of the many proven effective best practices for creating and using performance and balanced scorecards.

Table 7-2 Checklist of Best Practices for Creating Performance and Balanced Scorecards

- ☐ Identify the organization's
  - Vision
  - Mission
  - Values
  - Goals or objectives
- ☐ Choose three to five organizational goals or objectives.
- ☐ Clarify strategies to achieve goals.
- ☐ Divide or break down strategies into performance areas and metrics.
- ☐ Develop a map or weave a golden thread between the key actions, performance areas and metrics, and strategy.
- ☐ Select performance metrics for each performance area to achieve organizational goals or objectives.
- ☐ Choose three to five performance areas and related metrics.
- ☐ Communicate all aspects of the scorecard to all organizational team members.
- ☐ Tie each individual's performance plan to the scorecards.

Conducting Individual Performance Assessments

Form 7-2 provides an effective tool for buying or selling team leaders to use in working with team members to establish team member objectives and expected results that will contribute to business success. The buying or selling leader and team member can use **Form 7-2** throughout the year to assess individual performance results and business results, whether positive or negative. There is no secret formula for conducting individual performance assessments; it is all about the basics of communication.

Conducting individual performance assessments should be easy at the mid-point and end of each year, if the supervisor and employee did the following actions: (1) established and documented clear, specific, and measurable goals at the start of the year; (2) provided feedback to one another throughout the year; (3) adjusted the plan as needed; and (4) provided honest feedback.

Form 7-2 Team Member Objectives and Assessment Tool

Employee name:________________ Location:________________
Date: _____ Fiscal year: From:____________ To:____________
Project team name: __________ Organization:________________

Individual Business Objectives	Actual Results and Effect on Business	Supervisor Assessment
Desired Teamwork Behaviors	**Demonstrated Behaviors and Effect on Business**	**Supervisor Assessment**
Leadership Characteristics	**Actual Results and Effect on Business**	**Supervisor Assessment**
Professional Development Objectives	**Actual Results and Effect on Business**	**Supervisor Assessment**

Employee comments:____

____

☐ Objectives ☐ Quarterly assessment ☐ End-of-year assessment

Employee signature:____
Employee name (printed):________________________ Date:__________

Employee supervisor signature:____________________________
Supervisor name (printed):________________________ Date:__________

Selected Interview

Name: John E. Stuart

Job Title: Deepwater Aviation, Senior Program Manager—Subcontracts

Organization: Lockheed Martin Maritime Systems and Sensors

Location: Rosslyn, Virginia

Key Responsibilities: Responsible for ensuring that programmatic, technical, contractual, and measurement system requirements are fully integrated into a subcontract management strategy and subcontract execution plan for the air assets of the Integrated Deepwater Systems Program, the multibillion-dollar 20-year recapitalization program for the U.S. Coast Guard. Direct and manage the subcontract program management activities required to ensure successful execution of the Deepwater Air Domain subcontract plan, currently valued at more than $750 million. Provide leadership and manage and direct the activities of domain-specific asset teams of subcontract managers; subcontract administrators; and technical, logistics, and quality assurance functional personnel in the day-to-day execution and performance of the program's technical, cost, schedule, subcontract management, and administration activities.

Brief Resume: Professional experience in program contracts and procurement in the U.S. government, in international and commercial contracting, in program management, subcontract and supply-chain management, in pricing, and in business development. Work experience in both government and the private sector includes research and development, production, systems integration, and support of major weapons systems and component hardware involving aircraft and space technologies. Thirty years of experience with aerospace contract formation, subcontract management, pricing, negotiation, review and approval, and administration; 25 years at the director and manager level—directing, controlling, formulating and executing policy and procedures, and managing and allocation resources.

Education and Certification:

M.B.A. with honors in management and finance, University of Missouri

B.A. in political science and international economics, University of Colorado

Executive Program Management, Defense Systems Management College

Air War College, US Air Force–Air University

Education with industry (Rockwell International), Air Force Institute of Technology

Fellow and Certified Professional Contracts Manager, National Contract Management Association

Questions and Answers

Question: What are the core competencies of a successful buying or selling team leader?

Answer: You cannot successfully sell or buy what you don't have knowledge of! Leadership core competencies:

- Possession of detailed knowledge of the marketplace in which you are operating, whether as buyer or seller.
- In-depth knowledge of and understanding of the products and services being offered or acquired and sound understanding of contract and subcontract performance requirements, schedules, cost, and risk management. Being successful in the "gizmo" world does not necessarily translate to success in the "widget" world.

This basic business foundation is a necessity for the leader to ascertain the required skills and functional expertise required to assemble, mold, and direct a strong buying or selling team with their core competencies. Leaders need to understand what's required to be successful.

Question: What are the most significant challenges you must overcome to be a successful buying or selling team leader?

Answer: One team, one face, and one voice. The most significant challenge for team dynamics and success:

- Getting individual members aligned to become strong and productive members of the team as a whole performing at their best.
- Establishing and maintaining a common focus and end objective that all team members can relate to and believe in.
- Establishing an open and communicative environment within the team while ensuring that external communications carry a common message and position.
- Establishing clearly defined roles, responsibilities, and authority for all team members.

Question: In regard to the S3 leadership process, which step do you believe is the most important? Why?

Answer: The most important is Step 4, Execute Performance Plan—performance, performance, performance.

One cannot be a success, if one cannot perform and achieve.... The end objective of a competent leader must be to achieve excellence in performance, with "performance" being defined as achieving and exceeding the stated objective or plan. A leader can think the talk, dress the part, and walk the talk, but the measure of success is performance and achievement of the stated objective or plan. Likewise, excellence has no intrinsic value unless it is inherent to meeting and achieving the performance plan.

Question: Please provide a brief personal experience that you believe best illustrates leadership in buying or selling.

Answer: Leading by Example:

By far the most demanding and highly stressful environment in the buying or selling life cycle is the proposal stage. It is the stage that stresses the limits and capabilities of any team and places the highest demands on the skills and competencies of the leader.

A "Red Team" review of a billion-dollar proposal resulted in the need for a major and significant rewrite of several of the proposal sections. Meeting milestone schedule events of executive reviews, approvals, printing, and submittal would require full days, long nights, and weekend work for an already stretched team. True leadership skills were displayed by the proposal manger by re-energizing the team with a focused zeal to perform and achieve success. The key ingredient to success was leadership presence during the whole time the team was at work—not just showing up during normal work times to check on progress. This single action of being present in the trenches resulted in the team meeting the performance plan and winning the contract.

Selected Interview

Name: Janice Smets

Job Title: Contract Specialist

Organization: USAF Space Missile Center, Los Angeles Air Force Base

Location: El Segundo, California

Key Responsibilities: Pre- and post-award contracting duties such as preparing synopses, preparing solicitations, analyzing proposals, performing cost-price reviews, negotiating contracts and contract modifications, facilitating with other government officials in an Internet protocol telephony environment, staying current on all regulations and policies, mentoring junior military and civilian personnel, instructing an on-base contracting class, maintaining contractor's performance reviews, and performing award fee contract actions.

Brief Resume: My highest level of education is a master's degree in acquisition and contract management from the accredited West Coast University (1994). I have a total of 29 years with the government and, of those years, a total of 21 years in procurement. I have worked at the Los Angeles Air Force Base, El Segundo, California, for 15 years, and before that I worked for the Navy at Port Hueneme, California, and at the Air Force Plant Representative Office.

Along with fixed-price and cost-type contracts, I have also managed space and missile contracts (systems), and global positioning system, architect and engineering, and hazardous waste contracts.

As a part-time adjunct professor for the University of California–Los Angeles and Upper Iowa University Web-based curriculums, I teach marketing principles and marketing research. In the classes, I am required to help students form groups for group projects; in many instances, this is their first time being involved in group projects. I teach team building in my online courses.

Questions and Answers

Question: What personal leadership characteristics are most important for building successful buying or selling teams?

Answer: Being able to communicate effectively and get on a personal level, knowing when to lead and when to follow, being a good role model by having the experience base and skills required, and being able to help team members succeed in their careers, to make good and sound decisions, to keep up team morale and motivate the members, to be proactive, and to keep commitments.

Question: What are the most significant challenges you must overcome to be a successful buying or selling team leader?

Answer: A leader must overcome diversity of cultures, beliefs, and experience-based gaps between the senior and junior levels and must learn individual goals among the team members. Also, a reward may not be seen from the same perspective by everyone on the team.

Question: In regard to the S3 leadership process, which step do you believe is the most important? Why?

Answer: Step 4, Execute Performance Plans. When developing performance plans, you must devise the plan so that the results will be positive, not negative. One detailed plan usually doesn't fit all. Therefore, an individual performance plan must be flexible enough to help motivate in a positive way for different personalities and to help an individual overcome any historical bad experiences from prior performance plans.

A group performance plan must be focused on the mission while helping members grow within the team. A good plan can take an unsatisfactory worker and help develop his or her self-confidence and self-esteem to where the individual wants to work within the team and do his or her part.

A plan should never be unreachable by an individual or group; such plans will end up in frustration and failure. A good leader and a good plan turns non-performers into valued team members and high performers, regardless of age. Sometimes this process takes extra time by a leader, but it is truly a worthwhile investment. Finding the right fit for members within the team is a critical step for a successful leader. Getting buy-in from all team members as to what the plan should entail can only help a team function efficiently and effectively.

Question: Please provide a brief personal experience that you believe best illustrates leadership in buying or selling.

Answer: When organizations, or groups, within the government or a private concern merge to become larger entities and offices involved in the merger shrink, there are usually some people who are displaced or must compete for position. A merger is extremely difficult for loyal employees, and their opportunities for career growth are reduced. Also, there will be a turnover in supervisors, and close working relationships are changed or dissipate. This change can greatly affect the buying or selling capacity within a team or organization. Mergers fragment a team, and adjustments are needed. Managers may or may not be team leaders that are greatly affected by a merger.

Unfortunately, I am at present involved in such a scenario, and it is apparent that not all leaders have the knowledge or leadership skills to help make a smooth transition among the teams during a merger. There is no room for mistakes, because once trust in a leader is gone, there is usually insufficient time to reverse the damage in the working relationships. To lead people through a merger is the epitome of leadership within a team or organization. For success in the environment of the merger, only experienced leaders should be empowered to make the decisions and work directly with the new or displaced team member, to maintain the same high level of output within the team. Helping displaced team members accept change is a challenge, and the team leader must help the displaced team member establish new relationships either in another team or not in a team at all.

Summary

In this chapter, we focused on three primary performance areas: (1) using performance-based contracts between buyers and sellers and the five critical components, (2) using performance and balanced scorecards within buying and selling organizations, and (3) conducting individual performance assessments. Said simply, we have provided a holistic view of performance planning at three levels—the contract (between parties), the organization (team), and the individual. To achieve consistent high performance in buying and selling, you must do performance planning and execution at all three levels.

In the next chapter, we discuss the need to build leaders at every level of the organization. We also focus on understanding that leadership is not necessarily tied to a job title. Sometimes the real leaders are not the people who are supposed to be in charge.

Questions to Consider

1. What do you consider to be the most important component of a performance-based contract?
2. Does your organization have a balance scorecard program?
3. Does your organization effectively link or map organizational vision, mission, values, and goals to your team and individual objectives?

---

[1] Mohan Nair, *Essentials of Balanced Scorecard,* (New York: Wiley, 2004).

[2] Bain & Co., "Benchmarking Study: Use of Balanced Scorecards," London, 2003.

[3] Michael Tracy and Fred Wiersema, *Discipline of Market Leaders* (Boston: HBS Press, 2003).

[4] Nair, *Essentials of Balanced Scorecard,* op cit.

[5] Robert Kaplan and David Norton, *Balanced Scorecard* (Boston: HBS Press, 2001).

Chapter 8

Leadership Step 5: Build Leaders at Every Level

"Endeavors succeed or fail because of the people involved. Only by attracting the best people will you accomplish great deeds."

—Colin Powell

Introduction

In *The 21 Irrefutable Laws of Leadership,* John C. Maxwell, best-selling author and motivational speaker, states that he has been conducting informal surveys to find out what prompted people to become leaders.[1] The results of Maxwell's surveys are shown in **Table 8-1.**

Table 8-1 How They Became Leaders

Natural gift	10 percent
Result of crisis	5 percent
Influence of another leader	85 percent

Source: John C. Maxwell, *The 21 Irrefutable Laws of Leadership* (Nashville, TN: Thomas Nelson Inc., 1998).

While many people believe leadership is an inherited trait, Maxwell's survey results indicate otherwise. Certainly, we have all encountered some natural-born leaders, who seem to have a gift to navigate their way through life and business, building leaders along the way. Likewise, we have probably all met someone who was compelled to step up to a leadership role as a result of a crisis. But the vast majority of all leaders we meet have emerged as leaders because of the influence of established leaders who took the time to mentor them. Said differently, it takes a leader to build a leader.[2]

People naturally are attracted to and follow leaders stronger than themselves. Some people believe only strong leaders can develop strong leaders. It is very difficult for people to build in others skills that they themselves do not possess. However, not all strong leaders take the time to help develop leadership skills in others. It is possible to be perceived as a strong leader by others, yet still be insecure. Our experience and research has shown that only very secure leaders take the time and energy away from their followers and primary mission and goals to help build leadership in others. Only secure leaders truly empower others.

The best leaders in life and business make the development of other leaders one of their highest priorities. The best leaders know an organization depends on the strength of the entire leadership pipeline. Leadership does not begin at the vice president or general manager level. Leadership is essential at every level of every organization.

Leaders have often been compared to eagles. Eagles do not often flock together—they tend to fly alone and soar high! Yet eagles, like leaders, must be taught how to fly in an environment that provides a vision, incentives, encouragement, risk-taking, and accountability In this chapter, we discuss the importance of succession planning and numerous best practices to create a leadership-rich culture in an organization. Specifically, we discuss the need for leaders to coach others to (1) focus on mastering the five leadership competencies; (2) understand the Six Steps to Success (S3) leadership process; (3) learn the power of reading themselves, people, and the situation; and (4) develop leadership succession plans at every level of an organization. We believe leadership is the ultimate competitive differentiator in life and in business.

Coaching Others to Focus on Mastering the Five Leadership Competencies

Some people love to coach, teach, or mentor, while others do not. In business, as in most sports, a certain level of education and formal training is required. However, much of success in both business and sports is determined by how you are coached and trained to master the basic skills. Truly exceptional performers are people who have learned to master the required competencies of their professions. While some superstars may find apparent shortcuts to success, all have found a way to master the necessary skills.

Likewise, all superstars have learned when, where, and how to apply their skills to achieve outstanding results.

As discussed in Chapter 2, five key leadership competencies or specialized skill areas (SSAs) are required to become a successful buying or selling team leader:

1. Decision-making
2. Communications (verbal and nonverbal)
3. Integrity
4. Buying and selling business acumen
5. Interpersonal relations

An effective coach, teacher, or mentor will help an individual—whether a new salesperson, novice purchasing manager, experienced contract manager, senior contracts director, supply-chain general manager, or vice president of sales—to realistically assess his or her skills and determine what actions to take to further master the fundamental leadership skills.

Some bosses like to say no one is perfect. While this statement is true, it provides no help. An effective coach or mentor will sit down with you, either in person or through a teleconference, a net meeting, e-mail, or some other means, to discuss your level of mastery of each of the five leadership SSAs. Next, an effective coach or mentor will ask what you plan to do to improve your skills in the areas in which you have mutually agreed you need to improve. Then, an effective coach or mentor will ask you to develop an action plan that lists what you plan to do and when. Later, an effective coach will periodically ask how you are doing in executing your personal leadership action plan. Finally, an effective coach will provide timely and honest assessments of your performance and try to find innovative ways to stimulate your performance through rewards, penalties, guilt, and so forth.

As a coach, one must learn that what works for some does not work for all. Thus, a coach must be flexible in advice and approach, tailoring each to the individual situation. Of course, the manner in which one coaches also sends a strong message to followers, either good or bad. A good coach knows when to apply more pressure on an individual and when to back off. Yet an essential element of building leaders is testing, seeing how an individual will respond under pressure in various situations.

Coaching is a process for enhancing performance characterized by

- A dual commitment to development,
- A series of conversations over time, and

- A focus on maximizing potential and on clarifying and achieving the coachee's goals.

When successful, coaching can enhance employee attitudes, inspire commitment to excellence, and foster the development of a leader. **Table 8-2** describes coaching further.

Table 8-2 What Is Coaching?

Coaching is	**Coaching is not**
• A means of developing talent • About guiding someone toward his or her goals • About sharing experiences and opinions to create agreed-on outcomes • About inspiring and supporting another.	• About reprimanding someone or "fixing them" • About directing or ordering someone to do something to meet goals • About being the expert or consultant with all the answers • About solving all problems for someone.

Source: Interaction Associates Inc.

Coaching can occur in several contexts and across different roles in organizations.

- **Manager with direct reports.** Leaders with managerial responsibilities and authority.
- **Peer to peer.** Colleagues with similar standing in the organization.
- **Outside professional with client.** People contracted to provide coaching services relative to a particular project or goal.

Table 8-3 provides a checklist of coachable moments.

Table 8-3 Coachable Moments: Checklist of Dos and Don'ts
Do use coaching skills when you want to
☐ Develop an employee who is a reasonable performer into an excellent performer,
☐ Address a specific competency development,
☐ Motivate and maintain a talented employee,
☐ Help someone clarify his or her thinking,
☐ Enhance an employee's level of confidence, and
☐ Coach others to lead or coach.
Don't use coaching when
☐ You are delegating an assignment with specific ends and means,
☐ A person has received feedback numerous times about a performance issue and there still is no change in behavior,
☐ There is a clear violation of company policy, organizational values, or common business sense, and
☐ A person is new or inexperienced in a role—often she or he will need more direction, modeling, or assistance on a task.

So, as a coach, how do you help others improve their buying and selling leadership skills? The answer is, of course, it depends. **Table 8-4** provides a checklist of some of the many common actions to help people improve their buying or selling leadership skills.

Table 8-4 16 Actions to Improve Buying or Selling Leadership Skills
▪ Volunteer to serve as a leader for a special project, within your organization.
▪ Attend formal buying or selling educational seminars (sales, contracts, purchasing, supply-chain management, contract negotiation, and so forth).
▪ Obtain professional certification.
▪ Certified purchasing manager (CPM)
▪ Certified professional contracts manager (CPCM)
▪ Certified federal contracts manager (CFCM)

Table 8-4 16 Actions to Improve Buying or Selling Leadership Skills, continued

- Certified commercial contracts manager (CCCM)
- Certified project management professional (PMP)
- Certified public accountant (CPA)

- Complete ethics and compliance training courses.
- Complete leadership training seminars.

- Complete a 360° leadership assessment survey (with feedback from supervisors, peers, and employees).
- Read a thought-provoking book on leadership and then create a personal action plan.
- Receive informal feedback from your supervisor on your leadership strengths and areas needing improvement.
- Complete communications skills training courses: effective writing skills, public speaking, and so forth.
- Work with a coach or mentor to develop a personal leadership action plan.
- Serve as a leader of a professional organization at a local, regional, national, or international level (e.g., National Contract Management Association, Project Management Institute, Institute of Supply Management, International Association of Commercial and Contract Managers, or Association of Proposal Management Professionals).
- Serve as a leader in your church or community.
- Coach others to help them improve their leadership skills.
- Tape (audio or video) one of your presentations, and then review it with your coach to identify strengths and areas needing improvement.
- Write a paper or article for a professional magazine or journal.
- Volunteer to speak at an organizational meeting or professional conference.

Selected Interview

Name: Rita L. Wells

Job Title: Associate Administrator

Organization: Federal Transit Administration (FTA), U.S. Department of Transportation

Location: Washington, D.C.

Key Responsibilities: Executive leadership for procurement, human resources, the administrative budget, competitive sourcing, management planning, information technology, and facilities and property management for FTA headquarters and 10 regions.

Brief Resume:

2003–present: Associate Administrator, Federal Transit Administration

1998–2003: Deputy Executive Director and Chief Operating Officer, Committee for Purchase from People Who Are Blind or Severely Disabled

1974–1998: Department of Defense acquisition positions, including contracting officer, program manager, instructor, and contract price analyst in U.S. and overseas locations.

Education:

Ph.D., Ohio State University; M.B.A., Southern Illinois University; B.A., University of Illinois; diploma, Industrial College of the Armed Forces; all Department of Defense acquisition courses for Defense Acquisition Workforce Improvement Act Level III certification.

Questions and Answers

Question: What personal leadership characteristics are most important for building successful buying or selling teams?

Answer: (1) Being proactive—It's the first step to tearing down stovepipes and building integrated buying teams. You have to reach out to people in other parts of the organization because they often won't come to you first. For example, instead of chastising an engineer for submitting a purchase request late, go to the engineering office in advance and help staff members develop their acquisition plan as a team.

(2) Confidently demonstrating a solid understanding of what the team needs to do—Team members need to have confidence that the leader knows what needs to be done and truly understands the challenges the team will face.

(3) Showing team members that they are valued—There will be ups and downs in every team effort. When the team members truly feel valued, they will do amazing things.

Question: What are the most significant challenges you must overcome to be a successful buying or selling team leader?

Answer: (1) Focusing on the right priorities. Many things can distract team members from the goals they need to achieve. In a changing and dynamic environment, it's important to be flexible but also to keep the team focused on accomplishing the right goals. You have to put out a lot of fires on a daily basis but make sure that you and your team members never lose sight of your goals.

(2) Making the most effective use of the resources you have. I've rarely met anybody who thought they had all the resources they needed. It's easy to fall into the trap of thinking that the team's performance is limited because "we just don't have enough people, travel

funds, ______ (fill in the blank)." Yet history is replete with examples of teams accomplishing amazing things despite resource constraints. The fun of leading a team is to keep the members focused on their possibilities—not their limitations.

(3) Keeping the team members at peak performance. The team is as good as the people on it. Train continuously—both formally and informally. If you are hiring, make an effort to get people with the best potential and attitude; they may or may not be the most experienced. Stay connected with the people on the team—actively listen to what they have to say and continuously communicate your vision for the team's success. If there are jerks on the team, deal with them or they'll drag down the team's performance. Show appreciation for the accomplishments of the team. Take time to celebrate victories—even the small ones.

Question: Please provide a brief personal experience that you believe best illustrates leadership in buying or selling.

Answer: As with many other government organizations, we had experienced the loss of many experienced contract specialists to retirements and more lucrative job opportunities with industry. We found it almost impossible to hire replacements with the same level of experience and training. Two years ago, we worked with our agency's human resources staff to develop a comprehensive and multifaceted workforce plan. We implemented a program to repay student loans of new hires. We found this program to be a terrific recruitment tool that attracted talented interns with outstanding academic credentials. In addition to attending college job fairs, we also expanded our job outreach to other segments of the population. For example, we developed a memorandum of agreement with a local office that assists people with disabilities in finding jobs. We actively recruited veterans and industry purchasing agents. We hired new contract specialists who had no federal procurement experience but had superb analytical and communication skills. We set aside funding in our budget specifically for formal acquisition training and developmental assignments for the contract specialist interns. Senior staff members became personally available as mentors for the new hires. We launched an internal training program in which the new hires took turns researching topics, such as warranties or commercial contracting, and then taught them to the other employees. Today, more than half of the employees in the procurement office have fewer than two years of experience. Energy levels are high. The work is getting done correctly and on time. Our customers have never been more pleased.

A Personal Story: Coaching the Good, the Bad, and the Beautiful

Gregory A. Garrett

Over the years, I have learned three things about coaching or mentoring others to be leaders. First, I have learned that I really enjoy the challenge and the opportunity to make a positive difference in the lives of others. Second, the more experience that I have as a coach, the better leader I have become. The business results from the teams I support prove this to be true. Third, each individual you decide to coach or mentor is unique, and individuals range from low to high maintenance—so be prepared.

Typically, I coach 10 to 12 individuals beyond my job responsibilities. Often these are former team members or people I have met through professional associations or former students.

The good apprentice is the individual who is willing to learn, is easy to talk with, is open and receptive to constructive feedback, is dedicated to personal improvement, does not take a lot of your time, and is not looking for an inappropriate relationship or seeking favoritism. The bad apprentice is one who is difficult to talk to (always talking), is not receptive to constructive feedback, is not really dedicated to personal improvement, is not willing to make any personal sacrifices (wants everything for nothing), and is looking for preferential treatment or an inappropriate relationship. Plus, the bad apprentice wants to consume a lot of your time while increasing his or her visibility to other senior leaders.

The "beautiful apprentice" is a term I use that is not related to physical attractiveness or appearance but to the professional relationship that you develop that becomes a beautiful thing! The beautiful apprentice is a good apprentice with whom, over time, you create a high level of mutual respect and excellent quality of interaction, resulting in professional improvement for both the coach and the apprentice.

At any given time, of the 10 to 12 business professionals I coach or mentor, 80 percent are usually good apprentices, 10 percent are bad apprentices, and 10 percent are beautiful apprentices. On average, I spend 30 minutes or less a month with each of the good apprentices. I usually spend two or three hours a month with each of the bad apprentices, trying to help them evolve to good apprentices. I typically invest two or three months coaching bad apprentices—sometimes more, if I feel I can help them—but if I feel I can no longer help, I will drop the apprentice. I do not like to use the popular "You're fired." Finally, I spend as much time or as little time as needed with the beautiful apprentices. The beautiful apprentices are people I enjoy spending time with, and I am confident they are making a real, positive difference in the lives of others.

Lastly, I have learned over the years what a good coach does and does not do, from the numerous outstanding coaches and mentors I have been fortunate enough to work with, including

- Lt. General Edward P. Barry, Jr., U.S. Air Force (retired)
- W. Gregor Macfarlan, CPCM, past national president, National Contract Management Association (NCMA)

- Jack Carpenter, former president, Professional Systems and Services, Lucent Technologies
- Bernie Myers, Ph.D., senior vice president, Bechtel Corporation
- Dr. William C. Pursch, CPCM, president, Pursch Associates, and past national president, NCMA

Selected Interview

Name: Gail A. Parrott, CFCM

Job Title: eBusiness Lead, Core Contracts

Organization: The Boeing Company

Location: St. Louis, Missouri

Key Responsibilities: St. Louis site contracts lead of eBusiness projects, including electronic data interchange, wide area workflow, unique identification, radio frequency identification, and Web services.

Brief Resume: Joined McDonnell Douglas Corporation in 1997, now a subsidiary of The Boeing Company. Currently serves as the eBusiness lead for the core contracts organization in St. Louis, Missouri. Previously served in the accounting organization supporting numerous major aircraft programs, including F/A-18, AV-8, and others. Earned a B.S. degree in accounting from Southern Illinois University, an M.B.A. from Fontbonne University, and a certified federal contracts manager (CFCM) professional certification from the National Contract Management Association. A two-term president of the NCMA St. Louis Gateway chapter.

Questions & Answers

Question: What personal leadership characteristics are most important for building successful buying or selling teams?

Answer: There are many important leadership characteristics for building successful teams, but three stand out above all. First, a leader must be passionate about a vision or goal. Second, a leader must have the ability to inspire the team members to stretch beyond their comfort zones to develop new skills. Third, while maintaining the same level of passion and inspiration, a leader must have the determination to see it through, no matter what obstacles emerge.

Question: What are the core competencies of a successful buying or selling team leader?

Answer: Core competencies of a successful team leader begin with the ability to have a "big picture" vision, strategically develop an achievable plan, and inspire team members to enthusiastically support and take ownership of that vision. These characteristics require a leader to have excellent listening as well as oral and written communication skills and the ability to provide continuous encouragement. Most important, a successful leader is able to identify and position team members to draw on each member's strengths, while that member is developing new skills to improve his or her weaknesses.

Bottom line: a true leader has a genuine desire to help team members continuously develop new skills and evolve throughout their careers.

Question: In regard to the S3 leadership process, which step do you believe is the most important? Why?

Answer: Step 5, Build Leaders at Every Level, is the most important step. It is never too early to begin developing quality team members into leaders, nor should that developmental process ever end. Whether a person is fresh out of college and into the workforce or the chief executive officer of a Fortune 500 company, everyone has room for improvement, growth, and development. Developing effective leaders at every level of an organization does require time, effort, and money, but it should be considered an investment that improves not only the quality of the team members, but also their quality of life. Organizations that provide mentoring programs ensure that they retain the best workforce, while continuously developing an elite team of leaders.

Question: Please provide a brief personal experience that you believe best illustrates leadership in buying or selling.

Answer: After receiving several requests, I agreed to take on the role of president of the St. Louis Gateway Chapter for NCMA. My initial mind-set was simply to maintain the chapter's monthly meeting and annual educational seminar. At that time, there was no grand vision to grow the chapter; however, that soon changed, following my attendance at a Leadership Summit and the Aerospace and Defense Conference hosted by NCMA. After networking with other chapters and learning what NCMA truly represents, I formed a great vision to diversify the chapter membership to better represent the entire St. Louis market region, increase the educational programs, and create a more networking and mentoring environment. I knew that my vision would require a few years and many quality volunteers; however, my passion for it was so great that I was able to inspire both old and new members of the organization. Thus far, the St. Louis chapter has increased its membership by 35 percent, partners with two other not-for-profit organizations, provides three additional educational venues, and began tapping into the next generation of contract administrators and leaders by developing a university outreach program. Even though my presidency will end soon, the president-elect and other officers will continue to embrace, invest in, and develop this vision, as they too will continue to evolve as leaders and mentors.

Coaching Others to Understand the S3 Leadership Process

In addition to helping others improve their buying and selling leadership skills, it is important as a coach to help others understand, value, and execute all of the Six Steps to Success. It is our experience that most people understand, value, and execute only a few of the steps:

- Step 1: Think the Talk
- Step 2: Talk the Talk
- Step 3: Walk the Talk
- Step 4: Execute Performance Plans
- Step 5: Build Leaders and Every Level
- Step 6: Achieve Excellence with Integrity

As a good coach, you should seek to understand which of the S3 your apprentice truly understands, values, and effectively executes consistently. Helping others to truly think the talk, talk the talk, and walk the talk will then allow you to coach them to successfully execute performance plans, build leaders at every level of their organizations, and achieve excellence with integrity. The S3 leadership process has proven to be highly effective for thousands of people worldwide. We are now sharing it with you in hopes you will share it with others, to make a positive difference in everyone's life.

We have found that most buying and selling organizations seldom really think the talk. Instead, our experience and research shows that most buying and selling organizations focus heavily on talk the talk and, sometimes, walk the talk; inconsistently execute performance plans; do insufficient leadership succession planning at most levels of their organizations; and desire to achieve excellence with integrity, yet are not really sure what that is or how to get it! Chapter 10 provides excellent insights for both buying and selling organizations on key actions, proven effective processes, and best practices they should use to achieve success.

Coaching Others to Learn the Power of Reading Themselves, People, and the Situation

Intuition is a beautiful thing! In life and in business many people have learned to trust their gut instincts. We believe that the best leaders are people who have truly mastered the ability to read themselves, other people, and situations. Teaching others to read themselves, other people, and situations takes time, practice, and patience.

The ability to read themselves—their strengths, areas needing improvement, and state of mind—is vital to become effective buying or selling team leaders.[4]

Intuitive leaders can quickly assess other people and their hopes, concerns, fears, and personal integrity. Said differently, an intuitive leader can spot a liar and a fake from a mile away in the dark!

Contextual intelligence, or *zeitgeist* leadership, is an extremely valuable asset. Truly effective buying and selling business leaders are able to vary their strategy, tactics, style, and execution with the situation. Leaders who are able to read the situation understand that one size does not fit all. It is important to learn to adapt to the situation, to find a way to achieve a win-win scenario. In Chapter 9, we discuss this situational awareness and adaptive ability in more detail.

A Personal Story: Read the Situation!

William C. Pursch

In 1989, I led a group of NCMA educators and professionals to the People's Republic of China. Our mission was to assess the progress made in contract management education and training since our initial visit to China in 1986. The delegation was under the auspices of the Citizen's Ambassador People-to-People program.

We arrived in Beijing at the height of the student demonstration for democracy. We finished our five-day stay in Beijing and left for Xi'an for two days of meetings. We left Xi'an by overnight train to Wuhan on the Yangtze River. Upon arriving in Wuhan, we learned that "something terrible happened in Beijing," but we couldn't get any details. We were scheduled for three days of meetings in Wuhan, which we attended but not in the order they were originally scheduled. We found out from our guides that we were being steered around student demonstrations in Wuhan; that was why our meeting locations kept changing. By now rumors were really flying about what was going on in China.

Our final destination in China was Xiamen, a very progressive city in a designated Special Economic Zone, where joint ventures were being developed. During our 1986 visit to Xiamen, we visited three joint venture plants. Now, in 1989, there were 35 joint venture plants, and more were being constructed. We were scheduled to leave our hotel at 6:00 a.m. by van, cross the Yangtze River, and arrive at the airport. At 11:00 p.m., the night before our departure, I was advised to have everyone ready to go at 4:30 a.m. because the word on the street was that the students were going to barricade the bridge in protest over what had happened in Beijing. I quickly passed the word to the other delegates to be ready earlier, and we assembled in the hotel lobby at 4:30 a.m. The lobby was totally deserted—not even desk clerks were present, and no van was in sight.

In the Orient, patience is not only a virtue—it is a necessity! Our van finally arrived at 5:30 a.m., and we quickly loaded and left for the airport. As we crossed the far side of the bridge, there came the students in a solid mass, marching down the main street toward the bridge. We had to leave the main route and take side roads to get to the airport. The students proceeded to block the bridge, the only one over the river for 200 miles, for three days until they were finally persuaded to leave.

On arrival in Xiamen, which is located on the southern coast of China directly across the straits from Quemoy and Matsu Islands and Taiwan, I found a message waiting that the People-to-People program would call me that evening to discuss our early departure from China. During the day, we began our meetings in Xiamen. We saw no increased security and no evidence of any student demonstrations. It was a totally different atmosphere than at Wuhan.

The phone call from the People-to-People program was from a frantic director who informed me that he had been trying to reach me for several days. He wanted us out of China immediately and was sending a representative from Hong Kong to make arrangements for us to fly to Guangzhou and then go by train to Hong Kong. I informed the director that we were fine and that we had a direct flight to Hong Kong from Xiamen. Our guides had checked, and our plane reservations were still valid. I had already discussed the completion of the mission with the members of the delegation, and we agreed that we should stay with the original plan. I argued that to fly to Guangzhou would put us deeper into China and, in the absence of unrest in Xiamen, we wanted to finish the mission. The director told me that his representative would arrive in the morning, and we should listen to him. Then he hung up. We continued to follow our plans in Xiamen. When the representative from Hong Kong arrived, we learned that all flights from Xiamen to anywhere were fully booked. He and I agreed that the best course of action was to complete our mission and fly out to Hong Kong on schedule.

As we boarded our plane for the two-hour flight to Hong Kong, we waved goodbye to the representative from the People-to-People program. All flights out were fully booked, and now he was stranded in Xiamen. It was the classic case of top management being totally out of touch with what was really happening in the field. Sometimes higher management has to back off and have faith that the manager on the scene knows what he or she is doing. When we reached Hong Kong, we finally got the whole story of what really had happened in Beijing. We were the last People-to-People delegation to leave China.

Coaching Others to Develop Leadership Succession Plans at Every Level of the Organization

Let us begin with five key observations about leadership. First, it is important to remember that although everyone has the ability to become an effective and successful leader in life and in business, many people do not want the leadership responsibilities and challenges. Second, just because someone wants to be the leader, to be in charge, does not mean that person is prepared or is the right person at the right time. Third, every organization needs successful leaders at every level of the organization, not just at the top. Fourth, just because someone has a higher title or rank does not mean he or she is the real leader of the organization. In fact, many de facto, informal leaders really lead organizations as a result of the strength of their knowledge and expertise, outstanding communication skills, reputation for integrity, and so forth. Fifth, because no one can be the leader forever, leadership succession planning is essential to long-term organizational success.

According to *The Leadership Pipeline,* "Succession planning is perpetuating the enterprise by filling the pipeline with high-performing people to assure that every leadership level has an abundance of these performers to draw from, both now and in the future.[5]

Clearly, succession planning should be done on the basis of merit—skills and demonstrated performance—not who you know, how long you have been at an organization, some diversity quota, or where you went to school. Two of the most difficult aspects of succession planning are (1) racking and stacking your organization's talent and (2) deciding who is ready for a rotation or promotion.

In *The Leadership Pipeline,* Ram Charan, Stephen Drotter, and James Noel describe three categories of potential performance:[6]

- **Turn potential.** Able to do work at the next level in three to five years or sooner
- **Growth potential.** Able to do the work of bigger jobs at the same level in the near term
- **Mastery potential.** Able to do the same kind of work currently being done, only better.

The authors discuss and assess current performance in terms of three levels: high, medium, and low. Combining the three levels of potential with the three levels of performance creates a simple yet proven effective leadership development matrix **(Form 8-1)**.

The leadership development matrix helps supervisors at all levels evaluate talent. Clearly, not all high performers are ready or willing to be promoted. Likewise, many medium performers have the talent to become high performers if properly supported and given the right opportunity at the right time. People evaluated for a year or more in boxes 8 and 9 should be given another opportunity to excel in another organization!

Talent assessment and succession planning is a must in every organization. However, if you work in the business of buying and selling, where every dollar counts, then talent assessment and succession planning is even more critical to your ability to operate within budget and achieve profitability. If you want to create a true performance-based culture within your organization, you must begin by conducting performance-based talent assessments, providing performance-based pay, and making performance-based promotions. If not, then you are simply talking the talk, not walking the talk.

Form 8-1 Leadership Development Matrix

	High	Medium	Low
Turn (high) potential	Box 1	Box 3	Box 6
Growth (medium) potential	Box 2	Box 5	Box 8
Mastery (low) potential	Box 4	Box 7	Box 9

Source: Drotter Human Resources Inc.

Summary

In this chapter, we focused on Step 5, Build Leaders at Every Level. Specifically, we discussed the need for leaders to coach others to (1) focus on mastering the five buying and selling leadership competencies (Chapter 2); (2) understand the S3 buying and selling leadership process (Chapters 3–9); (3) learn the power of reading themselves, other people, and situations; and (4) develop leadership succession plans at every level of the organization. We have provided numerous checklists of best practices, two insightful interviews of buying and selling team leaders, and two personal stories, one about coaching and one about the leadership ability to read and adapt to the situation. We hope this chapter helps you become a more proactive and effective coach or mentor so that you can make a positive difference in the lives of others. In the next chapter, we focus on the sixth and final step of our leadership process—Achieve Excellence with Integrity.

Questions to Consider

1. Do you have an effective coach helping you improve your performance?
2. Are you currently coaching others? If so, how well are you doing?
3. What are the most important attributes of a good coach?

4. What are the most important attributes of a good apprentice?
5. Is it really important to build leaders at every level of the organization?

---

[1] John C. Maxwell, *The 21 Irrefutable Laws of Leadership* (Nashville, TN: Thomas Nelson Inc., 1998).

[2] Ibid.

[3] Ram Charan, Stephen Drotter, and James Noel, *The Leadership Pipeline: How to Build the Leadership Powered Company* (New York: Jossey-Bass, 2001).

[4] Ibid.

[5] Ibid.

[6] Ibid.

Chapter 9

Leadership Step 6: Achieve Excellence with Integrity

"To achieve excellence with integrity, you must care more than others think is wise, risk more than others think is safe, and do more than others believe is possible!"

—Gregory A. Garrett

Introduction

How much confidence do Americans have in their leaders? To find out, *U.S. News & World Report* and Harvard University's Center for Public Leadership commissioned a national survey on the state of U.S. leadership today. In telephone interviews conducted in September 2005, pollsters at The Segmentation Company, a division of the public opinion firm Yankelovich, asked a representative sample of 1,374 adults their views on a range of leadership questions. The poll yielded some striking findings:

- Americans are highly critical of the current state of the nation's leadership. Nearly two out of three believe their leaders have been corrupted by being in power.
- Military and medical leaders earn the highest marks, while, as in other surveys, respondents have the lowest confidence in the press.
- A large majority say the public shares responsibility for the nation's leadership woes. More than four in five agree that "Americans who don't keep up on important issues are a big part of today's leadership problem."

The full results and the survey methodology are available at **http://www.usnews.com/leaders.**

If your quest is to achieve excellence with integrity, then there are two fundamental questions. First, what is excellence? Second, what is integrity? Let us begin with the term "excellence." Excellence is defined as the fact or state of (1) excelling, surpassing, or being better than others and (2) being superior to others in some good or desirable quality, attainment, or performance.[1]

Next, let us examine the term "integrity." Integrity is defined as (1) soundness of moral principle and character; uprightness; honesty; (2) the state of being whole, entire, or undiminished; and (3) the state of being in sound, unimpaired, or perfect condition.[2]

Thus, if your quest is to achieve excellence with integrity in the business of buying or selling products, services, and solutions, your goals should include the following:

1. Develop a state of buying or selling that surpasses your competitors' performance (quality, cost, on-time delivery, etc.).
2. Execute your buying or selling practices with soundness of moral principle, character, and honesty.
3. Create a culture that seeks to develop and maintain a sound business environment that is based on respect.

With the two key definitions and three important goals in mind, one can build a highly successful game plan for oneself and one's organization to achieve excellence with integrity. In this chapter, we examine how you can draw on all of the previously discussed steps in the Six Steps for Success (S3) leadership process; focus your actions on the seven principles of leadership; and achieve the three goals of excellence with integrity.

Seven Principles of Leadership

From our experience and research, we have determined that there are seven principles of leadership that are essential to creating successful buying and selling team leaders **(Table 9-1).**

Table 9-1 Seven Principles of Leadership in Buying and Selling

1. The Principle of Respect	**5.** The Principle of Rewards and Penalties
2. The Principle of Vision	
3. The Principle of Best Value	**6.** The Principle of *Zeitgeist*
4. The Principle of Accountability	**7.** The Principle of Priorities

The Principle of Respect

When working in the business of buying and selling, you must realize that you cannot buy respect; it must be earned. You can earn respect through your thoughts, words, and demonstrated actions over time (Steps 1, 2, and 3 of the S3 leadership process). While most people initially will pay some respect to a person with a high-level position or title, that respect will diminish rapidly if the individual does not consistently demonstrate the abilities to think the talk, talk the talk, and walk the talk.

Respect can be further earned by leaders who work with their buying and selling team members to build individual and team performance plans. The individual and team performance plans should be linked to help the organization and its customers achieve excellence with integrity. Most people want to work for someone who is honest and does what is right for the right reason at the right time. Most people do not respect suck-ups; yes men; people with negative, "can't do" attitudes; people who don't care; people who are retired on the job; people who treat others like crap; or people who say one thing and mean another.

People do not follow others by accident. We believe that most individuals seek out people they respect. Generally, on a scale of 1 = weak leadership to 10 = strong leadership, a person who is an 8 in leadership does not look for a 6 to follow but instead seeks and follows a 9 or 10. In nearly all cases, the less skilled want to follow a more highly skilled leader.[3]

However, in life and in business, it is often the case that people in higher-level positions do not necessarily have higher levels of leadership. Thus, the leadership gap is the reason so many organizations suffer from poor to mediocre performance. Also, the leadership gap is the reason so many people are frustrated—because the people above them do not have the skills to coach them to a higher level of leadership.

Occasionally, a strong leader will choose to follow someone weaker. But when this happens, it is usually for a good reason. For example, the stronger leader may do it out of respect for the person's rank, office or title, or past accomplishments. Sometimes the stronger leaders may be following the organizational chain of command, out of a respect for duty. Yet it is widely proven that followers are attracted to people who are better leaders than themselves. It is also important to note that the more leadership skills an individual possesses, the more rapidly he or she recognizes leadership or lack thereof in others.

A key aspect of earning respect is being confident in your competence. Said differently, a leader must know that he or she knows and must make it clear to others that he or she knows! Some people consider such displays bragging. We disagree. We believe that displaying a strong sense of self-confidence in your knowledge and abilities is vital if others are to respect you. Of course, some people can and do go too far, thus becoming egomaniacs (a.k.a., Napoleons). In all things, balance is important to success. So, treat others with respect, show confidence in your knowledge and abilities, and seek out stronger leaders who will help you grow!

In buying and selling products, services, and solutions, it is important for the organization to create an ethical culture. The creation and use of codes of conduct and ethics and compliance training programs have proven very effective for many organizations. **Form 9-1** provides a simple yet effective checklist of sample ethics program metrics.

Form 9-1 Sample Ethics Program Metrics

☐ Presence of program	Yes or No?
☐ Part of values statement	Yes or No?
☐ Electronically available	Yes or No?
☐ Provided to customers and suppliers	Yes or No?
☐ Training program	Yes or No?
☐ Program reviewed and periodically updated	Yes or No?
☐ Effectiveness of training program	▪ Employee comments ▪ Supervisor comments

Source: Adapted from Jay Billings, "Enhancing Your Ethics Program," *Contract Management* (June 2005): 12.

A Personal Story: You Have to Know When to Transition

William C. Pursch

My first assignment as a field grade officer in the U.S. Army was as the materiel control officer for the Depot Maintenance Facility, Second Logistical Command, Okinawa. It was 1968, and our mission was to repair, if possible, battle-damaged and worn-out five ton, two and one-half ton, and three-fourths ton trucks coming out of Vietnam.

My boss was a full colonel who left no doubt in anyone's mind that he expected to make general officer, even if he had to pave the way with dog tags. He was the most absolute tyrant I have ever met, before or since. A person's very best was never good enough for him. He was a Theory X manager and an absolute jerk to every one of his junior officers. I watched him destroy the careers of more than a dozen junior officers and wondered when, not if, my time would come.

We were preparing for our annual inspection. The results of the inspection would really affect the colonel's efficiency report and therefore his chance at promotion to brigadier general. I had just received my efficiency report from him, which was acceptable, although not glowing, because it had been one year since my last report. Each division chief prepared a set of briefing charts to be used to brief the inspector general (IG) during the inspection. We then submitted the charts to the colonel for his review. It didn't take long for my phone to ring and the colonel to order "Get in here!"

When I arrived at his office, my charts were strewn over the table with red changes marked all over them. He said to me, "Take these charts and make the changes I have indicated." When I looked at the changes, I could see that he was fabricating and falsifying the data to make himself look good. I said, "Sir, I can't change the charts because the data came from my official records, and if the IG checks the charts with the data, it will be obvious the charts are wrong." He exploded with a string of expletives and ordered me again to do what he commanded. I requested his permission to talk to the commanding general about his order to falsify documents, and I thought he would come over his desk and hit me. He said I could talk to whomever I wanted, but the charts better be changed or my career was over.

Once again the phrase, "What are your actions and orders at this time?" flashed through my mind. I went home that night and sat down with my wife, laying out the entire scenario. We had been married only two years, and she expected to be an Army wife for a full career. I told her that I intended to go to the general rather than compromise my integrity and that by doing so I might be ending my Army career. At the very least, I would have to change my assignment or risk an adverse efficiency report that would kill my chances for promotion. Since I was stationed on Okinawa, the easiest assignment change would be to return to Vietnam for my second tour, and she and I would be separated for a year. Without any hesitation, she said, "You do what is right, whatever the outcome."

Imagine my dismay when I found the commanding general was backing the colonel. How dare this upstart major challenge the orders of a colonel? He raked me over the coals, up one side and down the other as he chewed me out like I had never been chewed out before. When he finished, it was perfectly evident to me that it was time to leave the command. That night I called my assignment officer in the Pentagon (because of the time difference it was daytime there) and told him what had transpired. Within seven days, my orders arrived, and I was on my way to Danang, Vietnam, and the most rewarding assignment of my Army career.

The IG found the falsified data in the colonel's charts, and the colonel never made general. The commanding general retired soon after. Today there are laws in place that are supposed to protect individuals who refuse to follow illegal orders.

The Principle of Vision

We have a slightly different perspective on the principle of vision than you may have read about in other books on leadership. We believe an effective buying or selling team leader needs to have a clear vision of the following key items:

1. How the organization should look and perform
2. How the buying or selling team should be structured
3. What is important to customers and to team members
4. What his or her future should be
5. Who his or her successor should be

First, a successful business leader should have a vision of how the organization should look and perform. One of the proven keys to success is the ability to foresee or anticipate the need for change before a crisis occurs. A successful buying or selling business leader should be continually evaluating the organizational structure, people, and performance goals and metrics. All organizations, small or large, must evolve to survive and thrive. The old model of business will not always work in the future. Thus, successful leaders always have one eye on where the organization needs to be in the future.

Second, a successful business leader should have a vision of how the buying or selling team should be structured. Today, the classic functional silos are largely dead. The business environment has driven the need to form integrated project teams or integrated solution teams to meet the multifunctional and multiparty needs of demanding customers. Serving as a value-added member of a larger team has also driven the importance of teamwork. Understanding the forces that affect teamwork and being able to foresee the right structure for the team is very important.

Third, a successful business leader should have a vision of what is important to customers and to team members. You must talk to your customers, not assume you know, and ask them what is important to their business. Then ask your customers how you can help them be successful. Likewise, ask your team members what is important to them and what you can do to help them be successful. After you ask, stop talking, listen, write down their responses, and then carefully consider what you can do to help them be successful. Next, inform them of your vision, and then do it!

Fourth, a successful business leader should have a vision of his or her own future. Many people realize now that we must take charge of our careers. We must create our own employability through our individual combination of education, experience, networking, and performance. For most people in business, the future is built piece by piece or project by project at a series of organizations or companies, small or large, in the public or private sector, over time. In the future, business professionals will understand that (1) learning is continuous, (2) self-reliance is essential, (3) each career consists of numerous mini-careers, (4) each mini-career consists of numerous projects, (5) communication is vital, (6) teamwork is fundamental, (7) people are talent, and (8) leadership talent drives success.[4]

Fifth, a successful business leader should have a vision of his or her successor. For you to move upward, you must help develop an appropriate successor for your current position. Thus, successful business leaders grow talent, especially to take over their current positions. Succession planning is vital to the health and long-term success of every organization. Clearly, our perspective on the principle of vision requires you to master a multivisionary ability to achieve success as a buying or selling team leader.

Selected Interview

Name: Gary Poleskey

Job Title: Vice President

Organization: Dayton Aerospace Inc.

Location: Dayton, Ohio

Key Responsibilities: Consultant on contracting and business strategy issues, including such areas as past performance, contract structure, and performance-based incentives.

Brief Resume: Thirty years of experience in contracting and acquisition management involving major weapon systems, research and development, and operational base–level contracting. Also responsible for acquisition policy formulation at the levels of major commands and the secretary of the Air Force with emphasis on source selection, past performance, and multi-year contracting policy.

Served as a principle business adviser to the commander and vice commander of Aeronautical Systems Center. Managed, in conjunction with the director, a contracting workforce of more than 1,000 professionals. Directed contracting operations of the Training System, System Program Office (SPO) with 34 people and annual contracting actions valued in excess of $2.5 billion. Developed contracting strategies for the C-17 air crew and maintenance training systems, the Special Operations Forces mission rehearsal devices, and the revamping of training systems for the C-130 and C-141. Structured, advocated within the Pentagon and Capitol Hill, and signed the first Air Force multi-year contract for 480 F-16s at $2.9 billion.

M.B.A., Northwestern University

B.S. in marketing, University of Illinois

Questions and Answers

Question: What personal leadership characteristics are most important for building successful buying or selling teams?

Answer: Honesty, integrated planning, and persistent project execution.

Question: What are the core competencies of a successful buying or selling team leader?

Answer: Having a clear vision of the future of the organization and leading with integrity.

Question: What are the most significant challenges you must overcome to be a successful buying or selling team leader?

Answer: Ensuring alignment of purpose between the buying team and the customer's needs.

Question: Please provide a brief personal experience that you believe best illustrates leadership in buying or selling?

Answer: A number of years ago, I took over as director of contracting for the Training System's buying office at Wright-Patterson Air Force Base at a time when it had a reputation for being unresponsive and uninspired. As a group, we established a vision for the organization and ensured that it aligned with Air Force and command leadership needs and objectives. We realigned our team structure and the team names to identify them closely with the program management teams. I asked teams and individuals to make integrated plans to complete their projects and then persist through to project completion. I never asked them to work harder than I did. I celebrated their successes and did my best to ensure that we had the right resources overall to accomplish our mission. As a result, at the end of my second year, the office accomplished the largest amount of work in its history, and we were picked as the best systems buying office at the Aeronautical Systems Center.

The Principle of Best Value

The term "best value" can have several meanings, depending on one's perspective. The U.S. government defines best value as the expected outcome of an acquisition that, in the government's estimation, provides the greatest overall benefit in response to the requirement. Best value is usually associated with the source selection process. However, the concept can also be applied to other situations.

In all situations, best value is a tool for the buyer and seller to establish a proper balance between factors such as price, quality, technical design, and performance. Best value applies to products and services already developed, as opposed to value engineering (also referred to as value analysis), which examines trade-offs during the design process.

Perhaps it would be more helpful to define best value in terms of what it is and what it is not. It is a disciplined, balanced approach, an assessment of trade-offs between price and performance; a team effort; an evaluation of qualitative and quantitative factors; and an integrated risk assessment. Best value is not price cutting; uncompensated overtime; accounting gimmicks; specials, one-time discounts; the shifting of all price and performance risk to the contractor; or an excuse not to define requirements properly.

For our purposes, best value is a determination of which offer presents the best trade-off between price and performance, where quality is considered an integral performance factor. The best-value decision can be made using a variety of qualitative and quantitative management tools.

Relation of best value to contract negotiations. Best-value contracting is intrinsically tied to the process of contract negotiations for several reasons. First of all, to be successful, negotiations must focus on some specific quantifiable objective. Best value offers a meaningful objective to each negotiation party. In addition, contract negotiation typically requires trade-offs among various interrelated factors. Using best-value techniques helps contract management professionals assess the effect of these trade-offs to ensure a successful negotiation session. These techniques also help determine the range of values (e.g., cost, production, quality requirements, life-cycle cost) for which trade-offs can be made while preserving the optimal balance between price, performance, and quality. Finally, best value establishes realistic negotiation objectives up front. For example, best-value contracting techniques can discourage the use of unrealistic initial negotiation positions by contractors seeking to win a contract with practices such as uncompensated overtime or unrealistically low initial prices.

To be successful, best-value contracting must be an integral part of the acquisition strategy planning process; therefore, early planning must occur. Best-value contracting also requires a team effort by various disciplines such as engineering, accounting, legal, manufacturing, and contracts to clearly identify all acquisition requirements and determine the optimum trade-offs among various factors.

Trade-offs in making a best-value decision should always consider the objectives of both the buyer and seller, as discussed previously. Trade-offs may have to be revisited as negotiations progress, since the needs of the buyer and seller will be revealed (usually incrementally) during the course of negotiations.

The level of analysis in a best-value trade-off decision depends on the complexity of the particular procurement. Low-technology procurements usually require a simple, straightforward trade-off approach, since price is normally the primary factor. However, high-technology procurements usually require more sophisticated trade-off analysis tools, because price is usually secondary to technical and quality concerns.

Because of the many types of contracting situations, there is no single preferred way to determine best value. Rather, a combination of techniques should be used, preferably integrating quantitative and qualitative factors.

The use of a team approach helps one make the necessary trade-offs rationally **(Figure 9-1)**.

Figure 9-1 Sample: Best-Value Proposal Evaluation Process

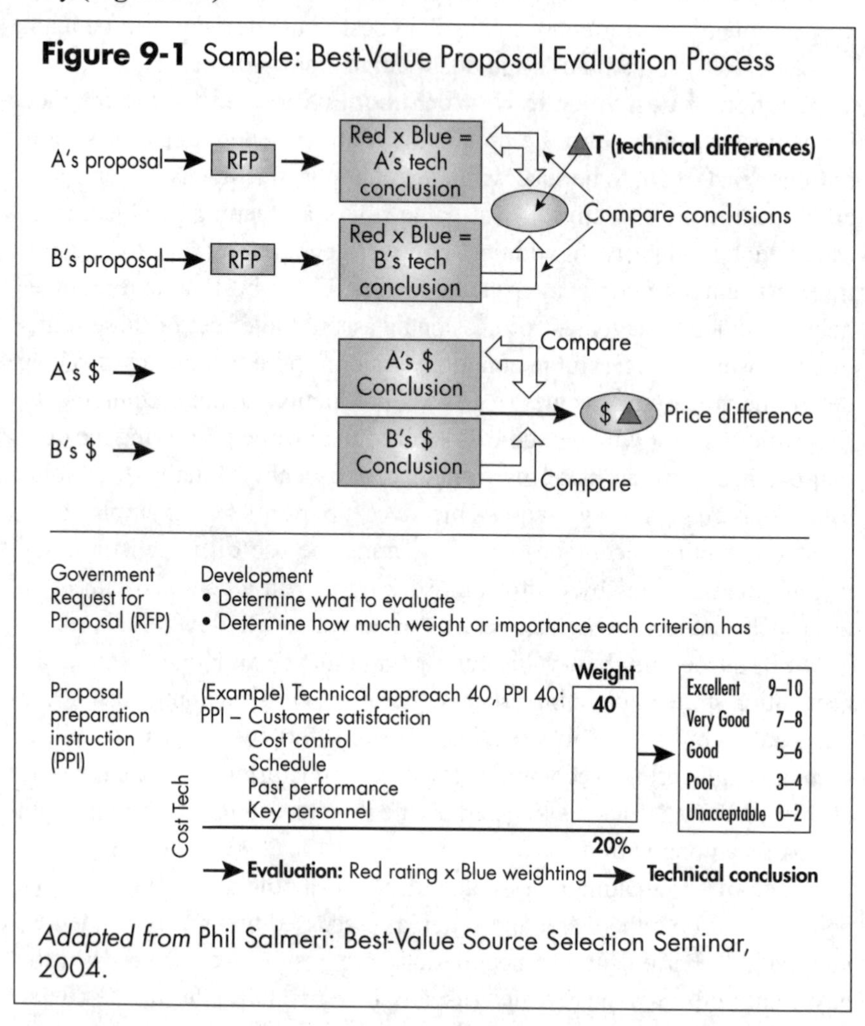

Adapted from Phil Salmeri: Best-Value Source Selection Seminar, 2004.

The evolution of best-value negotiation. The practice of best-value contracting has continued to grow in importance over the past decade. The federal regulatory environment has continually evolved, gradually allowing for increased best-value contracting techniques. Government contractors have responded to these changes by offering best-value pricing as a part of an overall value-based cost and technical approach, thus making them more efficient and competitive. In addition, the items and services to be purchased have continued to become more technical and complex (e.g., sophisticated consulting, advanced hardware, software, and professional services). As a result, quality and past performance factors often are more important than price-related factors. Also, the emphasis on making best-value purchasing decisions will increase as the government refines its attempts to obtain more value for its money. Finally, the continual improvement in the professional qualifications and credentials of both government and industry acquisition workforce personnel has fostered the use of best value on both sides.

The commercial sector has long used best-value contracting techniques as a means to remain competitive and profitable. The federal government has not had the same degree of flexibility to employ best-value techniques because it must comply with various requirements that have no material bearing on the business aspects of the contract but are mandated by law to be included in all federal acquisitions as a matter of public policy. As a result, best-value implementation has not achieved its full potential in the government contracting arena. See **Tables 9-2** and **9-3** for lists of best-value dos and don'ts.

Table 9-2 Best-Value Negotiation Dos

Do
▪ Develop or obtain proven best-value contracting tools.
▪ Select best-value measurement tools that are easy to understand and use.
▪ Ensure that quality factors do not become secondary to cost issues, except for noncomplex acquisitions.
▪ Consider using automation tools for best-value decision support during source selection.
▪ Tailor best-value measurement tools to specific procurement situations, realizing that complexity increases with the size and scope of the acquisition.
▪ Use a contract type that allocates risks fairly.
▪ Provide contract incentives for superior (quality) performance.
▪ Implement guidance throughout the agency or company.
▪ Continue to improve techniques.
▪ Make each best-value decision a team effort among contracts, engineering, production, quality assurance, and other related offices.
▪ Ensure a best-value approach supports the overall negotiation strategy.
▪ Realize that the best-value approach works only if you know what you're buying. Thus, all relevant price and performance-related issues need to be researched.
▪ Document the rationale for best-value decisions.
▪ Allow flexibility for trade-offs.

Source: Richard J. Hernandez, *Negotiating a Quality Contract* (McLean, VA: NCMA, 1992).

Table 9-3 Best-Value Negotiation Don'ts

Don't
▪ Use (1) the low bid or (2) the lowest-cost, technically acceptable offer as a substitute for best value, when best value is applicable. ▪ Expect to make a good best-value decision without clearly defining your approach up front. ▪ Attempt to implement best-value contracting without properly training acquisition personnel. ▪ Forget to research all relevant issues, especially technical factors. ▪ Make best-value decision tools unnecessarily complex. ▪ Allow for such practices as buy-in or uncompensated overtime. ▪ Use auctioning, technical leveling, or technical transfusion techniques as a substitute for best-value contracting. ▪ Forget to formalize the elements of the best-value agreement as soon as possible after contract negotiations. ▪ Allow an offeror's low initial price to overshadow life-cycle cost considerations. ▪ Expect to obtain the maximum level of economy when buying noncommercial off-the-shelf items.
Source: Richard J. Hernandez, *Negotiating a Quality Contract* (McLean, VA: NCMA, 1992).

The Principle of Accountability

Unfortunately, today far too many people want to receive awards without being held accountable for the results, especially if the results are bad. Many people in business like to play the lie-and-blame game or finger-pointing game. It appears that many people have been brought up not being held accountable for their actions, always being allowed to make up excuses or pass the blame for failure to others. In fact, we may have an entire generation of people now in the business world who practice the art of Teflon® management, where nothing sticks to them, anything that goes wrong is not their fault, and someone else is to blame.

We believe that to become a leader one must accept authority, responsibility, and accountability. Likewise, team members must show respect for authority, accept responsibilities assigned, and be accountable for their actions and inactions. One of the most common terms used in business today is "push-back." Push-back occurs when you as a leader have not obtained respect, support, and buy-in from your team members or business partners. A certain level of push-back is natural and expected. Regrettably, many organizations are unable to move beyond mediocrity because of the high level of push-back encountered anytime anyone tries to do nearly anything different from the status quo.

We believe that an effective buying or selling team leader must stand up to push-back by implementing a game plan to overcome or work around the obstacles. Push-back is common at mid-management levels in many organizations. Thus, team leaders can conduct all-hands meetings, focus group meetings, or teleconferences to try to inform all of their team members about what needs to be done, why it is important to them, and how it will help the organization. A true business leader must be persistent in driving the principle of accountability through words and actions. It can take weeks, months, and sometimes years to overcome deep-seated organizational push-back, Teflon management, and accountability-free people. Of course, you may need to remove one or more people who are the biggest obstacles if they do not see the value of accountability.

In contracts, the individual accountable for the contract award, contract modifications, contract termination, or contract closeout should be formally designated or appointed in writing. In all contract management actions, roles and responsibilities must be well defined, documented, and understood by all parties involved in the deal to ensure success.

The Principle of Rewards and Penalties

We believe individuals must motivate themselves and be accountable for the responsibilities that they are assigned or agree to perform. However, we believe team leaders are responsible for stimulating individual's motivation through an appropriate blend of rewards and penalties. People respond differently to various forms of rewards. Thus, some rewards are more effective than others in stimulating high performance. Some people are stimulated by being given large, complex projects, with high risk and high visibility, while others would consider such assignments a punishment. Some people truly appreciate a simple thank you, either in person or by phone. Many people value receiving a formal letter of appreciation on which senior organization leaders are copied. Yet most people believe the best way to reward high performance is with money, a bonus, a salary increase, or a promotion.

For a reward to be both affective and effective, the recipient must view the reward as positive and desirable, thus causing him or her to step up performance to achieve the reward. **Table 9-4** provides a list of various rewards that many buying or selling organizations provide to their people to stimulate high performance.

Table 9-4 List of Rewards

▪ Allow flexible schedule.	▪ Provide training.
▪ Provide better benefits.	▪ Provide coaching.
▪ Make people blush because of your praise.	▪ Provide travel opportunities.
▪ Just say thank you.	▪ Provide a bigger and better office.
▪ Send a thank you note.	▪ Promote the individual.
▪ Send a letter of appreciation.	▪ Provide more money—bonus or salary increase.
▪ Send a small, but appropriate gift.	▪ Provide stock—restricted stock or stock options.
▪ Provide challenging work.	▪ Provide a leadership development program.
▪ Increase visibility to senior leaders.	

While rewards can and do stimulate better performance for many people, rewards alone are not sufficient. In fact, many people are more significantly stimulated by the fear of penalties (negative incentives).

Table 9-5 List of Penalties

▪ Upset boss.	▪ Increased or decreased travel.
▪ Threat of being replaced.	▪ Increased micromanagement.
▪ Fear of being fired.	▪ Loss of certain benefits.
▪ Loss of reputation.	▪ Negative press.
▪ Loss of pay.	▪ No promotion opportunity.
▪ Loss of vacation days.	▪ No bonus.
▪ Fear of loss of face.	▪ No salary increase.
▪ Demotion.	▪ No stock.
▪ Increased or decreased workload.	▪ Forced relocation.
▪ Increased or decreased training.	

Table 9-5 provides a list of various penalties that many buying or selling organizations provide to stimulate high performance.

The key for any leader is to know his or her people and to apply an appropriate balance or blend of positive (rewards) and negative (penalties) incentives to stimulate consistent high performance.

The Principle of *Zeitgeist*

A leader's long-term success is derived from a combination of force of personality, breadth and depth of skills, and ability to adapt to changing business conditions. This combination is also known as *zeitgeist.* The notion of zeitgeist might be intangible, but the risks of contextual insensitivity are real and potentially significant. Clearly, zeitgeist—the ability to read the business landscape—is essential. If you cannot read the business landscape, you risk leading your organization in the wrong direction or choosing the wrong successors. An understanding of the zeitgeist and its implications has played a critical role in some of the greatest business victories of all time.

In business, especially in buying and selling, opportunities are deeply influenced by six contextual factors:

1. Demographics
2. Technology
3. Social mores
4. Government intervention
5. Labor
6. Global events

For buying or selling team leaders to be successful, especially at higher levels of an organization, they must have knowledge of these six contextual factors and the ability to adapt to changing situations. The best business leaders can see the writing on the wall or sense the winds of change and quickly adapt with the times.

For example, the U.S. government's enactment of the now infamous Sarbanes-Oxley Act of 2002 has dramatically affected American business in ways both good and bad. According to recent studies conducted by the International Association of Commercial and Contract Managers (IACCM), the Sarbanes-Oxley Act has had serious effects on U.S. buying and selling communities **(Figure 9-2).**

Figure 9-2 The Price of Regulatory Governance

IACCM 2005 survey results

- Sarbanes-Oxley Act has added about **10%** to the workload of the average commercial contracts professional in the United States.
- **80%** of IACCM U.S. members report a moderate to significant increase in the complexity of their work attributable to increased regulatory governance.
- **60%** struggle to explain and defend the Sarbanes–Oxley Act requirements to their overseas customers and suppliers.
- **40%** of the people surveyed report an increase in the cycle time to prepare and negotiate contracts.
- **25%** of the people surveyed highlight greater confrontation between the parties.

Source: International Association of Commercial and Contract Managers (IACCM), April 2005. (See www.iaccm.com.)

Case Study: General Electric

General Electric (GE) looks for potential compliance problems when it acquires a company. Last year, for example, GE discovered that representatives of InVision Technologies Inc., a Newark, California-based maker of bomb-detection equipment that GE had agreed to acquire, may have been making improper payments to obtain business in Thailand. U.S. laws prohibit companies from making such payments. GE alerted U.S. regulators, and InVision eventually agreed to pay $2.2 million in fines and disgorged profits as part of a settlement with the Justice Department and the Securities and Exchange Commission, without admitting wrongdoing.

Once the InVision acquisition was completed, GE embarked on a quicker-than-usual training program with InVision employees as part of the agreement with the government. At the same time, GE also re-screened outsiders who were doing business with InVision. Some InVision employees were dismissed, and GE also dropped some of InVision's distributors.

In most instances, GE employees undergo compliance training soon after joining the company. Like many companies, GE conducts much of the training online and tests employees on how to handle thorny issues such as unusual requests by a customer for money or requests to ignore a government regulation. The company also holds small group meetings in which employees are encouraged to ask questions and raise concerns over potentially improper behavior.

To reinforce its commitment to compliance, GE recently deployed a system to track how many employees are doing their homework. Every quarter, each business unit must tell the compliance department what percentage of its employees have completed the training sessions and what percentage have read and signed off on GE's *Spirit and Letter* ethics guide. The guide covers a range of issues, from determining when it is permissible to work with a competitor to checking customers against terrorist watchlists.

Case Study: United Technologies

United Technologies, of Hartford, Connecticut, whose units include Otis Elevators and Pratt & Whitney aircraft engines, is offering employees more specific training. Like GE, it is keeping tabs on managers to see what percentage of a manager's employees have completed compliance and ethics courses.

In 2007, the company will add a new wrinkle. It will evaluate managers and employees on specific behaviors reflective of good ethics, including whether the individuals have good communication skills, keep commitments, and maintain accountability. Additionally, United Technologies has a new online training module addressing the company's code of ethics.

The Principle of Priorities

The ability to rack and stack your organization's people, projects, and resources is critical to the success of the organization. Each buying or selling team leader must be able to effectively align the team's priorities to the strategic goals of the organization. While some people will argue that every aspect of business is potentially important, clearly some opportunities or projects are more important than others.

Unfortunately, many organizations in both the public and the private sector, suffer from managers who do a poor job of setting priorities. The common mistakes that managers tend to make are as follows:

- Lack of setting priorities
- Constantly changing priorities
- Outdated priorities
- Priorities not consistent with organizational strategies
- Failure to adequately communicate priorities

Stephen Covey, best-selling author of *The Seven Habits of Highly Effective People,* states you must "Put First Things First."[5] Too often people lose track of what is most important, often getting overly involved in solving minor issues. Likewise, too many managers spend too much time micromanaging team members. Thus, many managers find that they do not have the time to do the most important things because they spend too much time on the lesser things. Clearly, many buying and selling managers struggle to overcome such situations. The key to successfully executing priorities is to stay focused, plan your time appropriately, and spend your time wisely, which for most people is easy to say but difficult to accomplish.

Selected Interview

Name: Gregory C. Landon

Job Title: Customer Representative

Organization: U.S. Army

Key Responsibilities: Mr. Landon leads teams of contracting officers and contract negotiators. He also manages customer issues and acts as a joint partner for contracting issues with the Lockheed Martin Corporation.

Brief Resume: B.A. *cum laude* in history from Amherst College in 1971, M.A. in procurement management from Webster University in 1976, postgraduate courses in accounting and business at SUNY Binghamton and the Florida Institute of Technology.

Intern 1974–76 at Tank Automotive Command, Warren, Michigan. Contract specialist with the U.S. Army Materiel Command 1976–81, contracting officer with the U.S. Army 1981–85, supervisory contract specialist manager with the U.S. Army 1985–2005, various locations since 1976.

Member, National Contract Management Association, 1976–2005; president, local chapter, 2003–04

Certified Level III in Contracting, Defense Acquisition University 1994

Questions and Answers

Question: What personal leadership characteristics are most important for building successful buying or selling teams?

Answer: Demonstrates communication skills, including listening and the ability to build excitement and direction for the team, knows team member abilities and motivators, and acts the leader role clearly and with purpose.

Question: What are the core competencies of a successful buying or selling team leader?

Answer: The ability to define a goal and show a way to get there, the ability to inspire desire to reach the goal, and the ability to recognize contributions of others to fulfillment of the goal and instill the desire for more.

Question: In regard to the S3 leadership process, which step do you believe is the most important? Why?

Answer: In the long term, Step 6, Achieve Excellence with Integrity. If you cannot achieve the numbers without keeping to the organizational core values, your own team's success will be undermined, as will ultimately the success of the entire organization.

Question: Please provide a brief personal experience that you believe best illustrates leadership in buying or selling.

Answer: Early experiences often are the most influential in later life. While there are many, one of the most memorable experiences for me was as a very junior contract specialist in the conduct of two large, hotly contested competitive procurements, one for the development of prototypes and the other for production of another item. It was my assignment to satisfy our procurement staff, my customer of several levels, and members of industry simultaneously over a period of several weeks. The greatest satisfaction was to hear the compliments from the unsuccessful offeror or bidders for a successful process. The lesson was to be prepared, honest, unafraid, and willing to make those around you be the same.

Summary

In this chapter we discussed the key definitions of the words "excellence" and "integrity," the importance of focusing your actions on the seven principles of leadership, and the need to achieve the three goals of excellence with integrity. We believe that if you execute the S3 leadership process and practice the seven principles of leadership while doing so, you will

1. Develop a state of buying or selling that surpasses your competitors' performance (quality, cost, on-time delivery, etc.).
2. Execute your buying or selling practices with soundness of moral principle, character, and honesty.
3. Create a culture that seeks to develop and maintain a sound business environment that is based on respect.

In the next chapter, we go beyond individual leadership to discuss the need to benchmark your buying or selling organization's performance.

Questions to Consider

1. How does your organization define "excellence"?
2. How do you define or describe "integrity"?
3. Which of the seven principles of leadership are most important?
4. Is it possible to consistently achieve excellence without integrity?
5. What are your biggest challenges to achieve excellence with integrity?

[1] *The American College Dictionary* (New York: Random House, 1998).
[2] Ibid.
[3] Tom Peters, *Talent* (New York: DK Publishing, 2005).
[4] Ibid.
[5] Stephen R. Covey, *The Seven Habits of Highly Effective People* (New York: Free Press, 1989).

Chapter 10

The Contract Management Maturity Model and Buying and Selling Assessment Tools

"True leaders...invariably see a great challenge as an opportunity to excel!"

—The USAF Officer's Motto

Introduction

Now that we have fully discussed the individual buying and selling leadership levels, competencies, and the Six Steps to Success (S3) leadership process, it is time to focus on the buying and selling organizations. This chapter provides an insightful discussion of buying and selling organizational maturity. Plus, this chapter offers assessment tools to allow you to benchmark your buying or selling organization's strengths and areas that need improvement. The Contract Management Maturity Model (CMMM) and assessment tools allow you to lead your organization to a higher level of performance.

"Maturity," according to the *Random House Dictionary,* means "full development or a perfected condition."[1] Maturity also implies knowledge and understanding of what it takes to prevent problems and achieve success. In terms of contract management, it relates to organizational capabilities that can consistently produce successful business results for buyers and sellers of products, services, and integrated solutions.

The CMMM was developed by Dr. Rene G. Rendon and Gregory A. Garrett and first published by NCMA in the book *Contract Management Organizational Assessment Tools* (2005).[2] The CMMM creates a vision of excellence to help buying and selling organizations focus on the key areas of process improvement. It provides its users with a framework or a guide for improving their level of performance. It is envisioned that the model and survey assessment tool will serve as the foundation for ongoing discussion and further development within the contract management profession. The CMMM provides a visual tool to help an organization assess the six major actions that it must accomplish when buying or selling products, services, and integrated solutions in either the public or the private business sectors. The maturity levels reflected in the model allow an organization to assess its level of capability for each of the six major actions in its buying or selling process.

This chapter describes the development and creation of the CMMM as a systematic approach for assessing and improving the capability maturity level of an organization's contract management process for buying and selling. The development of the CMMM entailed the following two research objectives:

1. To develop an organizational contract management process capability maturity model for both buyers and sellers
2. To develop an appropriate assessment tool for buyers and sellers for measuring organizational contract management maturity

This chapter discusses these two research objectives. For the purpose of this discussion, the following terms and definitions are used:

- **capability maturity model:** An evolutionary road map for implementing the vital practices for one or more domains of organizational processes. It contains the essential elements of effective processes for one or more disciplines. It describes an evolutionary improvement path from an ad hoc, immature process, to a disciplined, mature process with improved quality and effectiveness.[3]
- **competency:** An underlying characteristic that is causally related to effective or superior performance, as determined by measurable, objective criteria, in a job or in a situation.[4]
- **contract management:** The art and science of managing contractual agreements throughout the contracting process.[5]
- **maturity:** A measure of effectiveness in any specific process.[6]
- **maturity level:** A level of organizational capability created by the transformation of one or more domains of an organization's processes. It is an evolutionary plateau on an organization's improvement path from ad hoc practices to a state of continuous improvement.[7]

- **process capability:** The inherent ability of a process to produce planned results.[8]

Objective 1: To Develop an Organizational Contract Management Process Capability Maturity Model for Both Buyers and Sellers

This research objective focused on answering the question, "How might a model be developed for determining the maturity level of an organization's contract management process?" The research objective consisted of two phases. The first phase involved reviewing current maturity models and identifying model characteristics that could be adopted in developing a contract management maturity model. The second phase involved developing the basic structure of the model.

Phase 1: Review of Current Maturity Models

In conducting this research, Dr. Rene G. Rendon and Gregory A. Garrett reviewed existing process capability maturity models to determine which features and characteristics should be adopted for the CMMM. The maturity models reviewed included the Software Engineering Institute's Capability Maturity Model,[9] Kerzner's Project Management Maturity Model,[10] Project Management Solutions Inc.'s Project Management Maturity Model,[11] the People Capability Maturity Model,[12] and the Berkeley Project Management Process Maturity Model.[13] Thus, the majority of maturity models reviewed were project management maturity models. They were appropriate models to review because the project management process is closely related to the procurement and contracting process.

Most of these models consisted of a five-level maturity model, with each level building on the previous maturity level. In almost all of the models, the first level of maturity reflected processes considered ad hoc, chaotic, inconsistent, and ill defined. These models labeled the first maturity level "initial" or "ad hoc." Kerzner's model described the first level of maturity by focusing on the use of a common language of project management as well as on the sporadic use of a project management methodology. Kerzner labeled the first maturity level in his model "common language," which focuses on project management education and knowledge at both the individual level and organizational level.[14]

The maturity models were generally in agreement in describing the second maturity level. This level described the processes as structured, common, planned, or managed. At this level of maturity, the processes reflect basic, structured processes and standards in place. The Berkeley Model reflected lack of project control processes or lessons learned at this level of maturity.[15]

The maturity models differed slightly in describing the third maturity level. Some of the models described this level as processes that were defined, standardized, and institutionalized throughout the organization and thus used a single methodology. The Berkeley Model described the third maturity level as "managed," reflecting both systematic planning and control characteristics, while the other models described this maturity level as processes having an institutional and organizational focus. These models labeled this maturity level as "organizational standards and institutionalized process," "singular methodology," "managed," and "defined."[16]

For the most part, the maturity models were also consistent in describing the fourth maturity level. The models described this level as organizations having integrated corporate processes, focusing on evaluation of practices and gauging process performance in terms of effectiveness and reduced variation. The labels used for this maturity level included "managed," "benchmarking," "integrated," and "quantitatively managed." The processes at this maturity level reflected integration with other corporate processes and were measured or evaluated against some standards. Kerzner labeled this maturity level "benchmarking," reflecting the fact that at this level organizations realize that existing methodologies can be improved.[17]

There was also strong consistency in describing the fifth and highest maturity level. The models reviewed characterized this level of maturity as processes focused on continuous improvement, establishing lessons learned and best-practice databases. The processes of transferring knowledge between organizations, making adjustments to processes, eliminating common failure, continuing efforts to improve, and encouraging innovative process capability were reflective of this level of maturity. Project Management Solutions Inc.'s maturity model reflected the use of efficiency and effectiveness metrics and a focus on continuous improvement in describing this level of maturity. The maturity models that were reviewed labeled the fifth maturity level "optimizing," "continuous improvement," and "learning."[18]

Thus, in total, the maturity models that were reviewed reflect an evolutionary increase in maturity from an ad hoc level (Level 1); to a basic, disciplined process capability (Level 2); to institutionalized and repeatable processes (Level 3); to processes integrated with other corporate processes, resulting in synergistic corporate benefits (Level 4); and finally, to processes focused on continuous improvement and adoption of lessons learned and best practices (Level 5).[19]

Another important characteristic of these maturity models was that most project management maturity models centered on the project management methods and processes outlined in *A Guide to the Project Management Body of Knowledge* published by the Project Management Institute (2000).[20] The models used the Project Management Body of Knowledge (PMBOK®) processes as a basis for identifying key processes and practices within project management. It should be noted that some of the project management maturity models did include the procurement process as a key process area within the model. This omission is reflective of the inclusion of the procurement process within the overall framework of the project management process. For example, the Project Management Solutions Inc. model did include the procurement process; however, this model and its related assessment tool did not break down the procurement process to a level of detail that would provide adequate insight and visibility to key organizational contract management (buying and selling) processes and practice activities. The Kerzner and Berkeley models also included the procurement process in their project management focus; however, the models and their related assessment tools did not provide sufficient detail or visibility in the contract management (buying and selling) processes and activities.[21]

This research also identified lack of granularity and specificity as a common criticism of current maturity models.[22] This criticism refers to the lack of detailed information in the focus area of the maturity model. To combat this criticism in the development of the CMMM, Dr. Rene G. Rendon and Gregory A. Garrett applied a strong focus to breaking down the contract management process into its specific subprocesses, thus allowing visibility into the more detailed contract management processes and practices. The purpose of this research was to develop a contract management maturity model specifically designed to focus on the detailed contract management processes and activities, thus giving organizations sufficient insight into their contract management processes. This work was the challenge of phase 2 of this research objective.

Phase 2: Development of the Basic Structure of the CMMM

This phase consisted of developing the contract management process maturity levels, as well as the key process areas and practice activities. This research entailed reviewing current contract management, procurement, and purchasing textbooks, journals, and other documents in the body of knowledge to identify generally accepted key contract management processes and activities.

On the basis of the results of the phase 1 research, a five-level maturity model was developed: ad hoc, basic, structured, integrated, and optimized. The CMMM is fully described in **Table 10-1.**

Table 10-1 Contract Management Maturity Model (CMMM): Narrative
Level 1: Ad hoc ▪ The organization acknowledges that contract management processes exist, that these are accepted and practiced throughout various industries, and that the organization's management understands the benefit and value of using contract management processes. ▪ Although no basic contract management processes are established organizationwide, some established contract management processes exist and are used within the organization but are applied only on an ad hoc and sporadic basis to various contracts. ▪ Informal documentation of contract management processes may exist within the organization, but it is used only on an ad hoc and sporadic basis on various contracts. ▪ Organizational managers and contract management personnel are not held accountable for adhering to or complying with any contract management processes or standards.
Level 2: Basic ▪ Some basic contract management processes and standards have been established within the organization, but they are required only on selected complex, critical, or high-visibility contracts, such as contracts meeting certain dollar thresholds or contracts with certain customers. ▪ Some formal documentation has been developed for these established contract management processes and standards. ▪ The organization does not consider these contract management processes or standards established or institutionalized throughout the entire organization. ▪ There is no organizational policy requiring the consistent use of these contract management processes and standards other than on the required contracts.

Table 10-1 Contract Management Maturity Model (CMMM): Narrative, continued

Level 3: Structured

- Contract management processes and standards are fully established, institutionalized, and mandated throughout the entire organization.
- Formal documentation has been developed for these contract management processes and standards, and some processes may even be automated.
- Because these contract management processes are mandated, the organization allows the tailoring of processes and documents, allowing consideration for the unique aspects of each contract, such as contracting strategy, contract type, terms and conditions, dollar value, and type of requirement (product or service).
- Senior management is involved in providing guidance, direction, and even approval of key contracting strategy decisions, related contract terms and conditions, and contract management documents.

Level 4: Integrated

- The procurement project's end-user customer is an integral member of the procurement team.
- Basic contract management processes are integrated with other organizational core processes, such as cost control, schedule management, performance management, and systems engineering.
- Management uses efficiency and effectiveness metrics to make procurement-related decisions.
- Management understands its role in the procurement management process and executes the process well.

Table 10-1 Contract Management Maturity Model (CMMM): Narrative, continued

Level 5: Optimized

- Contract management processes are evaluated periodically using efficiency and effectiveness metrics.
- Continuous process improvement efforts are implemented to improve the contract management process.
- Lessons learned and best-practice programs are implemented to improve contract management processes, standards, and documentation.
- Initiatives to streamline the procurement process are implemented as part of the process improvement program.

An important characteristic of the project management maturity models is that most focus on the project management methods and processes that are universally established and accepted in the project management profession. For most of the models, the project management methods and processes adopted were those from Project Management Institute's PMBOK. These models used the PMBOK processes as a basis for identifying key processes and practices within the project management area.[23] The most significant problem in developing the CMMM was the lack of an established, universally accepted contract management process, including sufficient visibility into the subprocesses and related activities. Thus, one of the first steps in developing the CMMM was selecting an appropriate standard for the contract management process. Various procurement and purchasing models were reviewed, resulting in the selection of a representative contract management process. This review and selection process is summarized below.

In 1972, the Commission on Government Procurement (COGP) published its model of the procurement process, which has been accepted as representative of the federal procurement process. The COGP procurement model consists of six phases: (1) needs and funding, (2) planning, (3) solicitation, (4) selection, (5) award, and (6) contract administration.[24] This model was developed to reflect the various federal procurement statutes and regulations as well as to focus on the procurement workforce. Although this model was developed for the federal procurement process, it is also somewhat reflective of procurement processes used by commercial organizations. One limitation of this model is its lack of granularity on the contract termination and contract closeout phase of the procurement process. The COGP model combines the termination and closeout phases with the contract administration phase. For this reason, the COGP model does not provide adequate visibility and insight into these two aspects of the procurement process.

Raedels describes the procurement and purchasing process as a nine-step process that focuses on acquiring materials and services of the right quality, in the right quantity, at the right price, at the right time, from the right source. This purchasing process consists of the following steps: (1) user identifies needs, (2) carry out requisition process, (3) identify potential sources, (4) develop solicitation proposal, (5) evaluate proposals, (6) evaluate suppliers, (7) develop contract, (8) manage contract, and (9) close contract.[25] The model seems to be inclusive and provides sufficient visibility and focus into the various phases of procurement. This model is unique in that it separates the proposal evaluation from the supplier evaluation. Although both evaluations are separate and have different objectives, most models combine these phases into one phase, usually called "source selection." The Raedels model is similar to the process described by Leenders and Fearon.[26] Both models consist of nine steps, but the Leenders and Fearon model reflects the process used for procuring small dollar value, commodity-type supplies, using mechanical steps such as "follow-up and/or expedite the order," "receipt of and inspection of goods," and "maintain records".[27]

With the procurement function moving toward a supply management perspective, **Burt, Dobler, and Starling** developed a model describing the four phases of supply management: (1) generation of requirements, (2) sourcing, (3) pricing, and (4) post-award activities.[28] Although much simpler than the other models discussed, the supply management model reflects strategic supply management activities such as the development of supply alliances, focusing on the total cost of ownership, supplier development, and supplier relationship management. As can be seen, this model does not delve very deeply into the processes of establishing procurement strategy, structuring and awarding a contract, and administering and closing out a contract.

An excellent depiction of the federal acquisition process is provided by Engelbeck, who uses an eight-step acquisition process model to illustrate the major events associated with the procurement of defense-related goods and services. These steps include (1) requirements determination, (2) acquisition planning, (3) solicitation, (4) source selection, (5) negotiation, (6) contract award, (7) contract performance, and (8) contract closeout.[29] Englebeck's model is primarily based on the Department of Defense system for managing major defense programs.

In 1997, Gregory A. Garrett developed a contract management model using three phases and six major actions covering all contract management activities for both the buyer and the seller.[30] This model captures all the contract management activities, beginning with the procurement strategy planning process and concluding with the contract termination or contract completion process. A unique aspect of Garrett's model is that it reflects not only the buyer's process of contract management but also the seller's process. The model that reflects the buyer's activities consists of the following major actions: (1) procurement planning, (2) solicitation planning, (3) solicitation, (4) source selection, (5) contract administration, and (6) contract closeout. The model that reflects the seller's activities consists of the following major actions: (1) presales activity, (2) bid and no-bid decision-making, (3) bid or proposal preparation, (4) contract negotiation and formation, (5) contract administration, and (6) contract closeout. Each phase in the seller's model coincides with the related phase in the buyer's process. Of all of the models reviewed, Garrett's model was the only one that focused on both the buyer's and seller's contract management activities. This approach reflects the perspective that contract management is about developing and maintaining professional business relationships between the buyer and the seller.[31]

Garrett's model is based on the project procurement management process established by Project Management Institute's PMBOK. The Project Management Institute has developed standards for the project management profession that have been accepted and adopted worldwide. Some consider the PMBOK to be the world's de facto standard for project management knowledge and practices in today's global marketplace. The PMBOK has established a standard process for each area of project management. These areas include management of integration, scope, time, cost, quality, human resource, communications, risk, and procurement. Garrett **(World-Class Contracting, 1997)** has expanded on the PMBOK project procurement management process by adding visibility to the buyer's, as well as the seller's, side of the contract management process.

On the basis of the review of these current procurement and contract management models, as well as other current procurement and contract management textbooks, including the NCMA's *Contract Management Body of Knowledge*[32] and the Institute for Supply Management's (formerly the National Association of Purchasing Management) *The Purchasing Handbook,*[33] a decision was made as to which contract management process to adopt in developing the CMMM. The review of these contract management bodies of knowledge also identified key practice activities for the contract management processes.[34] For the purpose of developing the CMMM, it was decided to adopt Garrett's three contract management phases and six steps or major actions.[35] This approach was based on Project Management Institute's PMBOK. Adopting a contract management model derived from a universally accepted Project Management Institute standard, which provided the level of detail needed in establishing the process capability maturity model, proved beneficial in accomplishing this research objective.

These contract management key practice activities were integral to the development of the Contract Management Maturity Assessment Tool, which is discussed in the next section.

The Garrett model provided an established baseline of the contract management process for both buyers and sellers that could be expanded on in developing the CMMM. The CMMM that reflects the buyer's activities consists of the following six major actions: (1) procurement planning, (2) solicitation planning, (3) solicitation, (4) source selection, (5) contract administration, and (6) contract closeout. The CMMM that reflects the seller's activities consists of the following six key process areas: (1) presales activity, (2) bid and no-bid decision-making, (3) bid or proposal preparation, (4) contract negotiation and formation, (5) contract administration, and (6) contract closeout. The key process areas of contract administration and contract closeout are identical for the buyer and seller; that is, both the buyer and the seller perform identical contract administration and contract closeout functions during the management of a contractual relationship. These key process areas and practice activities were used in developing assessment tools for buyers and sellers to measure their organization's contract management process capability.

Figure 10-1 illustrates the CMMM, reflecting the five levels of maturity and the six key process areas selected for both buyers and sellers. These key process areas provide detailed insight and visibility into an organization's contract management process capability. **Tables 10-2** and **10-3** illustrate the key process areas and practice activities for the buyer. **Tables 10-4** and **10-5** illustrate the key process areas and practice activities for the seller. The next section discusses the second research objective, which involves the development of an appropriate assessment tool for buyers and sellers to measure organizational contract management maturity.

Figure 10-1 Contract Management Maturity Model

Maturity Levels		Contract Management Process Areas					
	Buyer	Procure-ment planning	Solicitation planning	Solicitation	Source selection	Contract administration	Contract closeout
	Seller	Presales activity	Bid or no-bid decision	Bid or proposal preparation	Negotiation and formation		
5 Optimized							
4 Integrated							
3 Structured							
2 Basic							
1 Ad Hoc							

Source: Dr. Rene G. Rendon and Gregory A. Garrett, *Contract Management Organizational Assessment Tools,* (McLean, VA: NCMA, 2005).

Table 10-2 Contract Management Key Process Areas: Buyer's Perspective

1. **Procurement planning:** The process of identifying which business needs can be best met by procuring products or services outside the organization. This process involves determining whether to procure, how to procure, what to procure, how much to procure, and when to procure.
2. **Solicitation planning:** The process of preparing the documents needed to support the solicitation. This process involves documenting program requirements and identifying potential sources.
3. **Solicitation:** The process of obtaining information (bids and proposals) from prospective sellers on how project needs can be met.
4. **Source selection:** The process of receiving bids or proposals and applying evaluation criteria to select a provider.
5. **Contract administration:** The process of ensuring that each party's performance meets contractual requirements.
6. **Contract closeout:** The process of verifying that all administrative matters are concluded on a contract that is otherwise complete. This process involves completing and settling the contract, including resolving any open items.

Table 10-3 Contract Management Key Practice Activities: Buyer's Perspective

1. Procurement planning

- The organization has an established process for effectively determining the scope of work or description of the product to be procured.
- The process for determining the scope of work or description of the product to be procured includes representatives from procurement, program management, technical, and other affected functional areas.
- Adequate resources to conduct procurement planning are obtained by the organization, either internally or externally.
- Effective market research is conducted as part of the procurement planning process for analyzing the types of products and services available in the marketplace, from whom, and under what terms and conditions.
- The procurement planning process considers other program team areas such as funds availability, preliminary cost and schedule estimates, quality management plans, cash flow projections, work breakdown structures (WBSs), risk management, and manpower resources.
- The procurement planning process provides an integrated assessment of contract type selection, risk management, and contract terms and conditions.
- The statement of work (SOW) adequately describes the buyer's requirement in sufficient detail to allow the prospective sellers to submit a bid or proposal.
- The result of the procurement planning process is a documented acquisition management plan that effectively provides a road map for the upcoming procurement.

Table 10-3 Contract Management Key Practice Activities: Buyer's Perspective, continued

2. Solicitation planning

- The solicitation planning process includes the use of standard procurement forms and documents such as solicitations, model contracts, item descriptions, terms and conditions, SOWs, WBSs, and data item descriptions.
- Solicitation planning processes have incorporated automated and paperless processes as much as possible within the organization, as well as with customers and contractors.
- The organization has obtained, either internally or externally, adequate resources to conduct solicitation planning.
- Solicitations are structured to facilitate accurate and complete responses from prospective contractors.
- Solicitations are rigorous enough to ensure consistent, comparable responses but flexible enough to allow consideration of contractor suggestions for better ways to satisfy the requirements.
- Solicitation documents include appropriate evaluation criteria that are consistent with the acquisition strategy of the project.
- The solicitation planning process allows for amendments to solicitation documents before the solicitation is issued.

Table 10-3 Contract Management Key Practice Activities: Buyer's Perspective, continued

3. Solicitation

- The organization maintains a qualified bidders list with information on prospective sellers, such as relevant experience, areas of expertise, and similar information.
- The organization conducts market research and advertising to identify new sources of supplies and services as part of the solicitation process.
- Depending on the nature of the procurement, a presolicitation conference or a pre-bid conference may be conducted to ensure that all prospective contractors have a clear, common understanding of the technical and contractual requirements of the procurement.
- The organization solicits input from the industry to be used in developing solicitations for certain types of procurements.
- The organization uses a paperless process to the greatest extent possible in issuing solicitations and receiving proposals.

4. Source selection

- The organization uses evaluation criteria, evaluation standards, and a weighting system to evaluate proposals.
- Proposal evaluation focuses on management criteria, technical criteria, and price criteria.
- The evaluation criteria for selecting contractors, either lowest cost and technically acceptable or best value, are tailored to meet the objectives of the procurement plan.
- The price proposals are compared with the organization's independent cost estimate during the proposal evaluation process.
- Price evaluation includes a determination of price reasonableness in terms of realism and competitiveness.
- The organization takes into consideration a contractor's past performance on previously awarded contracts in evaluating proposals.
- The organization uses a team approach to conducting negotiations with potential contractors.
- If needed, the organization may conduct a pre-award survey on the potential contractor to verify the contractor's technical, managerial, and financial capability.
- The organization provides debriefings to the successful contractor as well as the unsuccessful contractors.

Table 10-3 Contract Management Key Practice Activities: Buyer's Perspective, continued
5. Contract administration ▪ The organization has an established method for assigning contracts to individuals or teams for managing the post-award phase of the contract. ▪ For applicable contracts, a pre-performance meeting is conducted to discuss buyer and seller contract administration responsibilities, as well as protocols for communication, performance management, and contract change management. ▪ The organization uses a team approach for monitoring the buyer's and seller's performance to ensure the fulfillment of contractual obligations by all parties to the contract. ▪ The organization has an established process for ensuring that only authorized individuals negotiate or agree to contract changes. ▪ The organization has an established process for managing seller invoices and payments. ▪ An established process for administering incentive fee and award fee provisions is used on applicable contracts. ▪ An established process for conducting periodic and integrated cost, schedule, and performance evaluations, such as earned value management, is used as part of the contract administration process. ▪ The organization encourages contract disputes to be resolved using alternative dispute resolution methods. ▪ An established process for maintaining a conformed copy of the contract is used to document all changes to contract requirements.
6. Contract closeout ▪ The organization has an established process for closing out contracts that ensures completion of work, complete documentation, and financial resolution of issues. ▪ The contract closeout process involves checklists, templates, and forms for ensuring proper documentation of closed-out contracts. ▪ The closeout process requires obtaining the seller's release of claims as well as verifying final payment from the buyer.

Table 10-3 Contract Management Key Practice Activities: Buyer's Perspective, continued
▪ The organization has an established process for exercising a party's contractual right to discontinue performance completely or partially under a contract. ▪ The organization has an established process for exercising a mutual agreement of the parties to discontinue performance completely or partially under a contract. ▪ The contract termination process requires a written or oral notification to terminate a contract because of cause or default. ▪ The organization maintains a database of lessons learned and best practices for use in future projects and contracts.

Table 10-4 Contract Management Key Process Areas: Seller's Perspective
1. **Presales activity:** The process of identifying prospective and current customers, determining customer's needs and plans, and evaluating the competitive environment. 2. **Bid and no-bid decision-making:** The process of evaluating the buyer's solicitation, assessing the competitive environment and the risks against the opportunities of a potential business deal, and then deciding whether to proceed. 3. **Bid or proposal preparation:** The process of developing offers in response to a buyer's solicitation or based on perceived buyer needs, for the purpose of persuading the buyer to enter into a contract. 4. **Contract negotiation and formation:** The process of reaching a common understanding of the nature of the project and negotiating the contract terms and conditions for the purpose of developing a set of shared expectations and understandings. 5. **Contract administration:** The process of ensuring that each party's performance meets contractual requirements. 6. **Contract closeout:** The process of verifying that all administrative matters are concluded on a contract that is otherwise physically complete. This involves completing and settling the contract, including resolving any open items.

Table 10-5 Contract Management Key Practice Activities: Seller's Perspective

1. Presales activity

- The organization has an established process for effectively identifying prospective and current customers, determining customer's needs and plans, and evaluating the competitive environment.
- The process for identifying prospective and current customers involves an integrated and proactive sales management effort among the organization's marketing, sales, and other functional personnel and involves the customer's process needs, desires, budgets, and key decision-makers.
- The process for determining and influencing customer needs and plans includes conducting market research and benchmarking to determine who buys the types of products that the organization sells. This research and benchmarking enables the organization to stay abreast of technologies relevant to its products and services, the needs of its buyers, the strategies and activities of its competitors, and the dynamics of the market. The result of the market research and benchmarking is a prioritized list of potential and existing customers and their needs.
- The process for evaluating the competitive environment involves an objective analysis of the buyer, the seller, and the seller's competitors. This includes (1) a competitive analysis report of the strengths, weaknesses, opportunities, and threats of all players in the competitive environment and (2) a complete financial business case analysis assessing the expected costs, expected revenue, expected cost of money, desired margin, rate of return, and realized revenue of any potential sales opportunity.
- The results of presales activity consist of a formal, documented sales management plan that effectively provides a roadmap for obtaining and retaining customers. This sales management plan includes the prioritized list of potential and existing customers, the competitive analysis report, and the complete business case analysis.

Table 10-5 Contract Management Key Practice Activities: Seller's Perspective, continued

2. Bid and no-bid decision-making

- The organization has an established process for effectively evaluating the buyer's solicitation, assessing the competitive environment and the risks against the opportunities of a potential business deal, and deciding whether to proceed.
- The process for effectively evaluating the buyer's solicitation involves an integrated team effort by the organization's contracts, cost, program management, and other functional personnel.
- The process for effectively assessing risks involves identifying, analyzing, and mitigating the risks associated with a potential project, using practical risk management tools—surveys, checklists, models, and reports—all containing both quantitative and qualitative information. Software programs are often used in performing this risk assessment.
- The process for effectively assessing opportunities involves identifying and analyzing the opportunities that are potentially viable from the project by using standard forms, surveys, checklists, or models.
- The processes used to assess risks versus opportunities reflect a solid understanding of risk management and a designated risk management team process for identifying, analyzing, and mitigating risks.
- The bid and no-bid decision-making results in a final decision on whether to bid on the project and a formal document justifying the seller's reason for its decision.

3. Bid or proposal preparation

- The organization has an established process for effectively developing offers in response to a buyer's solicitation or in accordance with a perceived buyer's needs, for the purpose of persuading the buyer to enter into a contract.
- The process of developing proposals involves an integrated, coordinated, planned, and controlled team effort among the organization's contracts, cost, program management, and other functional personnel.

Table 10-5 Contract Management Key Practice Activities: Seller's Perspective, continued

3. Bid or proposal preparation, continued

- The organization conducts an in-depth analysis of the buyer's solicitation and develops a compliance matrix showing where it meets, exceeds, or fails to meet the buyer's stated requirements.
- The organization uses a competitive analysis report to compare the seller's strengths and weaknesses with those of its competitors.
- The organization has an established process for reviewing standard contract terms and conditions as a basis for developing terms and conditions tailored to a particular solicitation.
- The organization reviews past proposals as a tool to share lessons learned and maintains a database of lessons learned for documenting and sharing best practices in proposal preparation.
- Proposals are either supplemented or replaced with oral presentations to reduce cycle time, increase the quality of the products or services offered, and provide more information for better decision-making.
- The organization uses an external review team to objectively evaluate the proposal before submitting the proposal to the potential buyer.
- The bid or proposal preparation process results in a proposal or oral presentation with an executive summary and supporting documentation.

4. Contract negotiation and formation

- The organization has an established process for reaching a common understanding of the nature of the project and negotiating the contract terms and conditions for the purpose of developing a set of shared expectations and understandings.
- An integrated team approach consisting of highly skilled negotiators knowledgeable of market and industry practices is used for planning, conducting, and documenting the negotiation process.
- The negotiation team develops a solid and approved team negotiation plan and uses negotiation agendas, interim summaries, final negotiation summary, and negotiation reviews and approval as part of the organizational negotiation process.
- A documented transition and contract administration plan is used for transition to the contract administration phase of the project.

Table 10-5 Contract Management Key Practice Activities: Seller's Perspective, continued

4. Contract negotiation and formation, continued

- The organization maintains a database of documented lessons learned and best practices for use in planning future negotiations.
- The results are either a contract agreement acceptable to the seller's organization with supporting documentation (a negotiation memorandum) or a documented decision to walk away from a bad business deal.

5. Contract administration

- The organization has an established method for assigning contracts to individuals or teams for managing the post-award phase of the contract.
- For applicable contracts, a pre-performance meeting is conducted to discuss the contract administration responsibilities of the buyer and the seller, as well as protocols for communication, performance management, and contract change management.
- The organization uses a team approach for monitoring the contractor's performance to ensure the fulfillment of contractual obligations by all parties to the contract.
- The organization has an established process for managing and controlling contract changes to cost, schedule, and performance requirements, ensuring that only authorized individuals negotiate or agree to contract changes.
- The organization has an established process for managing contractor invoices and payments.
- An established process for administering contract incentive fee and award fee provisions is used on applicable contracts.
- An established process for conducting periodic and integrated cost, schedule, and performance evaluations of the contractor, such as earned value management, is used as part of the contract administration process.
- The organization encourages resolving contract disputes using alternative dispute resolution methods.
- An established process for maintaining a conformed copy of the contract is used to document all changes to contract requirements.

Table 10-5 Contract Management Key Practice Activities: Seller's Perspective, continued

6. Contract closeout

- The organization has an established process for closing out contracts, ensuring completion of work, completing documentation, and resolving financial issues.
- The contract closeout process involves checklists, templates, and forms for ensuring proper documentation of closed-out contracts.
- The closeout process requires obtaining the seller's release of claims as well as verifying final payment from the buyer.
- The organization has an established process for exercising a party's contractual right to discontinue performance completely or partially under a contract.
- The organization has an established process for exercising a mutual agreement of the parties to discontinue performance completely or partially under a contract.
- The contract termination process requires written or oral notification to terminate a contract for cause or default.
- The organization maintains a database of lessons learned and best practices for use in future projects and contracts.

Objective 2: To Develop an Appropriate Assessment Tool for Buyers and Sellers for Measuring Organizational Contract Management Maturity

This research objective focused on answering the question "What method can be used for assessing the maturity level of an organization's contract management process?" This effort expands on the research from the first objective. The information obtained while developing the CMMM was used to develop a tool for assessing an organization's contract management process capability maturity—the Contract Management Maturity Assessment Tool (CMMAT).

The review of literature on software management, workforce management, and project management maturity models indicates that the self-administered survey was an effective and timely assessment method for obtaining information on these business processes.[36] Therefore, the survey was selected as the assessment method for the CMMM. This survey would be used to obtain information about an organization's key process areas and practice activities. This information, in turn, would be used to assess the maturity level of the organization's contract management process capability. This objective consisted of two phases: (1) developing the survey statements and (2) structuring the survey response options. A discussion follows of how the survey statements were developed and the response options structured.

Phase 1: Development of the Survey Statements

The CMMAT consists of two self-administered surveys: one for buyers and one for sellers. The surveys contain specifically developed statements related to each of the key buying and selling contract management process areas and practice activities identified in the first research objective. The key process areas for the buyer (procurement planning, solicitation planning, solicitation, source selection, contract administration, and contract closeout) and for the seller (presales activity, bid and no-bid decision-making, bid or proposal preparation, contract negotiation and formation, contract administration, and contract closeout) were used as the basis for the maturity assessment tool. A separate set of survey statements was developed for each key process area.

Furthermore, for each key process area, survey statements were developed to address the key practice activities identified through the first research objective. The survey statements were constructed to obtain information on the extent to which the organization executed or implemented the various activities. Additionally, the survey statements were structured so that the extent of the implementation of each key practice activity by the organization indicated the maturity level for that specific key process area. Thus, the totality of the respondent's answers to specific survey statements would determine whether the organization was at the ad hoc, basic, structured, integrated, or optimized level of maturity for that specific process.

Phase 2: Structuring of the Survey Responses

The response protocol used for the maturity assessment tools was designed using a Likert scale. With this type of response structure, the respondent is asked to agree or disagree with each statement. The respondent has six response choices, ranging from "never" to "always," or "don't know" for each statement. Each response is given a numerical score to reflect its degree of attitude favorableness; for example, a response of "never" gets a score of 1, while a response of "always" gets a score of 5. The response option of "don't know" gets a score of 0. The rationale for assigning a value of 0 to the "don't know" response was that for an organizational process to be capable and effective, it must be well known, understood, and accepted throughout the organization. A "don't know" response indicates that the key process area or practice activity is not well established or understood throughout the organization. The Likert scale allows the optional responses to be correlated with different levels of the maturity model for that specific process area.

Thus, the response options chosen for each survey item will be used to determine the level of process capability maturity for that specific aspect of the contract management process. The scores for all of the survey statements for that key process area are then totaled, and the total score is converted to the maturity level of that process area. A conversion table was developed for converting the total scores for each contract management key process area into a specific maturity level. After the surveys for each of the six process areas were completed, an organizational maturity level assessment could be made for each key process area.

After completing the assessment tool, a test run of the survey was performed to ensure that the survey statements, optional responses, and overall mechanics of the assessment tool were understandable, clear, and effective. The results of the test run confirmed that the assessment methodology was appropriate and the survey statements were well understood, clear, and effective. The CMMATs for the buyer and the CMMAT for the seller are given in **Forms 10-1** and **10-2**. The conversion tables for the key process areas for the buyer and the seller are illustrated in **Forms 10-3** and **10-4.**

Form 10-1 Contract Management Maturity Assessment Tool: Buyer's Perspective

Procurement planning	Never	Seldom	Some-times	Usually	Always	Don't know
1.1 The organization has an established process for planning acquisitions and effectively determining the scope of work or description of the product to be procured.	1	2	3	4	5	DK
1.2 The acquisition planning process is standardized throughout the organization and mandatory for all procurements.	1	2	3	4	5	DK
1.3 The acquisition planning process is well documented, and some portions may be automated.	1	2	3	4	5	DK
1.4 The result of the acquisition planning process is a documented acquisition management plan that effectively provides a roadmap for the upcoming procurement.	1	2	3	4	5	DK
1.5 Senior organizational management, both functional and program, are involved in providing input and approval of key procurement decisions and documents.	1	2	3	4	5	DK
1.6 The team responsible for the acquisition planning process includes representatives from other functional areas of the program, as well as the end user.	1	2	3	4	5	DK

Form 10-1 Contract Management Maturity Assessment Tool: Buyer's Perspective, continued

Procurement planning, continued	Never	Seldom	Some-times	Usually	Always	Don't know
1.7 The acquisition planning process is fully integrated with other organizational processes, such as cost management, engineering, and program management.	1	2	3	4	5	DK
1.8 The acquisition planning process includes an integrated assessment of contract type selection, risk management, and contract terms and conditions.	1	2	3	4	5	DK
1.9 The organization uses efficiency and effectiveness metrics in periodic evaluations of the procurement planning process.	1	2	3	4	5	DK
1.10 The organization adopts lessons learned and best practices as methods for continuously improving the acquisition planning process.	1	2	3	4	5	DK

Form 10-1 Contract Management Maturity Assessment Tool: Buyer's Perspective, continued

Solicitation Planning	Never	Seldom	Some-times	Usually	Always	Don't know
2.1 The organization has an established process for developing solicitations and effectively documenting the requirements of the procurement.	1	2	3	4	5	DK
2.2 The process described in 2.1 is documented and standardized throughout the organization and mandatory for all procurements.	1	2	3	4	5	DK
2.3 The solicitation planning process uses standard procurement documents, such as formal requests for proposal, model contracts, and preapproved terms and conditions, and some portions may be automated or paperless.	1	2	3	4	5	DK
2.4 The result of the solicitation planning process is a solicitation document structured to facilitate accurate and complete responses from prospective offerors.	1	2	3	4	5	DK
2.5 Senior organizational management, both functional and program, are involved in providing input and approval of key solicitation decisions and documents.	1	2	3	4	5	DK

Form 10-1 Contract Management Maturity Assessment Tool: Buyer's Perspective, continued

Solicitation planning, continued	**Never**	**Seldom**	**Some-times**	**Usually**	**Always**	**Don't know**
2.6 The team responsible for preparing the various solicitation documents includes representatives from other functional areas of the program, as well as the end user.	1	2	3	4	5	DK
2.7 The solicitation planning process is fully integrated with other organizational processes, such as cost management, engineering, and program management.	1	2	3	4	5	DK
2.8 The resulting solicitations are rigorous enough to ensure consistent, comparable responses, but flexible enough to allow consideration of offeror suggestions for better ways to satisfy the requirement.	1	2	3	4	5	DK
2.9 The solicitation documents include appropriate evaluation criteria consistent with the acquisition strategy of the project.	1	2	3	4	5	DK
2.10 The organization uses efficiency and effectiveness metrics in periodic evaluations and adopts lessons learned and best practices for continuously improving the solicitation planning process.	1	2	3	4	5	DK

Form 10-1 Contract Management Maturity Assessment Tool: Buyer's Perspective, continued

Solicitation Planning	**Never**	**Seldom**	**Some-times**	**Usually**	**Always**	**Don't know**
3.1 The organization has an established process for issuing solicitations and requesting bids or proposals from prospective offerors.	1	2	3	4	5	DK
3.2 The solicitation process is standardized throughout the organization and mandatory for all procurements.	1	2	3	4	5	DK
3.3 The solicitation process is well documented, and some portions may be automated.	1	2	3	4	5	DK
3.4 The results of the solicitation process are accurate and complete bids or proposals from prospective offerors who have a clear common understanding of the technical and contractual requirements of the procurement.	1	2	3	4	5	DK
3.5 The solicitation process includes using established qualified bidders lists, conducting market research, advertising, and holding bidders' conferences.	1	2	3	4	5	DK
3.6 The team responsible for issuing solicitations as well as for the activities in 3.5 includes representatives from other functional areas of the program, as well as the end user.	1	2	3	4	5	DK

Form 10-1 Contract Management Maturity Assessment Tool: Buyer's Perspective, continued

Solicitation, continued	**Never**	**Seldom**	**Some-times**	**Usually**	**Always**	**Don't know**
3.7 The solicitation process, including the activities listed in 3.5, is fully integrated with other organizational processes, such as cost management, engineering, and program management.	1	2	3	4	5	DK
3.8 The solicitation process includes soliciting inputs from industry to be used in developing solicitations for certain types of procurements.	1	2	3	4	5	DK
3.9 The organization uses efficiency and effectiveness metrics in periodic evaluations of the solicitation process.	1	2	3	4	5	DK
3.10 The organization adopts lessons learned and best practices as methods for continuously improving the solicitation process.	1	2	3	4	5	DK
Source selection						
4.1 The organization has an established process for evaluating proposals and awarding contracts.	1	2	3	4	5	DK
4.2 The proposal evaluation and contract award process is standardized throughout the organization and mandatory for all procurements.	1	2	3	4	5	DK
4.3 The proposal evaluation and contract award process are well documented, and some portions may be automated.	1	2	3	4	5	DK

Form 10-1 Contract Management Maturity Assessment Tool: Buyer's Perspective, continued

Source selection, continued	Never	Seldom	Some-times	Usually	Always	Don't know
4.4 The organization uses evaluation criteria, evaluation standards, and a weighting system to evaluate proposals.	1	2	3	4	5	DK
4.5 The organization uses the appropriate selection criteria, such as lowest cost and technically acceptable or best value, to meet the objectives of the acquisition strategy.	1	2	3	4	5	DK
4.6 During the evaluation process, the organization compares cost proposals with independent, internal cost estimates.	1	2	3	4	5	DK
4.7 During the proposal evaluation process, the organization considers the offerors' past performance, as well as technical, managerial, and financial capability.	1	2	3	4	5	DK
4.8 The organization uses an integrated team approach, with representatives from other functional areas as well as the user, for evaluating proposals.	1	2	3	4	5	DK
4.9 The proposal evaluation and contract award process is fully integrated with other organizational processes, such as cost, engineering, and program management.	1	2	3	4	5	DK

Form 10-1 Contract Management Maturity Assessment Tool: Buyer's Perspective, continued

Source selection, continued	Never	Seldom	Some-times	Usually	Always	Don't know
4.10 The organization uses efficiency and effectiveness metrics in periodic evaluations and adopts lessons learned and best practices for continuously improving the source selection process.	1	2	3	4	5	DK
Contract administration						
5.1 The organization has an established process for assigning contracts to individuals or teams for managing the post-award contract activities.	1	2	3	4	5	DK
5.2 The contract administration process is standardized throughout the organization and mandatory for all procurements.	1	2	3	4	5	DK
5.3 The contract administration process is well documented, and some portions may be automated.	1	2	3	4	5	DK
5.4 The organization conducts pre-performance conferences with new contractors to discuss such issues as communication, contract change control, and performance monitoring procedures.	1	2	3	4	5	DK
5.5 The organization has an established process for managing contract changes, contractor invoices and payments, and contract incentive and award fees.	1	2	3	4	5	DK

Form 10-1 Contract Management Maturity Assessment Tool: Buyer's Perspective, continued						
Contract administration, continued	**Never**	**Seldom**	**Some-times**	**Usually**	**Always**	**Don't know**
5.6 The organization maintains a conformed copy of the contract, in electronic form or on hard copy, reflecting all changes to contract requirements.	1	2	3	4	5	DK
5.7 The organization uses a team approach, with representatives from other functional areas as well as the user, for managing the post-award contract activities.	1	2	3	4	5	DK
5.8 The organization uses a team approach for conducting periodic integrated cost, schedule, and performance evaluations.	1	2	3	4	5	DK
5.9 The contract administration process is fully integrated with other organizational processes, such as cost, engineering, and program management.	1	2	3	4	5	DK
5.10 The organization uses efficiency and effectiveness metrics in periodic evaluations and adopts lessons learned and best practices for continuously improving the contract administration process.	1	2	3	4	5	DK

Form 10-1 Contract Management Maturity Assessment Tool: Buyer's Perspective, continued

Contract closeout						
6.1 The organization has an established process for closing out contracts that ensures completion of work, complete documentation, and resolution of financial and contract performance issues.	1	2	3	4	5	DK
6.2 The contract closeout process is standardized throughout the organization and is mandatory for all procurements.	1	2	3	4	5	DK
6.3 The contract closeout process is well documented, involving checklists, templates, and standard forms, and some portions may be automated.	1	2	3	4	5	DK
6.4 The contract closeout process requires verifying final delivery and payment, as well as obtaining the seller's release of claims.	1	2	3	4	5	DK
6.5 The organization has an established process for resolving contract claims and disputes promptly and dispassionately.	1	2	3	4	5	DK
6.6 The organization uses a team approach, with representatives from other functional areas as well as the user, for managing the contract closeout activities.	1	2	3	4	5	DK

Form 10-1 Contract Management Maturity Assessment Tool: Buyer's Perspective, continued

Contract closeout, continued	**Never**	**Seldom**	**Some-times**	**Usually**	**Always**	**Don't know**
6.7 The contract close-out process is fully integrated with other organizational processes, such as cost, engineering, and program management.	1	2	3	4	5	DK
6.8 The organization uses efficiency and effectiveness metrics in periodic evaluations of the contract closeout process.	1	2	3	4	5	DK
6.9 The organization adopts lessons learned and best practices as methods for continuously improving the contract closeout process.	1	2	3	4	5	DK
6.10 The organization maintains a database of lessons learned and best practices for use in planning future procurements and contracts.	1	2	3	4	5	DK

Form 10-2 Contract Management Maturity Assessment Tool: Seller's Perspective

Presales activity	Never	Seldom	Some-times	Usually	Always	Don't know
1.1 The organization has an established process for effectively identifying customers, determining customer's needs and plans, and evaluating the competitive environment.	1	2	3	4	5	DK
1.2 The presales activity process is standardized throughout the organization and is mandatory for all major sales opportunities.	1	2	3	4	5	DK
1.3 The presales activity process is well documented, and some portions may be automated.	1	2	3	4	5	DK
1.4 The result of the presales activity process is a documented sales management plan that effectively provides a roadmap for obtaining or retaining customers.	1	2	3	4	5	DK
1.5 Senior organizational management, both functional and program, are involved in providing input and approval of key sales management decisions and documents.	1	2	3	4	5	DK
1.6 The team responsible for the presales activity process includes representatives from sales, marketing, and other functional areas of the organization.	1	2	3	4	5	DK

Form 10-2 Contract Management Maturity Assessment Tool: Seller's Perspective, continued

Presales activity, continued	Never	Seldom	Some-times	Usually	Always	Don't know
1.7 The presales activity process is fully integrated with other organizational processes, such as cost management, engineering, and program management.	1	2	3	4	5	DK
1.8 The presales activity process includes an integrated assessment of the market and industry, financial business case analysis, and the competitive environment.	1	2	3	4	5	DK
1.9 The organization uses efficiency and effectiveness metrics in periodic evaluations of the presales activity process.	1	2	3	4	5	DK
1.10 The organization adopts lessons learned and best practices as methods for continuously improving the presales planning process.	1	2	3	4	5	DK
Bid and no-bid decision-making						
2.1 The organization has an established process for effectively evaluating the buyer's solicitation, assessing the risks against the opportunities, and deciding whether to submit a proposal.	1	2	3	4	5	DK

Form 10-2 Contract Management Maturity Assessment Tool: Seller's Perspective, continued						
2.2 The bid and no-bid decision process is standardized throughout the organization and is mandatory for all major sales opportunities.	1	2	3	4	5	DK
2.3 The bid and no-bid decision process is well documented, and some portions may be automated.	1	2	3	4	5	DK
2.4 The result of the bid and no-bid decision process is a final decision on whether to bid on the project and a formal document justifying the reason for the decision.	1	2	3	4	5	DK
2.5 Senior organizational management, both functional and program, are involved in providing input and approval of key bid and no-bid decisions and documents.	1	2	3	4	5	DK
2.6 The team responsible for the bid and no-bid decision process includes representatives from sales, marketing, and other functional areas of the organization.	1	2	3	4	5	DK
2.7 The bid and no-bid decision process is fully integrated with other organizational processes, such as cost management, engineering, and program management.	1	2	3	4	5	DK

Form 10-2 Contract Management Maturity Assessment Tool: Seller's Perspective, continued

Bid and no-bid decision-making, continued	**Never**	**Seldom**	**Some-times**	**Usually**	**Always**	**Don't know**
2.8 The bid and no-bid decision process includes an integrated assessment of risks involving identifying, analyzing, and mitigating project risks.	1	2	3	4	5	DK
2.9 The organization uses efficiency and effectiveness metrics in periodic evaluations of the bid and no-bid decision process.	1	2	3	4	5	DK
2.10 The organization adopts lessons learned and best practices as methods for continuously improving the bid and no-bid decision process.	1	2	3	4	5	DK
Bid and proposal preparation						
3.1 The organization has an established process for effectively developing offers for the purpose of persuading the buyer to enter into a contract.	1	2	3	4	5	DK
3.2 The bid and proposal preparation process is standardized throughout the organization and is mandatory for all major sales opportunities.	1	2	3	4	5	DK
3.3 The bid and proposal preparation process is well documented, and some portions may be automated.	1	2	3	4	5	DK

Form 10-2 Contract Management Maturity Assessment Tool: Seller's Perspective, continued						
Bid and proposal preparation, continued	Never	Seldom	Some-times	Usually	Always	Don't know
3.4 The result of the bid and proposal preparation process is a proposal with supporting documentation, executive summary, and oral presentation.	1	2	3	4	5	DK
3.5 Senior organizational management, both functional and program, are involved in providing input and approval of key bid and proposal preparation process documents.	1	2	3	4	5	DK
3.6 The team responsible for the bid and proposal preparation process includes representatives from sales, marketing, and other functional areas of the organization.	1	2	3	4	5	DK
3.7 The bid and proposal preparation process is fully integrated with other organizational processes, such as cost management, engineering, and program management.	1	2	3	4	5	DK
3.8 The bid and proposal preparation process includes an integrated assessment of the buyer's solicitation using a compliance matrix and a competitive analysis report.	1	2	3	4	5	DK
3.9 The organization uses efficiency and effectiveness metrics in periodic evaluations of the bid and proposal preparation process.	1	2	3	4	5	DK

Form 10-2 Contract Management Maturity Assessment Tool: Seller's Perspective, continued						
3.10 The organization adopts lessons learned and best practices as methods for continuously improving the bid and proposal preparation process.	1	2	3	4	5	DK
Contract negotiation and formation						
4.1 The organization has an established process for reaching a common understanding of the nature of the project and negotiating the contract terms and conditions.	1	2	3	4	5	DK
4.2 The contract negotiation and formation process is standardized throughout the organization and is mandatory for all major sales opportunities.	1	2	3	4	5	DK
4.3 The contract negotiation and formation process is well documented, and some portions may be automated.	1	2	3	4	5	DK
4.4 The result of the contract negotiation and formation process is either a contract or a decision to walk away from a bad business deal, with supporting documentation.	1	2	3	4	5	DK
4.5 Senior organizational management, both functional and program, are involved in providing input and approval of key contract negotiation and formation process documents.	1	2	3	4	5	DK

Form 10-2 Contract Management Maturity Assessment Tool: Seller's Perspective, continued						
Contract negotiation and formation, continued	**Never**	**Seldom**	**Some-times**	**Usually**	**Always**	**Don't know**
4.6 The team responsible for the contract negotiation and formation process includes representatives from sales, marketing, and other functional areas of the organization.	1	2	3	4	5	DK
4.7 The contract negotiation and formation process is fully integrated with other organizational processes, such as cost management, engineering, and program management.	1	2	3	4	5	DK
4.8 The contract negotiation and formation process includes an integrated application of market and industry practices and the use of agendas, interim summaries, and reviews and approvals.	1	2	3	4	5	DK
4.9 The organization uses efficiency and effectiveness metrics in periodic evaluations of the contract negotiation and formation process.	1	2	3	4	5	DK
4.10 The organization adopts lessons learned and best practices as methods for continuously improving the contract negotiation and formation process.	1	2	3	4	5	DK

Form 10-2 Contract Management Maturity Assessment Tool: Seller's Perspective, continued

Contract administration						
5.1 The organization has an established process for assigning contracts to individuals or teams for managing the post-award contract activities.	1	2	3	4	5	DK
5.2 The contract administration process is standardized throughout the organization and mandatory for all procurements.	1	2	3	4	5	DK
5.3 The contract administration process is well documented, and some portions may be automated.	1	2	3	4	5	DK
5.4 The organization conducts pre-performance conferences with new contractors to discuss such issues as communication, contract change control, and performance monitoring procedures.	1	2	3	4	5	DK
5.5 The organization has an established process for managing contract changes, contractor invoices and payments, and contract incentive and award fees.	1	2	3	4	5	DK
5.6. The organization maintains a conformed copy of the contract, in electronic form or on hard copy, reflecting all changes to contract requirements.	1	2	3	4	5	DK

Form 10-2 Contract Management Maturity Assessment Tool: Seller's Perspective, continued

Contract administration, continued	Never	Seldom	Some-times	Usually	Always	Don't know
5.7 The organization uses a team approach, with representatives from other functional areas as well as the user, for managing the post-award contract activities.	1	2	3	4	5	DK
5.8 The organization uses a team approach for conducting periodic integrated cost, schedule, and performance evaluations.	1	2	3	4	5	DK
5.9 The contract administration process is fully integrated with other organizational processes, such as cost, engineering, and program management.	1	2	3	4	5	DK
5.10 The organization uses efficiency and effectiveness metrics in periodic evaluations and adopts lessons learned and best practices for continuously improving the contract administration process.	1	2	3	4	5	DK
Contract closeout						
6.1 The organization has an established process for closing out contracts, ensuring completion of work, complete documentation, and resolution of financial and contract performance issues.	1	2	3	4	5	DK
6.2 The contract closeout process is standardized throughout the organization and mandatory for all procurements.	1	2	3	4	5	DK

Form 10-2 Contract Management Maturity Assessment Tool: Seller's Perspective, continued

Contract closeout, continued	Never	Seldom	Some-times	Usually	Always	Don't know
6.3 The contract closeout process is well documented, involving checklists, templates, and standard forms, and some portions may be automated.	1	2	3	4	5	DK
6.4 The contract closeout process requires verifying final delivery and payment, as well as obtaining the seller's release of claims.	1	2	3	4	5	DK
6.5 The organization has an established process for resolving contract claims and disputes promptly and dispassionately.	1	2	3	4	5	DK
6.6 The organization uses a team approach, with representatives from other functional areas as well as the user, for managing the contract closeout activities.	1	2	3	4	5	DK
6.7 The contract closeout process is fully integrated with other organizational processes, such as cost, engineering, and program management.	1	2	3	4	5	DK
6.8 The organization uses efficiency and effectiveness metrics in periodic evaluations of the contract closeout process.	1	2	3	4	5	DK

Form 10-2 Contract Management Maturity Assessment Tool: Seller's Perspective, continued						
Contract closeout, continued	**Never**	**Seldom**	**Some-times**	**Usually**	**Always**	**Don't know**
6.9 The organization adopts lessons learned and best practices as methods for continuously improving the contract closeout process.	1	2	3	4	5	DK
6.10 The organization maintains a database of lessons learned and best practices for use in planning future procurements and contracts.	1	2	3	4	5	DK

Form 10-3 Maturity Score Conversion Table: Buyer's Activities	
Procurement planning 0–20 Ad hoc 21–30 Basic 31–40 Structured 41–45 Integrated 46–50 Optimized	**Source selection** 0–20 Ad hoc 21–30 Basic 31–40 Structured 41–45 Integrated 46–50 Optimized
Solicitation planning 0–20 Ad hoc 21–30 Basic 31–40 Structured 41–45 Integrated 46–50 Optimized	**Contract administration** 0–20 Ad hoc 21–30 Basic 31–40 Structured 41–45 Integrated 46–50 Optimized
Solicitation 0–20 Ad hoc 21–30 Basic 31–40 Structured 41–45 Integrated 46–50 Optimized	**Contract closeout** 0–20 Ad hoc 21–30 Basic 31–40 Structured 41–45 Integrated 46–50 Optimized

Form 10-4 Maturity Score Conversion Table: Seller's Activities	
Presales activity 0–20 Ad hoc 21–30 Basic 31–40 Structured 41–45 Integrated 46–50 Optimized	**Contract negotiation and formation** 0–20 Ad hoc 21–30 Basic 31–40 Structured 41–45 Integrated 46–50 Optimized
Bid or no-bid decision-making 0–20 Ad hoc 21–30 Basic 31–40 Structured 41–45 Integrated 46–50 Optimized	**Contract administration** 0–20 Ad hoc 21–30 Basic 31–40 Structured 41–45 Integrated 46–50 Optimized
Bid or proposal preparation 0–20 Ad hoc 21–30 Basic 31–40 Structured 41–45 Integrated 46–50 Optimized	**Contract closeout** 0–20 Ad hoc 21–30 Basic 31–40 Structured 41–45 Integrated 46–50 Optimized

Summary

In this final chapter, we introduced the CMMM and the buying and selling CMMATs. Together, the individual leadership competencies model, S3 leadership process, case studies, interviews, best practices, and organizational maturity model and assessment tools will help you to lead yourself and your team to achieve excellence with integrity.

Questions to Consider

1. Does your organization use any benchmarking tools to evaluate your buying and selling processes?
2. How well has your organization documented your buying and selling processes?
3. Has your organization evaluated the maturity level of other business processes?
4. Do you believe your business performance results can be improved via more effective buying and selling practices?

---

[1] *Random House Dictionary*, pg. 424.

[2] Rene G. Rendon and Gregory A. Garrett, *Contract Management Organizational Assessment Tools* (McLean, VA: NCMA, 2005).

[3] B. Curtis, W.E. Hefley, and S.A. Miller, *The People Capability Maturity Model* (Boston: Addison-Wesley, 2001).

[4] Curtis, Hefley, and Miller, op cit.

[5] Gregory A. Garrett, *World-Class Contracting* (Chicago, IL: CCH Inc., 2003).

[6] P.C. Dinsmore, *Winning in Business with Enterprise Project Management* (New York: AMACOM, 1998).

[7] Curtis, Hefley, and Miller, op cit.

[8] D.M. Ahern, A. Clouse, and R. Turner, *CMMI Distilled* (Boston: Addison-Wesley, 2001).

[9] Ahern, Clouse, and Turner, op cit, and Persse (2001).

[10] H. Kerzner, *Strategic Planning for Project Management Using a Project Management Maturity Model* (Hoboken, NJ: John Wiley and Sons, 2001).

[11] J.K. Crawford, *Project Management Maturity Model: Providing a Proven Path to PM Excellence* (New York: Marcel Dekker, 2001).

[12] Curtis, Hefley, and Miller, op cit.

[13] C.W. Ibbs, and Y.H. Kwak, "Assessing Project Management Maturity," *PM Journal* 31, no. 1 (2000): 32-43.

[14] Ahern, Clouse, and Turner, op cit; Crawford, op cit; Ibbs and Kwak, op cit; Foti (2002); and Kerzner, op cit.

[15] Ibid.

[16] Ahern, Clouse, and Turner, op cit; Carr (2001); Crawford, op cit; Dinsmore, op cit; Ibbs and Kwak, op cit; Foti, op cit; and Kerzner, op cit.

[17] Ahern, Clouse, and Turner, op cit; Crawford, op cit; Ibbs and Kwak, op cit; Foti, op cit; and Kerzner, op cit.

[18] Ibid.

[19] Ibid.

[20] Project Management Institute, *A Guide to the Project Management Body of Knowledge* (Newtown Square, PA: Project Management Institute, 2000).

[21] Crawford, op cit; Ibbs and Kwak, op cit; and Kerzner, op cit.

[22] K. Jugdev and J. Thomas, "Project Management Maturity Models," *PM Journal* 33, no. 4 (2002): 4-14.

[23] Ahern, Clouse, and Turner, op cit; Crawford, op cit; Ibbs and Kwak, op cit; Foti, op cit; and Kerzner, op cit.

[24] S.N. Sherman, *Contract Management: Post Award* (Gaithersburg, MD: Woodcrafters, 1987).

[25] A. R. Raedels, *The Supply Management Process* (Tempe, AZ: NAPM, 2000).

[26] M.R. Leenders and E. H. Fearon, *Purchasing and Supply Management* (Boston: McGraw-Hill Irwin, 1997).

[27] Ibid.

[28] D. N. Burt, D.W. Dobler, and S. L. Starling, *World-Class Supply Management* (New York: McGraw-Hill Irwin, 2003).

[29] R. Englebeck, *Acquisition Management* (Vienna, VA: Management Concepts, 2002).

[30] Gregory A. Garrett, *World-Class Contracting* (Arlington, VA: ESI International, 1997).

[31] Ibid.

[32] D.L. Bruce, M. Norby, and V. Ramos, *Guide to the Contract Management Body of Knowledge* (McLean, VA: NCMA, 2002).

[33] Joseph L. Cavinato and Ralph G. Kauffman, *The Purchasing Handbook: A Guide for the Purchasing and Supply Professional* (New York: McGraw-Hill, 1999).

[34] Burt, Dobler, and Starling, op cit; Gregory A. Garrett (2001); Huston (1996); Leenders and Fearon, op cit.

[35] Garrett (1997), op cit.

[36] Carr, op cit; Curtis, Hefley, and Miller, op cit; Dinsmore, op cit; Foti, op cit; Kerzner, op cit; and Persse, op cit.

Appendix A

U.S. Government Accountability Office

Framework for Assessing the Acquisition Function at Federal Agencies

September 2005

Preface

Federal agencies are relying increasingly on contractors to perform their missions. With hundreds of billions of tax dollars spent each year on goods and services, it is essential that federal acquisition be handled in an efficient, effective, and accountable manner. The Government Accountability Office (GAO), however—as well as other accountability organizations, inspectors general, and the agencies themselves—continue to identify systemic weaknesses in key areas of acquisition. In fact, the acquisition function at several agencies has been on GAO's high-risk list, which identifies areas in the federal government with greater vulnerability to fraud, waste, abuse, and mismanagement. In January 2005, we added interagency contracting to this list.

Far too often, the result of poor acquisitions has been an inability to obtain quality goods and services on time and at a fair price. We can no longer afford such outcomes. Given current fiscal demands and the fiscal challenges we are likely to face in the 21st century, the federal government must improve its ability to acquire goods and services in a cost-effective manner.

GAO developed this framework to enable high-level, qualitative assessments of the strengths and weaknesses of the acquisition function at federal agencies. Such assessments can

- ✓ help senior agency executives identify areas needing greater management attention, and
- ✓ enable accountability organizations (including GAO) to identify areas requiring more focused follow-up work.

The framework consists of four interrelated cornerstones that our work has shown are essential to an efficient, effective, and accountable acquisition process: (1) organizational alignment and leadership, (2) policies and processes, (3) human capital, and (4) knowledge and information management. The framework supports an integrated evaluation approach, but each of these cornerstones can stand alone so users of this framework may tailor evaluations to an agency's specific needs. The table on page A-v provides an overview of the framework. Using the table, readers can see at a glance how the framework is structured and can quickly identify specific areas that may be of interest.

In developing the framework, GAO consulted with federal government and industry experts in the areas of human capital, information management, financial management, and acquisition practices. Additionally, we drew upon decades of experience within GAO in reviewing each of these areas.

We welcome any feedback you might have to enhance the usefulness of this framework. Please send comments by e-mail to frameworkcomments@gao.gov. I can also be reached at (202) 512-4841.

The framework was prepared under the direction of Bill Woods. Key contributors to this product were Lily Chin, Christina Cromley, Timothy DiNapoli, and Shannon Simpson.

Signed by

Katherine V. Schinasi
Managing Director
Acquisition and Sourcing Management

Framework for Assessing the Acquisition Function

Cornerstones	Elements	Critical Success Factors
Organizational Alignment and Leadership	Aligning Acquisition with Agency's Missions and Needs	• Assuring Appropriate Placement of the Acquisition Function • Organizing the Acquisition Function to Operate Strategically • Clearly Defining and Integrating Roles and Responsibilities
	Commitment from Leadership	• Clear, Strong, and Ethical Executive Leadership • Effective Communications and Continuous Improvement
Policies and Processes	Planning Strategically	• Partnering with Internal Organizations • Assessing Internal Requirements and the Impact of External Events
	Effectively Managing the Acquisition Process	• Empowering Cross-Functional Teams • Managing and Engaging Suppliers • Monitoring and Providing Oversight to Achieve Desired Outcomes • Enabling Financial Accountability
	Promoting Successful Outcomes of Major Projects	• Using Sound Capital Investment Strategies • Employing Knowledge-Based Acquisition Approaches

Cornerstones	Elements	Critical Success Factors
Human Capital	Valuing and Investing in the Acquisition Workforce	• Commitment to Human Capital Management • Role of the Human Capital Function
	Strategic Human Capital Planning	• Integration and Alignment • Data-Driven Human Capital Decisions
	Acquiring, Developing, and Retaining Talent	• Targeted Investments in People • Human Capital Approaches Tailored to Meet Organizational Needs
	Creating Results-Oriented Organizational Cultures	• Empowerment and Inclusiveness • Unit and Individual Performance Linked to Organizational Goals
Knowledge and Information Management	Identifying Data and Technology that Support Acquisition Management Decisions	• Tracking Acquisition Data • Translating Financial Data into Meaningful Formats • Analyzing Goods and Services Spending
	Safeguarding the Integrity of Operations and Data	• Ensuring Effective General and Application Controls • Data Stewardship

Table of Contents

Executive Summary

What this framework is
✓ General guidance to evaluate an agency's acquisition function and to identify areas that need improvement; ✓ Consistent with and integrates existing guidance and standards.

What this framework is not
✓ A tool to evaluate specific acquisition actions, contracts, compliance with contracting laws and regulations, or a source of detailed assessment questions; ✓ A substitute or replacement for existing standards.

Federal agencies have responsibility for a vast array of missions—assuring national defense, building and maintaining the nation's infrastructure, assessing and collecting tax revenue, advancing scientific knowledge, and promoting the health and well-being of the nation's citizens, among many others. To achieve these various missions, federal agencies use a variety of approaches and tools, including contracts to acquire goods and services needed to fulfill or support the agencies' missions. Federal agencies award contracts worth over $300 billion annually. Acquiring these goods and services in an efficient, effective, and accountable manner is therefore essential. However, our work—as well as the work conducted by the inspectors general, other accountability organizations, and the agencies themselves—continues to identify systemic weaknesses in key areas, which often result in cost, schedule, and performance problems on individual procurements.

GAO has developed this framework to provide senior acquisition executives, as well as GAO and other accountability organizations, an ability to assess at a high level the strengths and weaknesses of agencies' acquisition functions. This framework comprises four interrelated cornerstones that our work has shown promote an efficient, effective, and accountable acquisition function: (1) organizational alignment and leadership, (2) policies and processes, (3) human capital, and (4) knowledge and information management. These four cornerstones are summarized below.

CORNERSTONE 1: ORGANIZATIONAL ALIGNMENT AND LEADERSHIP

Organizational alignment is the appropriate placement of the acquisition function in the agency, with stakeholders having clearly defined roles and responsibilities. There is no single, optimal way to organize an agency's acquisition function. Each agency must assess whether the current placement of its acquisition function is meeting its organizational needs. Committed leadership enables officials to make strategic decisions that achieve agencywide acquisition outcomes more effectively and efficiently.

CORNERSTONE 2: POLICIES AND PROCESSES

Implementing strategic decisions to achieve desired agencywide outcomes requires clear and transparent policies and processes that are implemented consistently. Policies establish expectations about the management of the acquisition function. Processes are the means by which management functions will be performed and implemented in support of agency missions. Effective policies and processes govern the planning, award, administration, and oversight of acquisition efforts, with a focus on assuring that these efforts achieve intended results.

CORNERSTONE 3: HUMAN CAPITAL

The value of an organization and its ability to satisfy customers depends heavily on its people. Successfully acquiring goods and services and executing and monitoring contracts to help the agency meet its missions requires valuing and investing in the acquisition workforce. Agencies must think strategically about attracting, developing, and retaining talent, and creating a results-oriented culture within the acquisition workforce.

CORNERSTONE 4: KNOWLEDGE AND INFORMATION MANAGEMENT

Effective knowledge and information management provides credible, reliable, and timely data to make acquisition decisions. Each stakeholder in the acquisition process—program and acquisition personnel who decide which goods and services to buy; project managers who receive the goods and services from contractors; commodity managers who maintain supplier relationships; contract administrators who oversee compliance with the contracts; and the finance department, which pays for the goods and services—need meaningful data to perform their respective roles and responsibilities.

The framework is built on a foundation of strong internal control. Agency management is responsible for establishing and maintaining effective internal control, which includes the plans, methods, and procedures used to meet missions, goals, and objectives. Internal control serves as the first line of defense in safeguarding assets and preventing and detecting errors and fraud. The five standards of internal control—control environment, risk assessment, control activities, information, and communications—support the framework's four interrelated cornerstones.

Using the Framework

The main sections in this guide focus on the four interrelated cornerstones. To assist the user in applying the framework, each cornerstone is broken down into elements and critical success factors. Each element is integral to effective stewardship at an organization and depends on critical success factors. The presence of critical success factors—which focus on program results and mission accomplishment—can enhance the likelihood of consistently achieving desired acquisition outcomes. Conversely, the absence of these critical success factors can point to areas embodying high degrees of risk or those needing greater management attention.

To help users discover whether their organizations are employing critical success factors, we offer three indicators: questions to ask, situations to look for, and caution signs to be aware of. These indicators can be found by looking for the following symbols throughout this framework—

? KEY QUESTIONS

What to ask when trying to identify the presence or absence of critical success factors.

LOOK FOR

Indicators of practices and activities that facilitate good acquisition outcomes.

CAUTIONS

Indicators of practices and activities that hinder good acquisition outcomes.

Organizational Alignment & Leadership

Elements	Critical Success Factors
Aligning Acquisition with Agency's Missions and Needs	• Assuring Appropriate Placement of the Acquisition Function • Organizing the Acquisition Function to Operate Strategically • Clearly Defining and Integrating Roles and Responsibilities
Commitment from Leadership	• Clear, Strong, and Ethical Executive Leadership • Effective Communications and Continuous Improvement

? * !

In This Chapter

We focus on two elements and five critical success factors that can be used to assess the placement of an agency's acquisition function and the effectiveness of its leadership.

Organizational Alignment and Leadership

Organizational alignment is the appropriate placement of the acquisition function in the organization, with stakeholders having clearly defined roles and responsibilities. For example, Congress requires certain civilian executive agencies to designate a chief acquisition officer to take primary responsibility for managing agency acquisitions. In establishing chief acquisition officers, Congress recognized that the person in charge of the agency's acquisition function must have a respected and well-defined role that is consistent with the role of acquisition in meeting the agency's missions. Executive leadership is key to obtaining and maintaining organizational support for executing the acquisition function. Executive leadership determines the relationship between the various functional departments and is key to strengthening the interaction between the agency's management and employees.

Although there is no single, optimal way to organize an agency's acquisition function, officials from leading companies tell us that effective organizational alignment enables them to implement a coordinated and strategically oriented approach to acquisition activities. Similarly, to move toward a more results-oriented government, agencies must ask themselves how they can use acquisitions strategically to help them achieve their goals.

Aligning Acquisition with Agency's Missions and Needs **ELEMENT**

The end goal of organizational alignment is to ensure that the acquisition function enables the agency to meet its overall missions and needs. The acquisition function needs proper management support and visibility within the organization to meet that goal.

Critical Success Factor Assuring Appropriate Placement of the Acquisition Function

In response to market and other pressures, leading companies have assessed the current placement of their acquisition function to determine if it is meeting organizational needs, including acquiring needed goods and services, supporting strategic decision making, and ultimately improving overall business performance. In many cases, these organizations cut across traditional boundaries that contributed to a fragmented approach to buying goods and services by restructuring their acquisition function and typically assigning it growing responsibility and authority. Similarly, each agency must assess the current placement of its acquisition function to determine if it is meeting the agency's needs.

? KEY QUESTIONS

- What percentage of the discretionary budget does the agency spend on the acquisition of goods and services?
- Where is the acquisition function currently placed in the agency?
- What are the roles and responsibilities of the acquisition function and acquisition personnel in the agency?
- Do agency leaders, management, and staff view the acquisition function as a strategic asset in achieving their missions or supporting the agency's operations at lowest possible cost?
- To what extent is the agency's acquisition spending managed or influenced by the agency's acquisition office?

LOOK FOR

- The acquisition function has been assigned the appropriate degree of responsibility and authority for strategic planning, management, and oversight of the agency's purchases of goods and services, and this responsibility is consistent with the significance of acquisition to the agency's missions.
- Agency leaders view the acquisition function as a strategic asset in support of core agency missions and business processes.
- Agency managers and staff view the acquisition function as a business partner rather than a support function.

- Acquisition of goods and services is viewed from an agency-wide perspective.

 **CAUTIONS**

- Disconnects exist between where the acquisition function is placed in the agency's hierarchy and its role in achieving the agency's missions or supporting its operations.
- Lack of coordination across the acquisition function results in redundancy, inconsistency, and an inability to leverage resources to meet common or shared requirements.
- Staff views the acquisition function merely as an administrative support function rather than as a business partner.

Organizing the Acquisition Function to Operate Strategically

CRITICAL SUCCESS FACTOR

How an agency organizes and manages its acquisition function affects its ability to operate strategically. Traditionally, the acquisition function has been fragmented among business units, as each was responsible for its own acquisition activities. We found that leading organizations transformed the acquisition function from one focused on supporting various business units to one that is strategically important to the bottom line of the whole company.

? KEY QUESTIONS

- Has the agency assessed the current structure of the acquisition function and related controls? If so, what were the results of the study?
- Has the agency experienced significant changes in its missions, budget, workforce, technology, or other internal or external factors? What changes, if any, did the agency make in response to such factors?
- Does the agency have mechanisms to anticipate, identify, and react to risks presented by changes in conditions that can affect agency-wide or acquisition-related goals?
- Does the agency have metrics related to acquisition efficiency, effectiveness, and results that are included as part of overall perfor-

mance plan and communicated regularly to senior leaders and management? Are these metrics linked to agency missions and goals?
- Does the agency use its strategic and annual performance plan to document the contribution that agency officials expect the acquisition function will make to the agency's missions, strategic goals, and annual goals?

LOOK FOR

- The acquisition function's mission is well-defined, and its vision for the future, core values, goals, and strategies are consistent with and support the agency's overall missions.
- The current structure of the acquisition function has been assessed in response to changes, such as in the missions, operating environment, budget, workforce, or technology.
- Outcome-oriented performance measures are used to assess the success of the acquisition function. These measures should be designed to gauge the contribution that the acquisition function makes to support the agency's missions and goals.

CAUTIONS

- The agency lacks a clear definition of the acquisition function's mission, vision, core values, goals, or strategies.
- The agency has not assessed the role of the acquisition function in response to significant changes.
- The agency lacks a mechanism for addressing risks that arise in response to changing conditions.
- Performance measures are not used to evaluate the usefulness of the acquisition function to support the agency's missions.

CRITICAL SUCCESS FACTOR Clearly Defining and Integrating Roles and Responsibilities

An acquisition function that is successful at effectively and efficiently meeting the agency's missions generally reflects a consistent, cross-functional, and multidisciplinary approach. This approach requires engagement by all relevant stakeholders, including representatives from program offices, contracting officials, financial managers, human capital officials, information technology officials, and other appropriate participants. An integrated approach helps agencies better define their needs and identify, select, and manage providers of goods and services.

KEY QUESTIONS

- What are the roles and responsibilities of stakeholders in the agency's acquisition process?
- Does the agency empower stakeholders to coordinate, integrate, and ensure consistency among acquisition actions?
- How are stakeholders held accountable for their actions?

LOOK FOR

- Each stakeholder in the acquisition process has clearly defined roles and responsibilities.
- There is a shared understanding of each participant's role in acquisition activities.
- Key stakeholders are empowered to coordinate, integrate, and implement decisions about acquisitions.
- Acquisition managers support the agency's strategic-planning and decision-making needs at field and headquarters levels.

CAUTIONS

- The acquisition function's role is unclear.
- Acquisition and other agency offices do not clearly communicate and cooperate.
- There is little integration of acquisition planning among the different agency entities with a role in acquisitions.
- Conflicts among stakeholders are left unresolved, thereby resulting in inefficient operations.
- The agency's acquisition office is frequently bypassed.

ELEMENT — Commitment from Leadership

Organizations recognized for their best practices cite leadership as the most critical factor in providing direction and vision and, if necessary, changing the organization's culture. Leaders have the responsibility to set the corporate agenda, define and communicate the organization's values and culture, and remove barriers that block organizational changes. Research has found that lack of senior leadership commitment is the cause of most reengineering failures.

Congress recognized the critical role leaders play in providing direction and vision by requiring certain civilian agencies to designate a chief acquisition officer to take primary responsibility for managing acquisitions. The officer's responsibilities include evaluating the performance of acquisition programs, advising the agency head on business strategies, and directing acquisition policy for the agency, among others.

CRITICAL SUCCESS FACTOR — Clear, Strong, and Ethical Executive Leadership

Powerful, visionary leaders can set the direction, culture, and perceptions of the agency. Clear, strong, and ethical executive leadership can enable staff across the agency to work in an integrated fashion toward common goals.

? KEY QUESTIONS

- Does the agency have a chief acquisition officer? Is the officer's primary responsibility managing acquisitions?
- Has senior leadership articulated a strategic, integrated, and agency-wide vision for the acquisition function?
- Is senior leadership actively involved in pursuing changes, if appropriate, to how the agency acquires goods and services?
- Are managers at all levels held accountable for their contributions to the acquisition process?
- Does agency leadership promote integration and coordination among the agency's budgetary processes and human capital, acquisition, and financial management functions?

- Does agency leadership and management have a positive and supportive attitude toward internal control?
- Has agency management recently reviewed its key acquisition-related internal controls? If so, what were the results? Are all aspects of the acquisition program covered in the internal control review?
- Does agency management take a proactive stance to correct any deficiencies identified in its acquisition-related internal controls?
- Has the agency established policies, such as a code of conduct, communicating appropriate ethical standards? How does the agency ensure that it interacts with the contractor community in a fair, equitable, and ethical fashion?

LOOK FOR

- The agency has a chief acquisition officer dedicated to managing acquisitions in the agency.
- Senior leadership provides direction and vision, facilitates the development of common processes and approaches, and is involved in identifying and assessing risks associated with meeting acquisition objectives.
- Senior leadership promotes a strategic, integrated, and agencywide approach to acquisition, as appropriate.
- Improvement initiatives involve stakeholders from across the agency.
- Senior leadership and management set a positive and supportive attitude toward internal control.
- Senior leadership and management support monitoring to assess the quality of internal control performance and to ensure that issues are promptly resolved.
- Senior leadership and management have assessed risks the agency faces from external and internal sources in relation to acquisition objectives.
- Actions taken to address risks are effectively implemented.

CAUTIONS

- There is no chief acquisition officer, or the officer has other significant responsibilities and may not have management of acquisition as his or her primary responsibility.

- Senior leadership has not defined a common direction or vision for the acquisition function.
- Senior leadership does not continually support efforts to develop common processes and approaches.
- Senior leadership does not adequately set and maintain the agency's ethical tone, provides little guidance for proper behavior, and fails to remove temptations for unethical behavior or provide discipline when appropriate.
- Senior leadership has not comprehensively identified risks and considered all significant interactions between the agency and other parties.
- Agency management does not have adequate resources and support to implement common process and approaches.
- Agency personnel do not understand the importance of developing and implementing good internal controls.

Critical Success Factor Effective Communications and Continuous Improvement

Agency leadership needs to effectively communicate to employees the agency's missions, values, and guiding principles. Leaders use meaningful metrics to measure the effectiveness of the acquisition function and to provide the foundation for continuous improvement. Leading organizations use performance measurements to gain insight into and make judgments about (1) an organization's current performance level, (2) the critical processes that require focused management attention, (3) realistic goals for improvement, and (4) results over time.

? KEY QUESTIONS

- How does agency leadership communicate the agency's missions, values, and guiding principles, as well as its vision and expectations for the acquisition function, to agency personnel?
- Have agency personnel been asked for their views on the effectiveness of this communication?
- Does agency leadership facilitate and support clear lines of communication among all parties?

- Have stakeholders been asked for their views on the effectiveness of the existing acquisition process and areas needing improvement?
- What metrics does the agency use to demonstrate the impact and value of the acquisition function in supporting the agency's missions?
- What process does the agency use to develop these metrics?
- Are control activities an integral part of the agency's planning, implementation, review, and accountability activities to ensure results and stewardship of government resources?
- Does the agency or an independent organization continuously monitor control activities for their effectiveness at ensuring acquisition objectives are met?

LOOK FOR

- Agency leadership listens to its program units and other affected parties' needs and concerns and remains open to revising acquisition processes as appropriate.
- Revisions to processes reflect appropriate incorporation of affected parties' needs and concerns.
- Metrics used by agency leadership are targeted at demonstrating the impact and value of the acquisition function and provide useful feedback to identify areas for improvement.

CAUTIONS

- There is inadequate communication from agency leadership regarding the effectiveness of the acquisition function and how it supports agency missions.
- There is no mechanism in place for stakeholders to provide suggestions for improvement to the acquisition process.
- Little change is made to acquisition processes based on the needs and concerns expressed by affected parties.
- Internal control monitoring does not occur in the course of normal operations, is not performed continually, and is not ingrained in the agency's operations.
- The agency has inadequate policies, procedures, techniques, and mechanisms in place to ensure effective implementation of management directives.

- The agency has not implemented a program to continuously measure and assess the acquisition function's performance in supporting the agency's missions or achieving acquisition goals.
- Performance measures are in place but are not consistently utilized or communicated.

QUICK RECAP: How Organizational Alignment and Leadership Can Enhance the Acquisition Function
✓ Where the acquisition function falls in the agency's hierarchy and how the function is perceived are in balance with the overall agency missions.
✓ Agency leadership views the acquisition function as a strategic asset.
✓ Staff views the acquisition function as a business partner rather than merely a support function.
✓ An integrated approach to acquisition-involving stakeholders from program, contracting, finance, and human capital offices-helps agencies better define their needs and identify, select, and manage providers of goods and services.
✓ Agency leadership enables an integrated and agencywide approach to acquisition.
✓ Effective communications and use of measurements allow leaders to actively assess and continuously improve performance.
✓ Agency leadership establishes and maintains an environment that fosters a positive and supportive attitude toward internal control and conscientious management.

Learn more about organizational alignment and leadership by reading the reports found in appendix II.

Policies & Processes

In This Chapter

We discuss three elements and eight critical success factors that can be used to assess how well an agency is implementing the acquisition function.

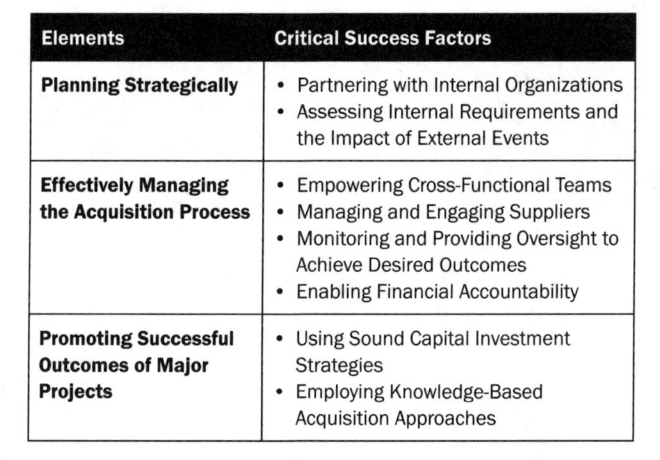

Elements	Critical Success Factors
Planning Strategically	• Partnering with Internal Organizations • Assessing Internal Requirements and the Impact of External Events
Effectively Managing the Acquisition Process	• Empowering Cross-Functional Teams • Managing and Engaging Suppliers • Monitoring and Providing Oversight to Achieve Desired Outcomes • Enabling Financial Accountability
Promoting Successful Outcomes of Major Projects	• Using Sound Capital Investment Strategies • Employing Knowledge-Based Acquisition Approaches

POLICIES AND PROCESSES

Policies and processes embody the basic principles that govern the way an agency performs the acquisition function. Ideally, policies and processes clearly define the roles and responsibilities of agency staff, empower people across the agency to work together effectively to procure desired goods and services, and establish expectations for stakeholders to strategically plan acquisitions and proactively manage the acquisition process. To be effective, policies and processes must be accompanied by controls and incentives to ensure they are translated into practice. Major acquisitions require special attention to promote successful outcomes. Policies and processes that fail to address these objectives contribute to missed opportunities to achieve savings, reduce administrative burdens, and improve acquisition outcomes.

Planning Strategically — ELEMENT

Planning strategically requires attention to the larger context within which acquisitions occur. First, it requires identifying and managing relationships among the parties involved in the acquisition process. Second, sufficient attention should be given to analyzing aggregate agency needs and devising strategic acquisition plans to meet those needs. Acquisition planning should also take into consideration the effects of the appropriations process and other external factors on the timing and execution of major contracts.

Partnering with Internal Organizations — CRITICAL SUCCESS FACTOR

Leading organizations have found that an acquisition function that successfully supports their missions generally employs a multidisciplinary approach. This approach requires engagement by all stakeholders, including contracting, finance, legal, and other appropriate participants to identify needs, assess alternatives, develop cost-effective acquisition approaches, and help ensure financial accountability.

KEY QUESTIONS

- Do end-users of the goods and services acquired work with the acquisition office to discuss requirements for meeting end-users' needs?
- Do stakeholders work together to develop a joint strategy for acquisitions?
- How receptive are stakeholders to evaluating different acquisition approaches and solutions and making trade-off decisions?
- How does the agency promote coordination among the stakeholders as an acquisition action moves through the various steps in the process?
- Do stakeholders work together to understand each other's needs?

LOOK FOR

- The agency has empowered stakeholders and holds them accountable for coordinating, integrating, and implementing effective acquisition decisions.
- Acquisition planning and strategy development support the agency's missions rather than focus on the needs of individual units.
- Stakeholders work on an ongoing basis to define key business and acquisition drivers and to understand each other's needs.
- Lessons learned are identified and shared among stakeholders.
- The agency has structures in place that require appropriate coordination among stakeholders developing and implementing acquisition strategies.

CAUTIONS

- There are only limited mechanisms for coordinating acquisitions in the agency.
- Stakeholders do not clearly communicate their needs or work together to identify solutions.
- Lack of integration across the acquisition function results in redundancy, inconsistency, and an inability to leverage resources to meet shared requirements.
- Acquisition and financial management executives do not partner to develop a shared vision.

Assessing Internal Requirements and the Impact of External Events

CRITICAL SUCCESS FACTOR

Successful acquisition strategies require sufficient attention to analyzing agencywide needs. Acquisition planning should include market research to identify appropriate products and services, determination of the extent of competition in the market, assessment of core competencies and opportunities to compete commercial-type activities, and identification of contract approaches that best meet end-users' needs. Additionally, past acquisitions should be reviewed to identify trends and opportunities for consolidating similar acquisitions planned in the coming year to leverage buying power and reduce administrative burdens.

Acquisition planning should take into consideration the effects of the appropriations process on the timing and execution of major contracts. Additionally, agencies must be cognizant of congressional mandates, administration initiatives, socioeconomic policy objectives, governmentwide fiscal imbalances, and other factors external to agencies. Additionally, acquisition processes should be sufficiently flexible to address unforeseen external events and emergencies.

? KEY QUESTIONS

- Does the agency strategically assess its needs and develop acquisition approaches to help it meet those needs?
- Does the agency leverage purchasing volume by identifying agencywide acquisitions of goods and services?
- Does the agency systematically identify and analyze agencywide acquisitions planned in the next 12 to 24 months?
- Are needs identified in the budget request submission consistent with planned acquisition strategies?
- Does the agency track the types of acquisition methods used for acquiring goods and services to ensure it is employing the most appropriate contract type?
- Does the agency have a mechanism to review planned acquisitions and identify opportunities for suppliers from the small or disadvantaged business community? Has the agency achieved its goals in each of the socioeconomic acquisition categories?

- Has the agency determined the type or extent of work that is and should be performed in-house and which could be contracted out?
- Has the agency assessed its core competencies and identified opportunities to compete commercial-type activities?
- Do agency officials track new or pending legislation that might affect acquisition policies and processes, training, and workload?
- Have agency officials assessed whether their acquisition processes are capable of responding to unforeseen external events and emergencies?
- Do agency officials carefully consider how to meet competing demands on the acquisition system?

LOOK FOR

- Strategic acquisition plans are current and reflect anticipated budgetary resources.
- The agency considers recurring purchases and develops acquisition plans that best leverage these acquisitions.
- The agency appropriately selects among contracting tools available, including commercial item acquisition, performance-based contracting, and government purchase cards to best meet end-user needs in a cost-effective manner.
- Adequate and relevant data are available and used to make strategic decisions about what work the agency should perform in- house and to identify opportunities to compete work with the private sector.
- The agency identifies opportunities for small and disadvantaged businesses and consistently achieves socioeconomic goals.
- There is an awareness of current and pending legislation and its potential implications on the agency's acquisition policies, processes, and practices.
- The agency has assessed and incorporated changes, as appropriate, to enable its acquisition processes to better respond to unforeseen external events and emergencies.
- There is an awareness of the agency's long-term budgetary outlook.

CAUTIONS

- The agency lacks a strategic acquisition plan.
- Acquisition planning is completed on a contract-by-contract basis rather than with consideration of agencywide needs.

- The agency lacks data on the types of contracts used on procurement actions.
- Frequent emergency or sole-source purchases are made to meet routine or recurring agency needs.
- The agency fails to achieve socioeconomic goals.
- Little knowledge exists of what work is contracted out and what work is performed in-house.
- The agency has not assessed its core competencies or identified opportunities to compete commercial-type activities.
- The agency makes frequent changes to acquisition plans due to unforeseen expenses or budgetary shortfalls.
- The agency is ill-equipped to purchase goods and services needed to respond to emergency situations.

Effectively Managing the Acquisition Process — ELEMENT

The role of the acquisition function does not end with the award of contracts. Acquisitions that help the agency meet its needs require continued involvement throughout contract implementation and closeout. In other words, agency processes need to ensure that contracted goods and services will be delivered according to the schedule, cost, quality, and quantity specified in the contract. Factors that can help an agency effectively manage its acquisition process include empowering cross-functional teams, managing and engaging external suppliers, providing effective monitoring and oversight, and implementing sound financial accountability measures.

Empowering Cross-Functional Teams — CRITICAL SUCCESS FACTOR

Leading organizations make extensive use of cross-functional teams to make sure they have the right mix of knowledge, technical expertise, and credibility. This approach helps organizations better define their needs and identify, select, and manage providers of goods and services, which in turn helps ensure that users' needs are met at the lowest total costs to the organization. Teams may vary in size but generally include representatives from the organization's purchasing unit, internal users of goods and services, and the budget or finance office. Teams are responsible for analyzing spending data, identifying and prioritizing potential opportunities for more detailed review, defining internal needs and requirements, and conducting market research.

? KEY QUESTIONS

- To what extent does the agency use cross-functional teams in performing acquisition activities? Are staff from field offices involved at any level? How?
- Do team members feel empowered to make decisions and are they invested in the project's outcome?
- Do the teams use a project plan to manage and control project implementation?
- Does the project plan include performance measurement baselines for schedule and cost, major milestones, and target dates and risks associated with the project?
- Do individuals outside the project team regularly review the status of cost, schedule, and performance goals?
- Are incentives in place to encourage teams to meet project goals?
- How are teams held accountable for meeting cost, schedule, and performance goals?
- Is there good communication among all stakeholders?

LOOK FOR

- The agency uses cross-functional teams to plan for and manage projects. These teams develop a project plan to implement projects effectively.
- The agency systematically monitors project performance and establishes controls and incentives for accountability.
- Open, honest, and clear communication is encouraged among all parties, including team members, program officials, and contractors.

CAUTIONS

- The agency makes limited use of cross-functional teams.
- Project team members do not feel empowered to make decisions or invested in the project outcome.

- Teams fail to use key elements of good project management techniques, including monitoring project performance and establishing controls and incentives to meet project goals.

Managing and Engaging Suppliers

CRITICAL SUCCESS FACTOR

Leading organizations have found that more cooperative business relationships with suppliers have improved their ability to respond to changing business conditions. Such relationships have led to lower costs, higher quality, and shorter product design and delivery times. Among the strategies employed by leading organizations are to establish commodity managers to oversee key goods and services and to establish an effective feedback system between the agency and its suppliers. Agencies can develop effective supplier relationships within the context of the Federal Acquisition Regulation by:

- ✓ establishing effective supplier relationship management as a core business strategy,
- ✓ employing rigorous supplier selection to create a strong supplier base,
- ✓ establishing commodity managers to more effectively manage key goods and services, and
- ✓ establishing and maintaining an effective communication and feedback system with suppliers.

? KEY QUESTIONS

- Does the agency have a process to identify key suppliers?
- Does the agency use a rigorous supplier selection process to create a strong supplier base?
- Has the agency established commodity managers for key goods and services?
- What is the role of the commodity manager?
- Has the agency embraced effective supplier relationships as a core business strategy?
- Does the agency train its acquisition workforce on how to manage supplier relationships?

- Has the agency established an effective communication and feedback system with its suppliers to continually assess and improve its own and its suppliers' performance?
- Does the agency foster an environment in which suppliers invest their intellectual capital—their ideas—into the venture?

LOOK FOR

- The agency uses stringent supplier selection criteria while maintaining an appropriate level of competition among suppliers.
- The agency has established commodity managers for key goods and services.
- Commodity managers are actively involved in defining requirements with internal clients, negotiating with potential providers of goods and services, and assisting in resolving performance or other issues after the contract is awarded.
- The agency has established an effective communication and feedback system with its suppliers, such as:
  - designating an authoritative person as a single interface with key suppliers;
  - using integrated teams to facilitate sharing of information;
  - establishing an objective basis for providing feedback by setting performance measures and expectations in terms of quality, responsiveness, timeliness, and cost;
  - providing periodic "report cards" and meeting formally with key suppliers to discuss issues; and
  - using surveys, supplier meetings, and formal agency-supplier councils or supplier advisory councils to assess existing customer-supplier working arrangements, identify problem areas, and report back to suppliers.

CAUTIONS

- Knowledge of its key suppliers is not shared across the agency.
- The agency does not take full advantage of the suppliers' intellectual capital, such as design or product ideas.
- The agency makes limited or no use of commodity managers to manage the acquisition of key goods and services.

- Commodity managers lack expertise, knowledge, or adequate training in the goods and services being procured.
- The agency is dependent on one or two suppliers for key goods or services.
- The agency continues to select the same suppliers without periodically assessing whether the goods and services offered are competitive in terms of price, quality, and performance.
- The acquisition workforce lacks the skills, knowledge, and expertise to manage supplier relationships effectively.

Monitoring and Providing Oversight to Achieve Desired Outcomes

CRITICAL SUCCESS FACTOR

Over the past decade, the federal government has increasingly relied on contractors to help carry out its missions. Consequently, agencies require effective oversight processes and staff with the right skills and training to ensure contractors provide the needed goods and services. Earned value management is one method to monitor large projects' progress toward cost, schedule, and performance goals.

? KEY QUESTIONS

- Does the agency track the types of acquisition methods used for acquiring goods and services to assess workload and training requirements?
- What tools, processes, and controls does the agency use to ensure effective oversight of contractor performance?
- What tools, processes, and controls does the agency use to ensure effective oversight of employees making purchases?
- What incentives does the acquisition workforce have to effectively monitor contractor performance?
- Does the agency clearly define the roles and responsibilities for those who perform contract management and oversight?
- What actions has the agency taken to ensure that it has adequate staff with the right skills, knowledge, and training to implement policies and processes and to oversee contractors?

- Do agency personnel or external parties with appropriate knowledge, skills, and responsibilities monitor internal control over the acquisition process on a continuous basis?
- Does the agency effectively use and require its contractors to use earned value management as an investment planning and control tool?

LOOK FOR

- The agency has undertaken a workforce-planning effort to ensure that individuals who award, manage, and monitor contracts have clearly defined roles and responsibilities and have the appropriate workload, skills, and training to perform their jobs effectively.
- The agency employs contract monitoring plans or risk-based strategies, and tracks contractor performance.
- The agency regularly reviews contract oversight processes, identifies areas needing improvement, and establishes and implements corrective action plans.
- The agency monitors the effectiveness of policies and processes, completes a cost benefit analysis when considering alternative policies and processes, and follows up on findings identified in monitoring efforts.
- The agency's suppliers have established earned value management systems, and the agency verifies that it and its suppliers effectively implement earned value management processes and procedures on all applicable programs.

CAUTIONS

- Personnel responsible for contract management have skills and knowledge gaps that inhibit their ability to properly oversee the types of contracts used by the agency.
- The agency does not monitor whether its contracts meet cost, schedule, performance, and quality requirements.
- A significant percentage of contracts fail to meet cost, schedule, performance, and quality requirements.
- The agency does not assign clear roles and responsibilities for overseeing contracts.
- There are material weaknesses and/or reportable conditions related to acquisitions in the agency's performance and accountability report.

- Earned value data are unavailable or unreliable, and earned value management principles are not properly implemented.

Enabling Financial Accountability

CRITICAL SUCCESS FACTOR

The need for organizations to deliver goods and services despite shrinking budgets requires agencies to spend their resources wisely. Throughout the acquisition process, financial information should be tracked and communicated in a way that enables effective evaluation and assessment of acquisition activities. When financial data are not useful, relevant, timely, or reliable, the acquisition function—as well as other functions across an organization—are at risk of inefficient or wasteful business practices.

? KEY QUESTIONS

- Does the acquisition workforce have access to and use timely contractual financial information to monitor and oversee individual acquisitions?
- Is the agency's financial management system integrated with its contract management system?
- Does the financial management system report frequently enough to provide reasonable assurance of accountability in acquisitions?
- Are financial data resulting from new contracts, task orders, and contract modifications clear and recorded properly?
- Does the agency measure how often erroneous or improper payments are made? Is a risk assessment process in place to address improper payments?

LOOK FOR

- The acquisition workforce has ready access to information on obligated and expended funds, with sufficient information to assure proper oversight and accounting at the contract level.
- Entries are made to the financial management system that update the contract management and property accountability systems.
- The agency reports frequently enough—monthly or quarterly—to ensure accountability in the acquisition function.

- Adjustments to contract accounting records are clearly reported and accurate; such adjustments represent a low percentage of financial transactions.
- Erroneous and improper payments and cost overruns are tracked and are not a significant problem.
- The agency takes appropriate corrective action when the contractor is not meeting expectations for cost, schedule, or performance.

CAUTIONS

- Acquisition and financial management staff lacks access to critical information, including fiscal year; appropriation/Treasury fund symbol; organization code; cost center; object classification; estimated amount; project code; program code; transaction date; action code; subject-to-funds-availability indicator; asset identifier code; contractor code/name; trading partner; trading partner code; award date; and amounts increased and/or decreased.
- Acquisition and financial management staff independently update the same types of data into independent financial and contract management systems.
- Financial management systems fail to provide transaction details to support account balances or identify the method of acquisition, lack evidence that the contractor's final invoice has been submitted and paid, or fail to perform other transaction processing and routine accounting activities adequately.
- Inadequate transaction processing, particularly improper payments, occur frequently.
- Financial management systems fail to include the taxpayer identification number for contractor identification and income reporting and debt collection purposes.
- The agency receives a qualified, disclaimed, or adverse audit opinion, which may indicate poor accountability.
- Auditors note weaknesses in the agency's acquisition or financial management function in the agency's audit report.

Promoting Successful Outcomes of Major Projects — ELEMENT

The federal government spends billions of dollars each year on major physical capital investment projects and to research, develop, and produce large custom projects. Capital investments and custom projects are generally expensive, span multiple years, and are crucial to the agency's strategy. Capital investments therefore usually require more analysis, support, and review than projects that cost less, have shorter time frames, or have less agencywide impact. Particular attention must be given to these long-term, capital-intensive projects.

Using Sound Capital Investment Strategies — CRITICAL SUCCESS FACTOR

Capital investment includes expenditures for water, power, and natural resource projects; construction and rehabilitation of Postal Service facilities and veterans' hospitals; major equipment; facilities for space and science programs; the air traffic control system; and information technology for the entire federal government.

To ensure an effective capital investment strategy, leading organizations:

- ✓ integrate organizational goals into the capital decision-making process;
- ✓ evaluate, select, and control capital assets using an investment approach; and
- ✓ balance budgetary control and managerial flexibility when funding capital projects.

Integrating organizational goals into the capital decision-making process

Leading organizations begin capital decision-making by defining the organization's mission in comprehensive terms and results-oriented goals and objectives. This process enables managers to identify resources needed to satisfy program requirements based on program goals.

KEY QUESTIONS

- Are the agency's capital investments linked to and driven by its missions and long-term strategic goals?
- Has the agency completed a comprehensive capital investment needs assessment?
- Does the agency thoroughly consider alternatives to capital investments?
- Does the agency perform an annual needs assessment on large capital investment projects lasting more than 1 year?
- Does the agency have an asset inventory? If so, does it contain assessments of the condition of the assets?
- Does the agency ensure it has the necessary resources available before beginning investments in capital projects?

LOOK FOR

- Capital and strategic plans are clearly linked.
- The agency has completed a comprehensive needs assessment that onsiders the overall missions and identifies the resources needed to fulfill immediate requirements and anticipated future needs.
- Gaps between current and needed capabilities have been identified.
- The agency tracks the use and performance of existing assets and facilities.
- The agency routinely evaluates alternatives, including noncapital options, and repair and renovation of existing assets, before choosing to purchase or construct a capital asset or facility.
- The agency annually assesses capital investment projects lasting more than 1 year to assess the continued viability, need, and size of the project.
- The agency has an asset inventory that includes condition assessments.
- The agency ensures it has adequate time, money, technology, and other resources in place before beginning major projects.

CAUTIONS

- Capital investment decisions are made without strategic consideration of what assets the agency already has and what it needs or the resources needed to fulfill its long-term and short-term goals and objectives.

- There is little consideration of alternatives to satisfy agency needs.

Evaluating and selecting capital assets using an investment approach

An investment approach builds on an agency's assessment of where it should invest its resources for the greatest benefit over the long term. Projects that are expensive, span multiple years, and are crucial to the agency's strategy usually require more analysis, support, and review than projects that cost less, have shorter time frames, or have less agencywide impact.

? KEY QUESTIONS

- Does the agency develop a decision or investment package, such as a business case, to justify capital project requests?
- Does the agency have preestablished criteria and a relative ranking of investment proposals?
- Does the agency develop a long-term capital plan that defines capital asset decisions?

LOOK FOR

- The agency develops an investment package that includes common categories of information, such as links to organizational objectives; solutions to organizational needs; project resource estimates and schedules; and project costs, benefits, and risks.
- The agency requires appropriate levels of management review and approval, supported by proper financial, technical, and risk analyses.
- Processes for ranking and selecting projects are based on preestablished criteria, a relative ranking of investment proposals and trade-offs, and an understanding of potential project risks.
- A long-term capital plan guides implementation of organizational goals and objectives and helps decision makers establish priorities in the long run.

CAUTIONS

- No framework exists to ensure appropriate levels of management review, analysis, and approval for capital investment projects before initiating projects.

- Projects are selected without using preestablished criteria and without consideration of project risks.
- Year-to-year changes are made in the absence of a long-term capital plan, without consideration of strategic decisions.

Balancing budgetary control and managerial flexibility

Leading organizations generally require that the total life cycle costs of a project be considered when making decisions to provide resources. In the federal environment, to mitigate the risks of unplanned changes in future budgets, agencies may budget for "useful segments" of capital projects.[1]

KEY QUESTIONS

- Does the agency budget for useful segments of capital projects?
- Do managers have the necessary information to plan for capital investment projects? For example, does the agency have systems to estimate the full cost of a project?
- Are alternatives to full up-front funding considered when they may be in the best economic interest of the government?

LOOK FOR

- The agency budgets projects in useful segments.
- Information and data systems are in place to develop estimates of the full cost of a project or segment early in the life of the project.
- The agency considers innovative approaches to full up-front funding, such as outsourcing capital-intensive services and developing public/private partnerships, when these are in the best economic interest of the government.

CAUTIONS

- Capital projects are not funded in useful segments, which leads to acquisitions that may not be fully analyzed or justified, cancellation of major projects, and loss of associated sunk costs.
- Agencies lack information to make strategic capital investment decisions.

1 The Office of Management and Budget has defined a "useful segment" as a component that (1) provides information that allows the agency to plan the capital project, develop the design, and assess the benefits, costs, and risks before proceeding to full acquisition (or canceling the acquisition) or (2) results in a useful asset for which the benefits exceed the costs even if no further funding is appropriated.

Employing Knowledge-Based Acquisition

CRITICAL SUCCESS FACTOR

The federal government spends billions annually to research, develop, and produce large custom projects, such as weapon systems, air traffic control systems, information technology, and space projects. Undesirable acquisition outcomes often occur, however, because agency officials proceed further into development or production without obtaining sufficient knowledge that the product will be able to meet established cost, schedule, performance, and quality targets.

The risk of undesirable acquisition outcomes can be significantly reduced. All product development efforts, whether for an automobile, airplane, missile, or satellite, go through a process of building knowledge. Ultimately, this process brings together and integrates the technology, components, and subsystems needed for the product to work and be reliably manufactured. GAO has identified three discrete points in the development process at which obtaining certain levels of knowledge promote successful outcomes. The attainment of each successive knowledge point builds on the preceding one. These knowledge points-technology maturity, design stability, and production process maturity-are defined in the following manner.

Knowledge point 1: A match between resources and needs occurs when the customer's requirements and the available resources—which are knowledge, time, and funding—correspond. Achieving a high level of technology maturity at the start of development is an important indicator of whether this match has been made.

Knowledge point 2: Design stability occurs when a program determines that a product's design is stable—that is, it will meet customer requirements and cost and schedule targets.

Knowledge point 3: Production process maturity occurs when it has been demonstrated that the product can be manufactured within cost, schedule, and quality targets and that the process is repeatable and sustainable.

KEY QUESTIONS

- Is a knowledge-based approach used to develop new products?
- What techniques does the agency use to match end-users' requirements with the technology resources available and the program's ability to meet cost and schedule predictions?
- Does the agency have an established metric or benchmark, such as the percentage of engineering drawings complete or similar criteria, to demonstrate that the product's design is stable?
- Is there an established metric or benchmark, such as having 100 percent statistical control over key manufacturing processes, to demonstrate that the product can be reliably produced and with high quality?
- Do program managers quantify the extent to which development efforts fail to achieve established benchmarks and assess whether those shortcomings are critical and correctable during the next phase?
- Does the agency measure the extent to which new product development activities meet the baseline cost, schedule, or performance requirements of the activities?
- Does the agency use lessons learned from programs that did not meet their baseline requirements to improve the agency's acquisition processes?

LOOK FOR

- The agency embodies a knowledge-based approach to acquisition that is reinforced in its policies, implemented in its processes, reflected in individual acquisition decisions, and demonstrated through knowledge-based deliverables.
- At knowledge point 1 or an equivalent milestone, the agency regularly matches requirements and technology resources before beginning product development.
- At knowledge point 2 or an equivalent milestone, agency policy requires the developer to demonstrate that the design is able to meet requirements. To do so, the agency uses an established benchmark, such as the release of at least 90 percent of its engineering drawings, as its criteria.

- At knowledge point 3 or an equivalent milestone, agency policy requires the developer to demonstrate that the production process is mature and uses an established benchmark, such as 100 percent statistical control of key manufacturing processes, as its criteria.

 **CAUTIONS**

- The agency does not use a knowledge-based process for developing new products.
- The agency does not use the necessary controls, such as demonstrating knowledge-based deliverables, to gauge whether adequate knowledge has been attained before deciding to move a product to the next phase of development.

QUICK RECAP: How Policies and Processes Can Enhance the Acquisition Function

✓ Effective partnering with internal organizations and awareness of external factors that could impact acquisitions are two keys to strategic acquisition planning.

✓ Effectively managing the acquisition process leads to improved acquisition outcomes and involves:
- empowered agencywide teams,
- a strategy for managing external suppliers,
- monitoring and oversight, and
- steps to ensure financial accountability throughout the acquisition process.

✓ Major acquisition projects, including capital investment and large custom projects, require special attention to achieve desired outcomes.

Learn more about policies and processes by reading the reports found in appendix II.

Human Capital

Elements	Critical Success Factors
Valuing and Investing in the Acquisition Workforce	• Commitment to Human Capital Management • Role of the Human Capital Function
Strategic Human Capital Planning	• Integration and Alignment • Data-Driven Human Capital Decisions
Acquiring, Developing, and Retaining Talent	• Targeted Investments in People • Human Capital Approaches Tailored to Meet Organizational Needs
Creating Results-Oriented Organizational Cultures	• Empowerment and Inclusiveness • Unit and Individual Performance Linked to Organizational Goals

? * !

In This Chapter

We present four elements and eight critical success factors to help agencies assess their human capital function in relation to acquisition.

Human Capital

People are assets whose value can be enhanced through investment. Leading organizations understand that the success of an organization and its ability to satisfy customers is dependent on the contributions of its people. Human capital policies and practices should support an organization's overall missions and performance goals.

Human capital permeates virtually every effort within an agency, including successfully acquiring goods and services and executing and monitoring contracts. Effective human capital management ensures that an agency has the right staff in the right numbers applying skills where needed to accomplish the mission effectively. Creating an acquisition workforce with the right skills and capabilities can be a challenge, given changes to acquisition processes, the introduction or expansion of alternative contracting approaches, and increased reliance on services provided by the private sector. In addition, agencies are facing a growing number of employees who are eligible for retirement, which could create an imbalance with regard to acquisition experience and skill sets.

Valuing and Investing in the Acquisition Workforce — ELEMENT

Successful acquisition efforts depend on agency leadership and management valuing and investing in the acquisition workforce.

Commitment to Human Capital Management — Critical Success Factor

In leading organizations, senior leadership is committed to developing better ways to invest in human capital and are personally committed to implementing change.

KEY QUESTIONS

- How does the agency's leadership demonstrate commitment to the acquisition workforce?
- What is the role of acquisition officials in developing the agency's human capital strategic plans?
- Does the agency have performance expectations for senior leaders and managers to foster collaboration within and across organizational boundaries and demonstrate a commitment to lead and facilitate change?
- How are senior leaders and managers held accountable for effectively managing the acquisition workforce?

LOOK FOR

- Acquisition officials play a significant role in developing the agency's overall human capital strategy and ensure that it reflects the goals of the acquisition function.
- Acquisition officials develop, implement, and evaluate human capital approaches designed to meet customer needs and improve overall business performance.
- Acquisition officials secure the support of managers at all levels for human capital approaches.
- Acquisition officials are held accountable for managing the acquisition workforce effectively.
- Acquisition employees are provided with resources for continuous learning efforts, competency-based appraisal systems, and retention and reward programs.

CAUTIONS

- Agency leadership views people as costs rather than as assets.
- Agency leadership makes decisions about the workforce without considering how the decisions affect mission accomplishment.
- Agency leadership and management are not held accountable for managing the acquisition workforce.
- Business decisions proceed without consideration of the human capital needs they entail or human capital approaches necessary for success.

CRITICAL SUCCESS FACTOR

Role of the Human Capital Function

The human capital function should incorporate a strategic approach for accomplishing the agency's missions and program goals. This requires the agency to elevate the role of human capital professionals from paperwork processors to trusted advisors and partners of senior leaders and acquisition managers. To accomplish this, agency leaders need to ensure that human capital professionals have the appropriate authority, competencies, and experience.

? KEY QUESTIONS

- What are the roles and responsibilities of human capital officials with respect to the acquisition workforce?
- How do acquisition managers collaborate with human capital personnel to make hiring and staffing decisions?

LOOK FOR

- Human capital professionals partner with the agency's leaders and managers, including acquisition officials, to develop strategic and workforce plans.
- Human capital professionals use streamlined personnel processes and other means to meet customer needs, including hiring and retaining an acquisition workforce with the right skills.

CAUTIONS

- Leaders view human capital management as a support or overhead function.
- Human capital management is largely process-oriented and compliance-focused.
- Acquisition and human capital officials do not coordinate with each other.

ELEMENT Strategic Human Capital Planning

By focusing on recruiting, hiring, training, and professional development, strategic workforce planning outlines ways to help the agency fill gaps in knowledge, skills, and abilities.

CRITICAL SUCCESS FACTOR Integration and Alignment

Leading organizations take human capital into account when developing ways to accomplish their missions, program goals, and results. These organizations assess the effectiveness of the integration and alignment effort by how well human capital approaches help to achieve organizational goals.

? KEY QUESTIONS

- Does the agency have a strategic human capital plan that incorporates the needs of the acquisition function? If not, does the acquisition function have its own plan?
- Does the agency's strategic human capital plan address the use of contractors that provide commercial-type services to the agency?
- Does the agency's succession planning and management of its acquisition workforce: receive active support from top leadership; link to strategic planning; identify people with critical skills; emphasize development assignments in addition to formal training; and address such human capital challenges as diversity, leadership capacity, and retention?
- Does the agency ensure that teams developing plans for the acquisition workforce consist of all stakeholders, such as customers or end-users, contracting officers, representatives from budget and finance, legal counsel, and human capital personnel?
- How does the agency track the effectiveness of human capital strategies for its acquisition workforce?

LOOK FOR

- Comprehensive strategic workforce planning efforts.
- A strategic workforce plan that reflects the needs of the acquisition function, including consideration of which functions to maintain in-house.
- Strategies for recruiting, retaining, and developing acquisition staff, including performance measures to evaluate the contribution these strategies make in supporting the agency's acquisition function and achieving its mission and goals.
- A knowledge and skills inventory is used to identify current and future weaknesses and needs in acquisition skills.

CAUTIONS

- The agency does not fully recognize the link between its human capital approaches and organizational performance objectives.
- The agency adopts human capital approaches without considering how well they support organizational and acquisition goals and strategies or how these approaches may be interrelated.

Data-Driven Human Capital Decisions

CRITICAL SUCCESS FACTOR

A fact-based, performance-oriented approach to human capital management is crucial to maximizing the value of human capital and to managing risk. Leading organizations use data to determine key performance objectives and goals, enabling them to evaluate the effectiveness of their human capital approaches.

KEY QUESTIONS

- Who is included in the acquisition workforce?
- How does the agency track data on the acquisition workforce?
- How does the agency determine the appropriate size of its acquisition workforce?
- Is the mix of entry-level, mid-level, and top-level executives appropriate given the agency's missions and role of the acquisition function?

- What training and professional certifications have current acquisition employees attained?
- How does the agency track the workload of the acquisition staff?
- Does the agency have a skills inventory for the acquisition workforce? How is it used to make human capital decisions?
- How long does the recruitment process take?
- What has the attrition rate been for the acquisition workforce?
- Does the agency conduct exit interviews with departing acquisition workforce employees to determine why people are leaving? If so, how are lessons learned used?
- What is the acceptance rate of applicants offered positions?
- How are training and development programs and results evaluated, and how does the agency track, report, and use this information?

⊛ LOOK FOR

- Data on the agency's acquisition workforce are reflected in strategic workforce-planning documents. This includes size and shape of the workforce; skills inventory; attrition rates; projected retirement rates and eligibility; deployment of temporary employee/contract workers; dispersion of performance appraisal ratings; average period to fill vacancies; data on the use of incentives; employee feedback surveys; and feedback from exit interviews, grievances, or acceptance rates of job candidates.
- Data are available on staff development, including the number of people receiving training; money spent on training; and measures to determine the real impact on the agency's goals and objectives (such as increased productivity, enhanced customer satisfaction, increased quality, and reduced costs and errors).
- The agency uses data to evaluate and continuously improve the effectiveness of training and development programs.

CAUTIONS

- Agency officials lack critical information with which to create a profile of the workforce or to evaluate the effectiveness of human capital approaches.

- Performance measures and goals for the agency's human capital programs, especially as they link to programmatic outcomes, have yet to be identified.
- The agency has little knowledge of what work is contracted out and what work is performed in-house.

Acquiring, Developing, and Retaining Talent **ELEMENT**

Recent trends in hiring and retirements in the federal government will leave many agencies with workforce imbalances in terms of skills, knowledge, and experience. Without sufficient attention given to acquiring, developing, and retaining talent, federal agencies could lose a significant portion of their contracting knowledge base.

Targeted Investments in People **CRITICAL SUCCESS FACTOR**

Leading organizations realize that investing in and enhancing the value of their acquisition staff benefits both employers and employees alike. For example, investing in training for the acquisition workforce is critical to ensuring adequate oversight of the quality, cost, and timeliness of goods and services delivered by third parties.

Industry and government experts recognize that training is a critical tool in successfully introducing and implementing new ways of doing business as well as reacting to change. An agency's overall training strategy—including planning, developing, implementing, and continuous improvement of its programs—is an important factor in ensuring staff has the necessary skills, knowledge, and experience to meet agency missions. The success of investment in training can be measured with balanced indicators that are results-oriented and client-based, encompass employee feedback, and incorporate multiple dimensions of performance.

? KEY QUESTIONS

- What process does the agency follow to determine the appropriate level of spending on training, recruiting, and retention efforts?
- Does the agency have individual training plans established for all employees?
- Do employees have opportunities for continuous learning- such as attending meetings, seminars, and summits-to hear about best practices or otherwise stay up-to-date on issues in their fields?
- What are the training requirements for new and current acquisition staff and related positions?
- How is staff trained regarding new practices in acquisition?
- Does the agency have a comprehensive training management system that can track the delivery of training? Does it identify and track the associated costs of specific training and development programs?
- Do managers consistently provide resources (funds, people, equipment, and time) to support training and development priorities for the acquisition staff?
- Does the agency actively work with colleges and universities to: (1) market the opportunities available for acquisition professionals and (2) include a federal acquisition course that will prepare students for careers in federal acquisition and help promote federal career possibilities?
- Are model career paths charted for acquisition staff?

LOOK FOR

- The agency demonstrates that it has prioritized the most important training initiatives; secured top-level commitment and provided resources; obtained and considered input on training and resource needs from management and staff; identified those needing training, and set training requirements; tailored training to meet the needs of the workforce; tracked training to ensure it reaches the right people at the right time; and measured the effectiveness of training.
- The agency targets investments in human capital to help it attract, develop, retain, and deploy talented, high-performing staff to accomplish its mission. These investments include training and professional development, recruiting bonuses, retention allowances, and skill-based pay.

- Goals, expectations, and criteria for investments in human capital development are clearly defined, transparent, consistently applied, and based on expected improvement in results.
- Agency investments are monitored and evaluated for effectiveness.

CAUTIONS

- Training and other human capital expenditures are minimized rather than viewed as an investment.
- Funding decisions are made without clearly defined objectives or adequate consideration of how they will impact the workforce.
- The agency does not establish priorities, provide adequate funding, or track investments in human capital.

Human Capital Approaches Tailored to Meet Organizational Needs

CRITICAL SUCCESS FACTOR

Existing laws, rules, and regulations provide the agency with flexibility to offer competitive incentives to attract skilled acquisition employees; to create performance incentives and training programs; and to build constructive labor-management relationships based on common goals. Such flexibility should enable agency officials to tailor their human capital approaches to their agency's specific needs and context.

When making decisions about the most appropriate approaches, the agency's acquisition officials should work with human capital professionals, managers, employees, and employee unions. Managers must be held accountable for applying these approaches in a fair and equitable manner across the agency.

? KEY QUESTIONS

- What human capital flexibilities have agency officials used over the past few years and with what results?
- What laws, regulations, or policies, if any, do agency officials view as limiting flexibility in human capital approaches?

 **LOOK FOR**

- The agency has a human capital strategy for the acquisition workforce, and it is based on the agency's missions.
- The agency explores opportunities to increase its competitiveness as an employer and eliminate barriers to building an effective, skilled acquisition workforce and takes appropriate action.

CAUTIONS

- Managers view improvements in the acquisition workforce as improbable.
- Managers fail to fully explore the range of tools and flexibilities available under existing laws and regulations.

ELEMENT Creating Results-Oriented Organizational Cultures

Leading organizations foster a work environment in which people are empowered and motivated to contribute to continuous learning and mission accomplishment.

CRITICAL SUCCESS FACTOR Empowerment and Inclusiveness

Getting employees directly involved in the planning process helps to develop goals and objectives from a front-line perspective. Leading organizations commonly seek employee input on a periodic basis and explicitly address and use it to adjust their human capital approaches.

KEY QUESTIONS

- Does the agency seek ideas from the acquisition workforce? Do employees feel a sense of ownership about policies and procedures?
- Do managers involve employees when planning and sharing acquisition performance information?

- Has the agency established a communication strategy to create shared expectations about the acquisition function and to report progress?

 **LOOK FOR**

- The agency obtains employees' ideas, involves employees in planning and sharing acquisition performance information, and incorporates employee feedback into new policies and procedures.
- Employee unions or councils are involved in major workplace changes, such as competitive sourcing or redesigning work processes.
- The agency has established a communication strategy to create shared expectations and report progress.
- Alternative dispute resolution programs are used effectively to resolve workplace disputes.

CAUTIONS

- Managers and staff rigidly adhere to standardized procedures.
- Relations between management and employees and their representatives appear adversarial.
- Substantial time and resources are consumed by reacting to workplace disputes and long-standing sources of conflict.

Unit and Individual Performance Linked to Organizational Goals

CRITICAL SUCCESS FACTOR

Leading organizations find that effective performance management systems can transform their cultures to be more results-oriented, customer-focused, and collaborative in nature. These systems are used to achieve results, accelerate change, and facilitate discussions about individual and organizational performance throughout the year. An effective performance management system links organizational goals to individual performance for all acquisition-related employees and creates a "line of sight" between individual activities and organizational results.

KEY QUESTIONS

- Has the agency recently assessed whether its performance management systems for the acquisition workforce adequately meet its needs?
- What efforts, if any, are underway to review or improve existing performance management systems?
- Does the agency's performance management system provide:
  - candid and constructive feedback to help individuals understand their contributions and help the organization achieve its goals;
  - objective information to reward top performers; and
  - documentation and information to deal with poor performers?

LOOK FOR

- Individual performance expectations are aligned with organizational and crosscutting goals.
- Performance information is routinely used to track and plan follow-up actions to address organizational priorities.
- Competencies are used that enable fuller assessments of performance.
- Pay is linked to individual and organizational performance.
- Meaningful distinctions in performance are made.
- Roles and responsibilities are defined and enable staff to maintain a consistent focus on programmatic priorities even during organizational transitions.

CAUTIONS

- The agency has not aligned performance expectations with organizational goals.
- The agency does not use performance information to track progress at meeting organizational priorities.

QUICK RECAP: How Human Capital Can Enhance the Acquisition Function

- ✓ Agency leadership and managers value and invest in the acquisition workforce.
- ✓ Human capital professionals partner with acquisition managers to make staff development decisions.
- ✓ Acquisition managers take human capital approaches into account when developing ways to attain organizational goals.
- ✓ A strategic workforce plan profiles the current staff and projects staffing needs for the future.
- ✓ The agency invests in talented, high-performing staff.
- ✓ The agency fosters a work environment in which people are empowered and motivated to meet missions and goals.

Learn more about human capital by reading the reports found in appendix II.

Knowledge & Information Management

Elements	Critical Success Factors
Identifying Data and Technology that Support Acquisition Management Decisions	• Tracking Acquisition Data • Translating Financial Data into Meaningful Formats • Analyzing Goods and Services Spending
Safeguarding the Integrity of Operations and Data	• Ensuring Effective General and Application Controls • Data Stewardship

? * !

In This Chapter

We describe two elements and five critical success factors that focus on data essential to making good acquisition decisions.

Knowledge and Information Management

Knowledge and information management refers to a variety of technologies and tools that help managers and staff make well-informed acquisition decisions. Such decisions have a direct impact on many levels—program and acquisition personnel who decide which goods and services to buy; project managers who receive the goods and services from contractors; commodity managers who maintain supplier relationships; contract administrators who oversee compliance with the contracts; and the finance department, which pays for the goods and services. They all need meaningful data to perform their respective roles and responsibilities.

Identifying Data and Technology that Support Acquisition Management Decisions — ELEMENT

Leading organizations gather and analyze data to identify opportunities to reduce costs, improve service levels, measure compliance with supplier agreements, and provide better management of service providers. Information systems help managers learn how much is being spent with which service provider and for what supplies or services. Additionally, data collected in support of meaningful metrics can assist agencies track achievements in comparison with plans, goals, and objectives. They can also allow agencies to analyze differences between actual performance and planned results. Generating meaningful data, however, requires good data stewardship.

Tracking Acquisition Data — Critical Success Factor

When buying goods and services, many leading organizations have implemented comprehensive systems that integrate contracting, financial, and other data to support management decision making and external reporting requirements. These data:

- track events throughout the life of a contract;
- monitor contractor performance and work progress;
- record and validate the receipt of goods and services; and
- link to human capital systems to obtain information that monitors workload levels of contracting officers and contract specialists, and workforce training and education.

The agency's financial systems support the preparation of auditable financial statements, track financial events, and help to ensure correct and timely payments for goods and services acquired. Financial data can, in conjunction with contracting and other data, enable strategic decision making by supporting an analysis of the agency's buying patterns. External data are obtained from commercial sources or other federal organizations. Examples include market research information and supplier financial status and performance.

Additionally, metrics, when designed to measure outcomes rather than inputs, can be used to: evaluate and understand an organization's current performance level; identify critical processes that require focused management attention; obtain the knowledge needed to set realistic goals for improvement; and document results over time.

? KEY QUESTIONS

- What acquisition-related data does the agency collect? Are data kept current?
- Are the agency's financial (including budgetary), acquisition, operating, and management information systems integrated? Do the systems provide timely, accurate, and relevant information?
- Do stakeholders believe the agency's information systems meet their business needs?
- How does the agency make needed data available to stakeholders within the acquisition process, such as program officials, commodity managers, and contracting officers?
- How does the agency manage institutional knowledge and identify and share best practices?

- Has the agency established specific goals and metrics—and collected data in support of those metrics—to assess the performance of the acquisition function?

LOOK FOR

- Stakeholders generally agree that the agency's information systems provide credible, reliable, and timely information that they can use to make informed decisions.
- An effective agencywide system integrates financial, acquisition, operating, and management information and allows decision makers to access relevant information easily and perform ad-hoc data analysis.
- The agency's contracting management information system tracks events throughout the life of a contract, such as:
  - contract award;
  - period of performance;
  - contract modifications;
  - key milestones;
  - contractor performance, including cost and schedule status;
  - contract closeout;
  - identification of outstanding acquisition requests;
  - expected cost;
  - types of goods and services acquired;
  - receipt and acceptance of goods and services; and
  - trouble spots and progress in dealing with them.
- Financial data—such as budgetary resources and funds availability, status of obligations and expenditures on individual contracts, outstanding purchase requests, and payments for the receipts of goods and services—are readily available to stakeholders.
- Knowledge and information management systems support strategic planning and performance improvement by enabling:
  - real-time benchmarking;
  - sourcing and volume discount tracking;
  - complete vendor information;
  - contractors' past performance; and
  - "what-if" analysis and planning.

- Data are available on the agency's overall "health," internal capabilities, and the external environment. Useful sources include:
  - agency financial statements;
  - customer and employee satisfaction surveys;
  - knowledge and skills inventories;
  - workforce training and education data;
  - retention and recruitment reports; and
  - internal audit reports.
- Metrics have been established and are used to assess the effectiveness of the acquisition function, and measurements taken are credible.
- Metrics established allow the agency to assess the acquisition function's progress in meeting financial, customer satisfaction, and business operation objectives, as well as day-to-day activities, such as compliance with applicable laws, regulations, and best practices.

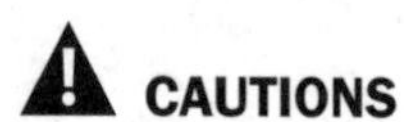

- The agency has not collected the full set of information or data to make effective and fact-based decisions.
- Incomplete data prevent the agency from maximizing information tools for strategic acquisition planning and analysis.
- Data are not current, reliable, complete, or accurate.
- The agency does not make needed data accessible to decision makers, leading them to rely on informal, ad-hoc systems to make acquisition decisions.
- Decisions are not supported by demonstrable, underlying information.
- Lack of integration among systems hinders a user's ability to access acquisition-related information in a timely manner.
- Metrics established measure only inputs rather than outputs.
- Measurements taken in support of metrics are not credible, leading to disagreements over numbers and the value of the assessment process.

Critical Success Factor Translating Financial Data into Meaningful Formats

New technology tools can generate volumes of data, but the data are meaningless unless they can be translated into relevant, understandable formats for acquisition officials. Financial information is meaningful for acquisition officials when it is relevant, timely, and reliable, and enables them to manage costs, measure performance, and make program funding decisions.

KEY QUESTIONS

- Do finance executives work with acquisition executives and managers to determine their information needs?
- What types of financial data or reports are regularly provided to acquisition officials?
- To what extent do acquisition personnel use financial information to support acquisition decisions?

LOOK FOR

- Finance executives work with acquisition executives and managers on an ongoing basis to determine business and acquisition information needed to manage and oversee the agency's missions and objectives.
- Relevant financial information pertaining to acquisition is presented with suitable detail in an understandable format. Multiple levels of detail are available to provide complete and consistent obligation and expenditure information for an agency's overall contracting activities and for individual contracts.
- Financial management staff and officials receive feedback from acquisition staff and officials to ensure the acquisition function's data and reporting needs are being met.

CAUTIONS:

- Financial information pertaining to acquisition is not of the proper scope, level of detail, timing, content, and presentation format to provide real value to users.
- Acquisition information received by financial management staff is not clear and understandable, impairing efficient processing of the information into management reports.

Critical Success Factor Analyzing Goods and Services Spending

Leading organizations continually analyze their spending on goods and services to answer basic questions about how much is being spent and where dollars are going. This approach is called "spend analysis." When organizations complete these analyses, they often realize they are buying similar goods and services from numerous providers, often at greatly varying prices.

? KEY QUESTIONS

- Does the agency regularly conduct and make use of spend analyses for key goods and services?
- What process does the agency use to conduct a spend analysis?
- Does the agency include purchases made with purchase cards in its spend analysis?
- If spend analyses have been conducted, how were the results used?
- Does the agency use a standard taxonomy to uniquely identify the products and services being analyzed?

LOOK FOR

- The agency makes regular use of spend analysis techniques to support strategic planning efforts.
- The agency knows how much it is spending using purchase cards and has considered this information in its spend analysis.
- The agency uses a variety of information, including financial data, to conduct a spend analysis. At a minimum, the agency's spend analysis identifies:
  - what types of goods and services are being acquired;
  - how many suppliers for a specific good or service the agency is using;
  - how much they are spending for that good or service, in total and with each supplier;
  - which units within the agency are purchasing the goods and services; and
  - what goods and services have been or could be purchased to meet socioeconomic supplier goals.

 **CAUTIONS**

- The agency does not conduct or make regular use of spend analysis.
- The agency information and financial management systems are unable to provide credible, reliable, and timely data needed to conduct a spend analysis.
- Information is not maintained in a standardized format or is of poor quality, thus hampering efforts to use the data to more effectively manage goods and services spending.

Safeguarding the Integrity of Operations and Data — ELEMENT

Internal controls—such as structures, policies, and procedures—promote efficiency, reduce the risk of asset loss, help ensure that financial and acquisition management systems issue reliable reports and that the organization is in compliance with laws and regulations. It is essential that acquisition management systems contain appropriate, cost-effective controls to safeguard assets, ensure accurate aggregation and reporting of information, and support the accomplishment of organizational objectives. Internal control actions and activities occur throughout an agency's operations and on an ongoing basis. Management must balance safeguards with the need to make accessible, timely, and accurate data available to managers and others needing acquisition information.

There are two broad groupings of information systems controls that can help safeguard the integrity of operations and data: general controls and application controls. Assessing general and application controls is a technical analysis and requires the assistance of persons knowledgeable in computer systems evaluation.

Ensuring Effective General and Application Controls — CRITICAL SUCCESS FACTOR

General control applies to all information systems and includes agency-wide security program planning, management control over data center operations, system software, acquisition and maintenance, access security, and application system development and maintenance. Application control is designed to help ensure the completeness, accuracy, authorization, and validity of all transactions during application processing. General and application controls over computer systems are interrelated. General control supports the functioning of application control, and both are needed to ensure complete and accurate information processing.

KEY QUESTIONS

- When was the last information systems control review performed?
- What documentation exists of the reviews?
- What issues or problems did the reviews identify?
- How were the issues and problems addressed?
- What are the unresolved issues or problems?
- What is the impact of the unresolved issues and problems?
- What practices and procedures does the agency use to ensure that hardware and software are reliable, secure, and user-friendly?

LOOK FOR

- Evidence in general controls that the structure, policies, and procedures—which apply to all or a large segment of the agency's information systems—help to ensure proper operation, data integrity, and security.
- Evidence in application controls that the structure, policies, and procedures that apply to individual application systems—such as inventory or payroll—produce outputs that are complete, accurate, authorized, consistent, timely, relevant, and useful for its intended purpose.

CAUTIONS

- The agency has not recently reviewed the internal controls governing its major systems.
- The agency has not addressed all identified major internal control issues or established corrective action plans.

Data Stewardship

Critical Success Factor

Data stewardship ensures that data captured and reported are accurate, accessible, timely, and usable for acquisition decision making and activity monitoring. Effective stewardship provides the structure, oversight, and assurance that data can be accurately translated into meaningful information about organizational activities. Taking the time to manage quality of data ultimately helps support the agency's acquisition management needs.

? KEY QUESTIONS

- How does the agency ensure that data reflected in its knowledge and information management systems have the following properties:
  - integrity of data;
  - synchronization of data collection;
  - reduced data redundancy;
  - accessibility of data;
  - transferability of data; and
  - flexibility in the data management process?

LOOK FOR

- The agency's internal controls provide reasonable assurance that data are accurate, complete, timely, and reliable.
- There is consistency among data definitions, sources, controls, and edit routines.
- Managers group data into logical categories and collect data according to commonly accepted reporting time frames.
- Data are redundant only when necessary. Inconsistencies are eliminated.
- Data are accessible to authorized users when needed.
- Data can be transferred to other systems for operational, analytical, and forecasting processes.

CAUTIONS

- Data are unreliable, incomplete, or unsuitable for efficient and effective management decisions.

- Users have little or no confidence in the credibility of the data and outputs from information systems.
- Management does not periodically test the reliability of its data.

QUICK RECAP: How Knowledge and Information Management Can Enhance the Acquisition Function
✓ Acquisition personnel should track data on the contracting, financial, and external environment when developing an integrated acquisition information system. ✓ Data are relevant, timely, reliable, and presented with suitable detail in understandable formats. ✓ Spend analyses answer basic questions about how much is being spent and where the money is going. ✓ Hardware and software are safeguarded to ensure the integrity of operations and acquisition data.

Learn more about knowledge and information management by reading the reports found in appendix II.

Appendix I: Scope and Methodology

The purpose of this framework is to provide a systematic method for evaluating the acquisition function within federal agencies. The framework can be used to identify opportunities for improvements in acquisition processes as well as to highlight specific risks faced by each agency.

To develop the evaluation framework, we made use of the experience, knowledge, and expertise within GAO, the executive branch, state agencies, the private sector, and academia to develop key cornerstones that comprise an integrated acquisition function. The outline of the evaluation framework was then further refined in discussions with:

- federal officials from a procurement executive council working group set up to assist GAO in assessing the acquisition function;
- individuals with acquisition expertise from the private sector and academia; and
- senior acquisition executives at a forum held at GAO in March 2004.

To provide us with a broad understanding of the weaknesses, issues, and potential reforms of the acquisition function, we consulted studies and reports from organizations such as Rand Corporation, the National Academy of Public Administration, the Australian National Audit Office, the National Association of State Purchasing Officials, the PricewaterhouseCoopers Endowment for the Business of Government, the Corporate Executive Board's Procurement Strategy Council, the Center for Advanced Purchasing Studies, and audit reports from GAO and various federal agency inspector general offices.

We also consulted guides on acquisition, human capital, financial management, and information technology from the Department of Defense, Office of Management and Budget, Office of Personnel Management, Department of Veterans Affairs, Department of Energy, Department of Transportation, Department of Treasury, Joint Financial Management

Improvement Program, and GAO. Many of these resources are listed in appendix II.

To verify the accuracy of the information provided and improve the technical usefulness of the information reported, we asked acquisition, human capital, financial management, and information technology experts to review a draft of the evaluation framework. We incorporated their comments to create an exposure draft, which was distributed to obtain comments from interested parties of the federal, state and local acquisition community, acquisition experts from associations, academia, and professional organizations. We then incorporated these additional comments as appropriate in this publication.

Appendix II: Additional Sources of Information

To download GAO reports, please visit our Web site at www.gao.gov and enter the report numbers specified below.

Cross-cutting information

U.S. Department of Energy, Office of Contract Management, Office of Procurement & Assistance Management. *Acquisition & Financial Assistance Self-Assessment Checklist.* Revised March 2005.

GAO. *21st Century Challenges: Reexamining the Base of the Federal Government.* GAO-05-325SP Washington, D.C.: February 2005.

GAO. *Financial Management: Effective Internal Control Is Key to Accountability.* GAO-05-321T. Washington, D.C.: February 16, 2005.

GAO. *High-Risk Series: An Update.* GAO-05-207. Washington, D.C.: January 2005.

U.S. Department of Energy, Office of Procurement and Assistance Management. *Balanced Scorecard: Performance Measurement and Performance Management Program.* Revised January 2005.

U.S. Department of Transportation. *Department of Transportation's Procurement Performance Management System, Guidance Manual.* Revision 3, October 2004.

GAO. *Highlights of a GAO Forum: Workforce Challenges and Opportunities for the 21st Century: Changing Labor Force Dynamics and the Role of Government Policies.* GAO-04-845SP Washington, D.C.: June 2004.

GAO. *Transportation Security Administration: High-Level Attention Needed to Strengthen Acquisition Function.* GAO-04-544. Washington, D.C.: May 28, 2004.

GAO. *Highlights of a GAO Forum on High-Performing Organizations: Metrics, Means, and Mechanisms for Achieving High Performance in the 21st Century Public Management Environment.* GAO-04-343SP Washington, D.C.: February 13, 2004.

Rand Corporation. *Project AIR FORCE Research Brief Speeding Acquisition Reform in the U.S. Air Force.* RB-119-AF. Full report: MR-1711-AF. 2004.

U.S. Department of Energy. *Office of Procurement and Assistance Management, Balanced Scorecard Performance Measures Information Document.* Revised April 22, 2005.

Department of Veterans Affairs. *Procurement Reform Task Force Report.* May 2002.

GAO. *Best Practices: Taking a Strategic Approach Could Improve DOD's Acquisition of Services.* GAO-02-230. Washington, D.C.: January 18, 2002.

GAO. *Internal Control Management and Evaluation Tool.* GAO-01-1008G. Washington, D.C.: August 2001.

Australian National Audit Office, Commonwealth of Australia. *Contract Management: Better Practice Guide.* February 21, 2001.

Schooner, Steven L. *Fear of Oversight: The Fundamental Failure of Business-like Government.* Washington, D.C.: American University Law Review, Vol. 50, No. 3, 2001.

GAO. *Standards for Internal Control in the Federal Government.* GAO/AIMD-00-21.3.1. Washington, D.C.: November 1999.

Procurement Executives' Association. *Guide to a Balanced Scorecard Performance Management Methodology.* Chartered 1998.

Organizational Alignment and Leadership

GAO. *Military Transformation: Clear Leadership, Accountability, and Management Tools Are Needed to Enhance DOD's Efforts to Transform Military Capabilities.* GAO-05-70. Washington, D.C.: December 17, 2004.

GAO. *HUD Management: Actions Needed to Improve Acquisition Management.* GAO-03-157. Washington, D.C.: November 15, 2002.

GAO. *Business Process Reengineering Assessment Guide.* GAO/AIMD-10.1.15. Washington, D.C.: May 1997, Version 3.

GAO. *Reengineering Organizations: Results of a GAO Symposium.* GAO/NSIAD-95-34. Washington, D.C.: December 13, 1994.

Policies and Processes

GAO. *Defense Acquisitions: Assessments of Selected Major Weapon Programs.* GAO-05-301. Washington, D.C.: March 31, 2005.

GAO. *Best Practices: Using Spend Analysis to Help Agencies Take a More Strategic Approach to Procurement.* GAO-04-870. Washington, D.C.: September 16, 2004.

GAO. *Contract Management: Guidance Needed to Promote Competition for Defense Task Orders.* GAO-04-874. Washington, D.C.: July 30, 2004.

GAO. *Information Technology: DOD's Acquisition Policies and Guidance Need to Incorporate Additional Best Practices and Controls.* GAO-04-722. Washington, D.C.: July 30, 2004.

GAO. *The Federal Acquisition Streamlining Act of 1994--Fair opportunity procedures under multiple award task order contracts.* B302499. Washington, D. C.: July 21, 2004.

GAO. *Acquisition/Financial Systems Interface Requirements: Checklist for Reviewing Systems under the Federal Financial Management Improvement Act.* GAO-04-650G. Washington, D.C.: June 2004.

GAO. *Contract Management: Impact of Strategy to Mitigate Effects of Contract Bundling on Small Business Is Uncertain.* GAO-04-454. Washington, D.C.: May 27, 2004.

GAO. *Federal Acquisition: Increased Attention to Vehicle Fleets Could Result in Savings.* GAO-04-664. Washington, D.C.: May 25, 2004.

GAO. *Contract Management: Agencies Can Achieve Significant Savings on Purchase Card Buys.* GAO-04-430. Washington, D.C.: March 12, 2004.

GAO. *Defense Acquisitions: Stronger Management Practices Are Needed to Improve DOD's Software-Intensive Weapon Acquisitions.* GAO-04-393. Washington, D.C.: March 1, 2004.

GAO. *Financial Management: Some DOD Contractors Abuse the Federal Tax System with Little Consequence.* GAO-04-95. Washington, D.C.: February 12, 2004.

GAO. *Best Practices: Using a Knowledge-Based Approach to Improve Weapon Acquisition.* GAO-04-386SP Washington, D.C.: January 2004.

GAO. *Contracting for Information Technology Services.* GAO-03-384R. Washington, D.C.: February 14, 2003.

GAO. *HUD Management: Actions Needed to Improve Acquisition Management.* GAO-03-157. Washington, D.C.: November 15, 2002.

GAO. *Contract Management: Guidance Needed for Using Performance-Based Service Contracting.* GAO-02-1049. Washington, D.C.: September 23, 2002.

GAO. *DOE Contractor Management: Opportunities to Promote Initiatives That Could Reduce Support-Related Costs.* GAO-02-1000. Washington, D.C.: September 20, 2002.

GAO. *Contract Reform: DOE Has Made Progress, but Actions Needed to Ensure Initiatives Have Improved Results.* GAO-02-798. Washington, D.C.: September 13, 2002.

GAO. *Best Practices: Capturing Design and Manufacturing Knowledge Early Improves Acquisition Outcomes.* GAO-02-701. Washington, D.C.: July 15, 2002.

Gansler, Jacques S. *A Vision of the Government as a World-Class Buyer: Major Procurement Issues for the Coming Decade.* The PricewaterhouseCoopers Endowment for the Business of Government. January 2002.

GAO. *Information Technology: Leading Commercial Practices for Outsourcing of Services.* GAO-02-214. Washington, D.C.: November 30, 2001.

GAO. *Strategies to Manage Improper Payments: Learning from Public and Private Sector Organizations.* GAO-02-69G. Washington, D.C.: October 2001.

GAO. *Best Practices: DOD Teaming Practices Not Achieving Potential Results.* GAO-01-510. Washington, D.C.: April 10, 2001.

GAO. *Best Practices: Better Matching of Needs and Resources Will Lead to Better Weapon System Outcomes.* GAO-01-288. Washington, D.C.: March 8, 2001.

GAO. *Best Practices: A More Constructive Test Approach Is Key to Better Weapon System Outcomes.* GAO/NSIAD-00-199. Washington, D.C.: July 31, 2000.

GAO. *Executive Guide: Creating Value Through World-class Financial Management.* GAO/AIMD-00-134. Washington, D.C.: April 2000.

GAO. *Defense Acquisition: Best Commercial Practices Can Improve Program Outcomes.* GAO/T-NSIAD-99-116. Washington, D.C.: March 17, 1999.

GAO. *Executive Guide: Leading Practices in Capital Decision-Making.* GAO/AIMD-99-32. Washington, D.C.: December 1998.

GAO. *Best Practices: DOD Can Help Suppliers Contribute More to Weapon System Programs.* GAO/NSIAD-98-87. Washington, D.C.: March 17, 1998.

GAO. *Budget Issues: Budgeting for Capital.* GAO/T-AIMD-98-99. Washington, D.C.: March 6, 1998:

GAO. *Best Practices: Successful Application to Weapon Acquisitions Requires Changes in DOD's Environment.* GAO/NSIAD-98-56. Washington, D.C.: February 24, 1998.

Joint Financial Management Improvement Program. *Framework for Federal Financial Management Systems.* FFMSR-0. January 1995.

Human Capital

GAO. *Human Capital: Principles, Criteria, and Processes for Governmentwide Federal Human Capital Reform.* GAO-05-69SP Washington, D.C.: December 1, 2004.

GAO. *Posthearing Questions Related to Assessing Progress in Human Capital Management.* GAO-04-1072R. Washington, D.C.: September 3, 2004.

GAO. *Human Capital: Building on the Current Momentum to Transform the Federal Government.* GAO-04-976T Washington, D.C.: July 20, 2004.

GAO. *Human Capital: Increasing Agencies' Use of New Hiring Flexibilities.* GAO-04-959T Washington, D.C.: July 13, 2004.

GAO. *Human Capital: Key Practices to Increasing Federal Telework.* GAO- 04-950T Washington, D.C.: July 8, 2004.

GAO. *Human Capital: Selected Agencies' Use of Alternative Service Delivery Options for Human Capital Activities.* GAO-04-679. Washington, D.C.: June 25, 2004.

GAO. *Posthearing Questions Related to Agencies' Implementation of the Chief Human Capital Officers (CHCO) Act.* GAO-04-897R. Washington, D.C.: June 18, 2004.

GAO. *Human Capital: Additional Collaboration Between OPM and Agencies Is Key to Improved Federal Hiring.* GAO-04-797. Washington, D.C.: June 7, 2004.

GAO. *Human Capital: Status of Efforts to Improve Federal Hiring.* GAO-04-796T. Washington, D.C.: June 7, 2004.

GAO. *Highlights of a GAO Forum: Workforce Challenges and Opportunities For the 21st Century: Changing Labor Force Dynamics and the Role of Government Policies.* GAO-04-845SP Washington, D.C.: June 2004.

GAO. *Human Capital: Senior Executive Performance Management Can Be Significantly Strengthened to Achieve Results.* GAO-04-614. Washington, D.C.: May 26, 2004.

GAO. *Human Capital: Observations on Agencies' Implementation of the Chief Human Capital Officers Act.* GAO-04-800T Washington, D.C.: May 18, 2004.

GAO. *Human Capital: A Guide for Assessing Strategic Training and Development Efforts in the Federal Government.* GAO-04-546G. Washington, D.C.: March 2004.

GAO. *Human Capital: Selected Agencies' Experiences and Lessons Learned in Designing Training and Development Programs.* GAO-04-291. Washington, D.C.: January 30, 2004.

GAO. *Human Capital: Implementing Pay for Performance at Selected Personnel Demonstration Projects*. GAO-04-83. Washington, D.C.: January 23, 2004.

GAO. *Acquisition Management: Agencies Can Improve Training on New Initiatives.* GAO-03-281. Washington, D.C.: January 15, 2003.

GAO. *Acquisition Workforce: Status of Agency Efforts to Address Future Needs.* GAO-03-55. Washington, D.C.: December 18, 2002.

GAO. *Human Capital: Effective Use of Flexibilities Can Assist Agencies in Managing Their Workforces.* GAO-03-2. Washington, D.C.: December 6, 2002.

GAO. *Acquisition Workforce: Department of Defense's Plans to Address Workforce Size and Structure Challenges.* GAO-02-630. Washington, D.C.: April 30, 2002.

GAO. *A Model of Strategic Human Capital Management.* GAO-02-373SP Washington, D.C.: March 15, 2002.

U.S. Office of Personnel Management. *Human Resources Flexibilities and Authorities in the Federal Government.* Washington, D.C.: July 25, 2001.

GAO. *Managing For Results: Emerging Benefits From Selected Agencies' Use of Performance Agreements.* GAO-01-115. Washington, D.C.: October 30, 2000.

GAO. *Best Practices: DOD Training Can Do More to Help Weapon System Programs Implement Best Practices.* GAO/NSIAD-99-206. Washington, D.C.: August 16, 1999.

Knowledge and Information Management:

GAO. *Defense Acquisitions: Better Information Could Improve Visibility over Adjustments to DOD's Research and Development Funds.* GAO-04-944. Washington, D.C.: September 17, 2004.

GAO. *Best Practices: Using Spend Analysis to Help Agencies Take a More Strategic Approach to Procurement*. GAO-04-870. Washington, D.C.: September 16, 2004.

GAO. *Information Technology: DOD's Acquisition Policies and Guidance Need to Incorporate Additional Best Practices and Controls.* GAO-04-722. Washington, D.C.: July 30, 2004.

GAO. *Acquisition/Financial Systems Interface Requirements: Checklist for Reviewing Systems under the Federal Financial Management Improvement Act.* GAO-04-650G. Washington, D.C.: June 2004.

GAO. *Defense Acquisitions: Knowledge of Software Suppliers Needed to Manage Risks.* GAO-04-678. Washington, D.C.: May 25, 2004.

GAO. *Information Technology Investment Management: A Framework for Assessing and Improving Process Maturity.* GAO-04-394G. Washington, D.C.: March 2004, Version 1.1.

GAO. *Financial Management: Some DOD Contractors Abuse the Federal Tax System with Little Consequence.* GAO-04-95. Washington, D.C.: February 12, 2004.

GAO. *Best Practices: Using a Knowledge-Based Approach to Improve Weapon Acquisition.* GAO-04-386SP Washington, D.C.: January 2004.

GAO. *Best Practices: Improved Knowledge of DOD Service Contracts Could Reveal Significant Savings.* GAO-03-661. Washington, D.C.: June 9, 2003.

GAO. *Contracting for Information Technology Services.* GAO-03-384R. Washington, D.C.: February 14, 2003.

GAO. *Assessing the Reliability of Computer-Processed Data.* GAO-03-273G. Washington, D.C.: October 2002, External Version 1.

Joint Financial Management Improvement Program. *Acquisition/ Financial Systems Interface Requirements.* JFMIP-SR-02-02. June 2002.

Joint Financial Management Improvement Program. *Core Financial System Requirements.* JFMIP-SR-02-O1. November 2001.

GAO. *Executive Guide: Creating Value Through World-class Financial Management.* GAO/AIMD-00-134. Washington, D.C.: April 2000.

GAO. *Federal Information System Controls Audit Manual, Volume I - Financial Statement Audits.* GAO/AIMD-12.19.6. Washington, D.C.: January 1999.

GAO. *Assessing Risks and Returns: A Guide for Evaluating Federal Agencies' IT Investment Decision-making.* GAO/AIMD-10.1.13. Washington, D.C.: February 1997.

GAO. *Information Technology Investment: Agencies Can Improve Performance, Reduce Costs, and Minimize Risks.* GAO/AIMD-96-64. Washington, D.C.: September 30, 1996.

Joint Financial Management Improvement Program. *Framework for Federal Financial Management Systems.* FFMSR-0. January 1995.
GAO-05-218G: Download this publication from GAO's Web site: www.gao.gov/cgi-bin/getrpt?GAO-05-218G

GAO's Mission

The Government Accountability Office, the investigative arm of Congress, exists to support Congress in meeting its constitutional responsibilities and to help improve the performance and accountability of the federal government for the American people. GAO examines the use of public funds; evaluates federal programs and policies; and provides analyses, recommendations, and other assistance to help Congress make informed oversight, policy, and funding decisions. GAO's commitment to good government is reflected in its core values of accountability, integrity, and reliability.

Obtaining Copies of GAO Reports and Testimony

The fastest and easiest way to obtain copies of GAO documents at no cost is through GAO's Web site (www.gao.gov). Each weekday, GAO posts newly released reports, testimony, and correspondence on its Web site. To have GAO e-mail you a list of newly posted products every afternoon, go to www.gao.gov and select "Subscribe to Updates."

Order by Mail or Phone

The first copy of each printed report is free. Additional copies are $2 each. A check or money order should be made out to the Superintendent of Documents. GAO also accepts VISA and Mastercard. Orders for 100 or more copies mailed to a single address are discounted 25 percent. Orders should be sent to:

U.S. Government Accountability Office
441 G Street NW, Room LM
Washington, D.C. 20548

To order by Phone:
Voice: (202) 512-6000
TDD: (202) 512-2537
Fax: (202) 512-6061

To Report Fraud, Waste, and Abuse in Federal Programs

Contact:

Web site: www.gao.gov/fraudnet/fraudnet.htm
E-mail: fraudnet@gao.gov
Automated answering system: (800) 424-5454 or (202) 512-7470

Congressional Relations

Gloria Jarmon, Managing Director
JarmonG@gao.gov (202) 512-4400
U.S. Government Accountability Office
441 G Street NW Room 7125
Washington, D.C. 20548

Public Affairs

Paul Anderson, Managing Director
AndersonP1@gao.gov (202) 512-4800
U.S. Government Accountability Office
441 G Street NW Room 7149
Washington, D.C. 20548

Appendix B

Glossary of Key Terms

acceptance

(1) The taking and receiving of anything in good part and as if it were a tacit agreement to a preceding act, which might have been defeated or avoided if such acceptance had not been made. (2) Agreement to the terms offered in a contract. An acceptance must be communicated, and (in common law) it must be the mirror image of the offer.

acquisition cost

The money invested up front to bring in new customers.

acquisition plan

A plan for an acquisition that serves as the basis for initiating the individual contracting actions necessary to acquire a system or support a program.

acquisition strategy

The conceptual framework for conducting systems acquisition. It encompasses the broad concepts and objectives that direct and control the overall development, production, and deployment of a system.

act of God

An inevitable, accidental, or extraordinary event that cannot be foreseen and guarded against, such as lightning, tornadoes, or earthquakes.

actual authority

The power that the principal intentionally confers on the agent or allows the agent to believe he or she possesses.

actual damages

See *compensatory damages.*

affidavit

A written and signed statement sworn to under oath.

agency

A relationship that exists when there is a delegation of authority to perform all acts connected within a particular trade, business, or company. It gives authority to the agent to act in all matters relating to the business of the principal.

agent

An employee (usually a contract manager) empowered to bind his or her organization legally in contract negotiations.

allowable cost

A cost that is reasonable, allocable, and within accepted standards or that otherwise conforms to generally accepted accounting principles, specific limitations or exclusions, or agreed-on terms between contractual parties.

alternative dispute resolution

Any procedure that is used, in lieu of litigation, to resolve issues in controversy, including but not limited to settlement negotiations, conciliation, facilitation, mediation, fact finding, mini-trials, and arbitration.

amortization

The process of spreading the cost of an intangible asset over the expected useful life of the asset.

apparent authority

The power that the principal permits the perceived agent to exercise, although not actually granted.

as is

A contract phrase referring to the condition of property to be sold or leased. The phrase generally pertains to a disclaimer of liability; property sold in as-is condition is generally not guaranteed.

assign

To convey or transfer to another, as to assign property, rights, or interests to another.

assignment

The transfer of property by an assignor to an assignee.

audits

The systematic examination of records and documents or the securing of other evidence by confirmation, physical inspection, or otherwise for one or more of the following purposes: determining the propriety or legality of proposed or completed transactions, ascertaining whether all transactions have been recorded and are reflected accurately in accounts, determining the existence of recorded assets and inclusiveness of recorded liabilities, determining the accuracy of financial or statistical statements or reports and the fairness of the facts that they represent, determining the degree of compliance with established policies and procedures in terms of financial transactions and business management, and appraising an account system and making recommendations concerning it.

base profit

The money a company is paid by a customer that exceeds the company's cost.

best value

The best trade-off between competing factors for a particular purchase requirement. The key to successful best-value contracting is consideration of life-cycle costs, including the use of quantitative as well as qualitative techniques to measure price and technical performance trade-offs between various proposals. The best-value concept applies to acquisitions in which price or price-related factors are *not* the primary determinant of who receives the contract award.

bid

An offer in response to an invitation for bids (IFB).

bid development

All of the work activities required to design and price the product and service solution and accurately articulate it in a proposal for a customer.

bid phase

The period of time a seller of goods or services uses to develop a bid or proposal, conduct internal bid reviews, and obtain stakeholder approval to submit a bid or proposal.

bilateral contract

A contract formed if an offer states that acceptance requires only a promise to perform by the accepting party. In contrast, a *unilateral contract* is formed if an offer requires actual performance for acceptance.

bond

A written instrument executed by a seller and a second party (the surety or sureties) to ensure fulfillment of the principal's obligations to a third party (the obligee or buyer) that is identified in the bond. If the principal's obligations are not met, the bond ensures payment, to the extent stipulated, of any loss sustained by the obligee.

breach of contract

(1) The failure, without legal excuse, to perform any promise that forms the whole or part of a contract. (2) The ending of a contract that occurs when one or both of the parties fail to keep their promises. Such a breach of contract could lead to arbitration or litigation.

buyer

The party contracting for goods or services with one or more sellers.

capability maturity model

An evolutionary roadmap for implementing the vital practices for one or more domains of organizational processes. It contains the essential elements of effective processes for one or more disciplines. It describes an evolutionary improvement path from an ad hoc, immature process, to a disciplined mature process with improved quality and effectiveness.

cancellation

The withdrawal of the requirement to purchase goods or services by the buyer.

capture management

The art and science of winning more business.

capture management life cycle

The art and science of winning more business throughout the entire business cycle.

capture project plan

A document or game plan of who needs to do what, when, where, how often, and how much to win business.

change in scope

An amendment to approved program requirements or specifications after negotiation of a basic contract. It may result in an increase or decrease.

change order or purchase order amendment

A written order directing the seller to make changes according to the provisions of the contract documents.

claim

A demand by one party to contract for something from another party, usually but not necessarily for more money or more time. Claims are usually based on an argument that the party making the demand is entitled to an adjustment by virtue of the contract terms or some violation of those terms by the other party. The word does not imply any disagreement between the parties, although claims often lead to disagreements.

clause

A statement of one of the rights or obligations of the parties to a contract. A contract consists of a series of clauses.

collaboration software

Automated tools that allow for real-time exchange of visual information using personal computers.

collateral benefit

The degree to which pursuit of an opportunity will improve existing skill levels or develop new skills that will positively affect other or future business opportunities.

compensable delay

A delay for which the buyer is contractually responsible that excuses the seller's failure to perform and is compensable.

compensatory damages

Damages that will compensate the injured party for the loss sustained and nothing more. They are awarded by a court as the measure of actual loss, not as punishment for outrageous conduct or to deter future transgressions. Compensatory damages are often referred to as "actual damages." See also *incidental damages* and *punitive damages.*

competency

An underlying characteristic that is causally related to effective or superior performance, as determined by measurable, objective criteria, in a job or in a situation.

competitive intelligence

Information on competitors or competitive teams that is specific to an opportunity.

competitive negotiation

A method of contracting involving a request for proposals that states the buyer's requirements and criteria for evaluation; submission of timely proposals by a maximum number of offerors; discussions with those offerors found to be within the competitive range; and award of a contract to the one offeror whose offer, price, and other consideration factors are most advantageous to the buyer.

condition precedent

A condition that activates a term in a contract.

condition subsequent

A condition that suspends a term in a contract.

conflict of interest

A term that is used in connection with public officials and fiduciaries and their relationships to matters of private interest or gain to them. Ethical problems connected therewith are covered by statutes in most jurisdictions and by federal statutes at the federal level. A conflict of interest arises when an employee's personal or financial interest conflicts or appears to conflict with his or her official responsibility.

consideration

(1) The thing of value (amount of money or acts to be done or not done) that must change hands between the parties to a contract. (2) The inducement to a contract—the cause, motive, price, or impelling influence that induces a contracting party to enter into a contract.

contract management

The art and science of managing a contractual agreements throughout the contracting process.

contract negotiation

The process of unifying different positions into a unanimous joint decision regarding the buying and selling of products or services.

contract negotiation process

A three-phase approach composed of planning, negotiating, and documenting a contractual agreement between two or more parties to buy or sell products or services.

constructive change

An oral or written act or omission by an authorized or unauthorized agent of such a nature that it is construed to have the same effect as a written change order.

contingency

The quality of being contingent or casual, an event that may but does not have to occur, or a possibility.

contingent contract

A contract that provides for the possibility of its termination when a specified occurrence takes place or does not take place.

contra proferentem

A legal phrase used in connection with the construction of written documents, to the effect that an ambiguous provision is construed most strongly against the person who selected the language.

contract

(1) A relationship between two parties, such as a buyer and seller, that is defined by an agreement about their respective rights and responsibilities. (2) A document that describes such an agreement.

contract administration

The process of ensuring compliance with contractual terms and conditions during contract performance up to contract closeout or termination.

contract closeout

The process of verifying that all administrative matters are concluded on a contract that is otherwise physically complete—in other words, the seller has delivered the required goods or performed the required services, and the buyer has inspected and accepted the goods or services.

contract fulfillment

The joint actions taken by the buyer and seller to successfully perform and administer a contractual agreement and meet or exceed all contract obligations, including effective change management and timely contract closeout.

contract interpretation

The entire process of determining what the parties agreed to in their bargain. The basic objective of contract interpretation is to determine the intent of the parties. Rules calling for interpretation of the documents against the drafter and imposing a duty to seek clarification on the drafter allocate risks of contractual ambiguities by resolving disputes in favor of the party least responsible for the ambiguity.

contract management

The art and science of managing a contractual agreement throughout the contracting process.

contract type

A specific pricing arrangement used for the performance of work under the contract.

contractor

The seller or provider of goods or services.

controversy

A litigated question. A civil action or suit may not be instigated unless it is based on a "justifiable" dispute. This term is important in that the judicial power of the courts extends only to cases and controversies.

copyright

A royalty-free, nonexclusive, and irrevocable license to reproduce, translate, publish, use, and dispose of written or recorded material and to authorize others to do so.

cost

The amount of money expended in acquiring a product or obtaining a service or the total of acquisition costs plus all expenses related to operating and maintaining an item, once acquired.

cost of good sold (COGS)

Direct costs of producing finished goods for sale.

cost accounting standards

Federal standards designed to provide consistency and coherency in defense and other government contract accounting.

cost plus award fee (CPAF) contract

A type of cost reimbursement contract with special incentive fee provisions used to motivate excellent contract performance in such areas as quality, timeliness, ingenuity, and cost-effectiveness.

cost plus fixed fee (CPFF) contract

A type of cost reimbursement contract that provides for the payment of a fixed fee to the contractor. It does not vary with actual costs but may be adjusted if there are any changes in the work or services to be performed under the contract.

cost plus incentive fee (CPIF) contract

A type of cost reimbursement contract with provision for a fee that is adjusted by a formula in accordance with the relationship between total allowable costs and target costs.

cost plus a percentage of cost (CPPC) contract

A type of cost reimbursement contract that provides for a reimbursement of the allowable cost of services performed plus an agreed-on percentage of the estimated cost as profit.

cost reimbursement (CR) contract

A type of contract that usually includes an estimate of project cost, a provision for reimbursing the seller's expenses, and a provision for paying a fee as profit. CR contracts are often used when there is high uncertainty about costs. They normally also include a limitation on the buyer's cost liability.

cost-sharing contract

A cost reimbursement contract in which the seller receives no fee and is reimbursed only for an agreed-on portion of its allowable costs.

cost contract

The simplest type of cost reimbursement contract. Governments commonly use this type when contracting with universities and nonprofit organizations for research projects. The contract provides for reimbursing contractually allowable costs, with no allowance given for profit.

cost proposal

The instrument required of an offeror for the submission or identification of cost or pricing data, by which an offeror submits to the buyer a summary of estimated (or incurred) costs suitable for detailed review and analysis.

counteroffer

An offer made in response to an original offer that changes the terms of the original.

customer revenue growth

The increased revenues achieved by keeping a customer for an extended period of time.

customer support costs

Costs expended by a company to provide information and advice concerning purchases.

default termination

The termination of a contract, under the standard default clause, because of a buyer's or seller's failure to perform any of the terms of the contract.

defect

(1) The absence of something necessary for completeness or perfection. (2) A deficiency in something essential to the proper use of a thing. (3) Some structural weakness in a part or component that is responsible for damage.

defect, latent

A defect that existed at the time of acceptance but would not have been discovered by a reasonable inspection.

defect, patent

A defect that can be discovered without undue effort. If the defect was actually known to the buyer at the time of acceptance, it is patent, even though it otherwise might not have been discoverable by a reasonable inspection.

definite-quantity contract

A contractual instrument that provides for a definite quantity of supplies or services to be delivered at some later, unspecified date.

delay, excusable

A contractual provision designed to protect the seller from sanctions for late performance. To the extent that a delay is excusable, the seller is protected from default termination or liquidated damages. Examples of excusable delay are acts of God, acts of the government, fires, floods, quarantines, strikes, epidemics, unusually severe weather, and embargoes. See also *act of God, forbearance,* and *force majeure clause.*

depreciation

The amount of expense charged against earnings by a company to write off the cost of plant or machine over its useful life, giving consideration to wear and tear, obsolescence, and salvage value.

design specification

(1) A document (including drawings) setting forth the characteristics required of a particular component, part, subsystem, system, or construction item. (2) A purchase description that establishes precise measurements, tolerances, materials, in-process and finished product tests, quality control, inspection requirements, and other specific details of the deliverable.

direct cost

The costs specifically identifiable with a contract requirement, including but not restricted to costs of material and labor directly incorporated into an end item.

direct labor

All work that is obviously related and specifically and conveniently traceable to specific products.

direct material

Items, including raw material, purchased parts, and subcontracted items, directly incorporated into an end item, which are identifiable to a contract requirement.

discount rate

Interest rate used in calculating present value.

discounted cash flow (DCF)

Combined present value of cash flow and tangible assets minus present value of liabilities.

discounts, allowances, and returns

Price discounts and returned merchandise.

dispute

A disagreement not settled by mutual consent that could be decided by litigation or arbitration. Also see *claim.*

e-business

Technology-enabled business that focuses on seamless integration between each business—the company and its supply partners.

EBITDA

Earnings before interest, taxes, depreciation, and amortization, but after all selling, general, and administrative (SG&A) costs for products or services are accounted for. Sometimes referred to as operating profit.

EBITDARM

Earnings before interest, taxes, depreciation, amortization, rent, and management fees.

e-commerce

A subset of e-business: Internet-based electronic transactions.

electronic data interchange (EDI)

Private networks used for simple data transactions, which are typically batch processed.

elements of a contract

The items that must be present in a contract if the contract is to be binding, including an offer, acceptance (agreement), consideration, execution by competent parties, and legality of purpose.

enterprise resource planning (ERP)

An electronic framework for integrating all organizational functions, evolved from manufacturing resource planning (MRP).

entire contract

A contract that is considered entire on both sides and cannot be made severable.

e-procurement

Technology-enabled buying and selling of goods and services.

estimate at completion (EAC)

The actual direct costs plus indirect costs allocable to the contract, plus the estimate of costs (direct or indirect) for authorized work remaining.

estoppel
A rule of law that bars, prevents, and precludes a party from alleging or denying certain facts because of a previous allegation or denial or because of its previous conduct or admission.

ethics
(1) Of or relating to moral action, conduct, motive, or character (such as ethical emotion). (2) Treating of moral feelings, duties, or conduct; containing precepts of morality; moral. (3) Professionally right or befitting; conforming to professional standards of conduct.

e-tool
An electronic device, program, system, or software application used to facilitate business.

exculpatory clause
Contract language designed to shift responsibility to the other party. A "no damages for delay" clause would be an example of one used by buyers.

excusable delay
See *delay, excusable.*

executed contract
A contract that is formed and performed at the same time. If performed in part, it is partially executed and partially executory.

executed contract (document)
A written document, signed by both parties and mailed or otherwise furnished to each party, that expresses the requirements, terms, and conditions to be met by both parties in the performance of the contract.

executory contract
A contract that has not yet been fully performed.

express
Something put in writing—for example, "express authority."

fair and reasonable
A subjective evaluation of what each party deems equitable consideration in areas such as terms and conditions, cost or price, assured quality, timeliness of contract performance, and any other areas subject to negotiation.

Federal Acquisition Regulation (FAR)

The governmentwide procurement regulation mandated by Congress and issued by the Department of Defense, the General Services Administration, and the National Aeronautics and Space Administration. Effective April 1, 1984, the FAR supersedes both the Defense Acquisition Regulation (DAR) and the Federal Procurement Regulation (FPR). All federal agencies are authorized to issue regulations implementing the FAR.

fee

An agreed-to amount of reimbursement beyond the initial estimate of costs. The term "fee" is used when discussing cost reimbursement contracts, whereas the term "profit" is used in relation to fixed price contracts.

firm fixed price (FFP) contract

The simplest and most common business pricing arrangement. The seller agrees to supply a quantity of goods or to provide a service for a specified price.

fixed costs

Operating expenses incurred to provide facilities and keep an organization ready to do business without regard to actual volumes of production and sales. Examples of fixed costs are rent, property tax, and interest expense.

fixed price

A form of pricing that includes a ceiling beyond which the buyer bears no responsibility for payment.

fixed price incentive (FPI) contract

A type of contract that provides for adjusting profit and establishing the final contract price using a formula that is based on the relationship of total final negotiated cost to total target cost. The final price is subject to a price ceiling, negotiated at the outset.

fixed price redeterminable (FPR) contract

A type of fixed price contract that contains provisions for subsequently negotiated adjustment, in whole or in part, of the initially negotiated base price.

fixed price with economic price adjustment

A fixed price contract that permits an element of cost to fluctuate to reflect current market prices.

forbearance

An intentional failure of a party to enforce a contract requirement, usually done for an act of immediate or future consideration from the other party. Sometimes forbearance is referred to as a nonwaiver or as a one-time waiver, but not as a relinquishment of rights.

***force majeure* clause**

A contract clause that protects the parties in the event that a part of the contract cannot be performed for reasons outside the control of the parties that could not be avoided by exercise of due care. *Force majeure* means major or irresistible force. Excusable conditions for nonperformance, such as strikes and acts of God (e.g., typhoons), are contained in this clause.

fraud

(1) An intentional perversion of truth to induce another who relies on it to part with something of value belonging to him or her or to surrender a legal right. (2) A false representation of a matter of fact, whether by words or conduct, by false or misleading allegations, or by concealment of that which should have been disclosed, that deceives and is intended to deceive another so that he or she shall act on it to his or her legal injury. (3) Anything calculated to deceive.

free on board (FOB)

A term used in conjunction with a physical point to determine (a) the responsibility and basis for payment of freight charges and (b) unless otherwise agreed, the point at which title for goods passes to the buyer or consignee. *FOB origin*—The seller places the goods on the conveyance by which they are to be transported. Cost of shipping and risk of loss are borne by the buyer. *FOB destination*—The seller delivers the goods on the seller's conveyance at destination. Cost of shipping and risk of loss are borne by the seller.

functional specification

A purchase description that describes the deliverable in terms of performance characteristics and intended use, including those characteristics that at minimum are necessary to satisfy the intended use.

general and administrative (G&A)

(1) The indirect expenses related to the overall business: expenses for a company's general and executive offices, executive compensation, staff services, and other miscellaneous support purposes. (2) Any indirect management, financial, or other expense that (a) is not assignable to a program's direct overhead charges for engineering, manufacturing, material, and the like, but (b) is routinely incurred by or allotted to a business unit and (c) is for the general management and administration of the business as a whole.

general accepted accounting principles (GAAP)

A term encompassing conventions, rules, and procedures of accounting that are generally accepted and have substantial authoritative support. The GAAP have been developed by agreement on the basis of experience, reason, custom, usage, and to a certain extent practical necessity, rather than derived from a formal set of theories.

General Agreement on Tariffs and Trade (GATT)

A multinational trade agreement signed in 1947 by 23 founding nations.

gross profit margin

Net sales minus cost of goods sold. Also called gross margin, gross profit, or gross loss.

gross profit margin percent or ratio

Gross profit margin in dollars divided by net sales.

gross sales

Total revenues at invoice value before any discounts or allowances.

horizontal exchange

A marketplace that deals with goods and services that are not specific to one industry.

imply

To indirectly convey meaning or intent; to leave the determination of meaning up to the receiver of the communication based on circumstances, general language used, or conduct of those involved.

incidental damages

Any commercially reasonable charges, expenses, or commissions incurred in stopping delivery; in the transportation, care, and custody of goods after the buyer's breach; or in connection with the return or resale of the goods or otherwise resulting from the breach.

indefinite-delivery/indefinite-quantity (IDIQ) contract
A type of contract in which the exact date of delivery or the exact quantity—or a combination—is not specified at the time the contract is executed. Provisions are placed in the contract to stipulate these elements of the contract later.

indemnification clause
A contract clause by which one party engages to secure another against an anticipated loss resulting from an act or forbearance on the part of one of the parties or of some third person.

indemnify
To make good; to compensate; to reimburse a person in case of an anticipated loss.

indirect cost
Any cost not directly identifiable with a specific cost objective but subject to two or more cost objectives.

indirect labor
All work that is not specifically associated with or cannot be practically traced to specific units of output.

intellectual property
The kind of property that results from the fruits of mental labor.

interactive chat
A feature provided by automated tools that allow users to establish a voice connection between two or more parties and exchange text or graphics on a virtual bulletin board.

intranet
An organization-specific internal secure network.

joint contract
A contract in which the parties bind themselves both individually and as a unit.

liquidated damages
A contract provision providing for the assessment of damages on the seller for its failure to comply with certain performance or delivery requirements of the contract. The provision is used when the time of

delivery or performance is of such importance that the buyer may reasonably expect to suffer damages if the delivery or performance is delinquent.

mailbox rule

The idea that the acceptance of an offer is effective when deposited in the mail if the envelope is properly addressed.

marketing

Activities that direct the flow of goods and services from a producer to consumers.

market intelligence

Information on competitors or competitive teams operating in the marketplace or industry.

market research

The process used to collect and analyze information about an entire market to help determine the most suitable approach to acquiring, distributing, and supporting supplies and services.

maturity

A measure of effectiveness in any specific process.

maturity level

A level of organizational capability created by the transformation of one or more domains of an organization's processes. It is an evolutionary plateau on an organization's improvement path from ad hoc practices to a state of continuous improvement.

memorandum of agreement (MOA) or memorandum of understanding (MOU)

The documentation of a mutually agreed-on statement of facts, intentions, procedures, and parameters for future actions and matters of coordination. A memorandum of understanding may express mutual understanding of an issue without implying commitments by the parties to the understanding.

method of procurement

The process used for soliciting offers, evaluating offers, and awarding a contract.

modifications

Any written alterations in the specification, delivery point, rate of delivery, contract period, price, quantity, or other provision of an existing contract, accomplished in accordance with a contract clause. Modifications may be unilateral or bilateral.

monopoly
A market structure in which the entire market for a good or service is supplied by a single seller or firm.

monopsony
A market structure in which a single buyer purchases a good or service.

NCMA contract management body of knowledge (CMBOK)
Definitive descriptions of the elements making up the body of professional knowledge that applies to contract management.

negotiation
A process between buyers and sellers seeking to reach mutual agreement on a matter of common concern through fact-finding, bargaining, and persuasion.

net marketplace
A two-sided exchange in which buyers and sellers negotiate prices, usually through a bid-and-ask system, and prices move both up and down.

net present value (NPV)
The lifetime customer revenue stream discounted by the investment costs and operations costs.

net sales
Gross sales minus discounts, allowances, and returns.

North America Free Trade Agreement (NAFTA)
A trilateral trade and investment agreement between Canada, Mexico, and the United States, ratified on January 1, 1994.

novation agreement
A legal instrument executed by (a) the contractor (transferor), (b) the successor in interest (transferee), and (c) the buyer, by which, among other things, the transferor guarantees performance of the contract, the transferee assumes all obligations under the contract, and the buyer recognizes the transfer of the contract and related assets.

offer
(1) The manifestation of willingness to enter into a bargain, so made as to justify another person in understanding that his or her assent to that

bargain is invited and will conclude it. (2) An unequivocal and intentionally communicated statement of proposed terms made to another party. An offer is presumed revocable unless it specifically states that it is irrevocable. An offer once made will be open for a reasonable period of time and is binding on the offeror, unless revoked by the offeror before the other party's acceptance.

oligopoly
A market dominated by a few sellers.

operating expenses
Selling, general, and administrative (SG&A) costs plus depreciation and amortization.

opportunity
A potential or actual favorable event.

opportunity engagement
The degree to which a company or its competitors were involved in establishing the customer's requirements.

opportunity profile
A stage of the capture management life cycle during which a seller evaluates and describes an opportunity in terms of what it means to a buyer's customer, what it means to the buyer, and what will be required to succeed.

option
A unilateral right in a contract by which, for a specified time, the buyer may elect to purchase additional quantities of the supplies or services called for in the contract or may elect to extend the period of performance of the contract.

order of precedence
A solicitation provision that establishes priorities so that contradictions within the solicitation can be resolved.

organizational breakdown structure (OBS)
An organized structure that represents how individual team members are grouped to complete assigned work tasks.

outsourcing
A contractual process of getting another party to provide goods or services previously provided within an organization.

overhead

An accounting cost category that typically includes general indirect expenses necessary to operate a business but not directly assignable to a specific good or service produced. Examples include building rent, utilities, salaries of corporate officers, janitorial services, office supplies, and furniture.

overtime

The time worked by a seller's employee in excess of the employee's normal workweek.

parol evidence

Oral or verbal evidence; in contract law, the evidence drawn from sources other than the written instrument.

parol evidence rule

A rule that seeks to preserve the integrity of written agreements by refusing to permit contracting parties to attempt to alter a written contract with evidence of any contradictory prior or contemporaneous oral agreement (parol to the contract).

payments

The amount payable under the contract supporting data required to be submitted with invoices, plus other payment terms such as time for payment and retention.

payment bond

A bond that secures the appropriate payment of subcontracts for their completed and acceptable goods and services.

performance-based contract (PBC)

A documented business arrangement in which the buyer and seller agree to use a performance work statement, performance-based metrics, and a quality assurance plan to ensure that contract requirements are met or exceeded.

performance bond

A bond that secures the performance and fulfillment of all the undertakings, covenants, terms, conditions, and agreements contained in a contract.

performance specification

A purchase description that describes the deliverable in terms of desired operational characteristics. Performance specifications tend to be more restrictive than functional specifications, in that they limit alternatives that the buyer can consider and define separate performance standards for each such alternative.

performance work statement (PWS)
A statement of work expressed in terms of desired performance results, often including specific measurable objectives.

post-bid phase
The period of time after a seller submits a bid or proposal to a buyer through source selection, negotiations, contract formation, contract fulfillment, contract closeout, and follow-on opportunity management.

pre-bid phase
The period of time a seller of goods or services uses to identify business opportunities before the release of a customer solicitation.

pricing arrangement
An agreed-to basis between contractual parties for the payment of amounts for specified performance; usually expressed in terms of a specific cost reimbursement or fixed price arrangement.

prime or prime contractor
The principal seller performing under the contract.

private exchange
A marketplace hosted by a single company inside a company's firewall and used for procurement from among a group of preauthorized sellers.

privity of contract
The legal relationship that exists between the parties to a contract that allows either party to (a) enforce contractual rights against the other party and (b) seek remedy directly from the other party.

process capability
The inherent ability of a process to produce planned results.

procurement
The complete action or process of acquiring or obtaining goods or services using any of several authorized means.

procurement planning
The process of identifying which business needs can be best met by procuring products or services outside the organization.

profit
The net proceeds from selling a good or service when costs are subtracted from revenues. Profit may be positive or negative (loss).

program management
The planning and execution of multiple projects that are related to one another.

progress payment
An interim payment for delivered work in accordance with contract terms. Such payments are generally tied to meeting specified performance milestones.

project management
Planning and ensuring the quality, on-time delivery, and cost of a specific set of related activities with a definite beginning and end.

promotion
Publicizing the attributes of a good or service through media and personal contacts and presentations (e.g., technical articles and presentations, press releases, advertising, and sales calls).

proposal
Normally, a written offer by a seller describing its offering terms. Proposals may be issued in response to a specific request or may be made unilaterally when a seller feels there may be interest in its offer (also known as an unsolicited proposal).

proposal evaluation
An assessment of both a proposal and the offeror's ability (as conveyed by the proposal) to successfully accomplish the prospective contract. An agency shall evaluate competitive proposals solely on the factors specified in the solicitation.

protest
A written objection by an interested party to (a) a solicitation or other request by an agency for offers for a contract for the procurement of property or services, (b) the cancellation of the solicitation or other request, (c) an award or proposed award of the contract, or (d) a termination or cancellation of an award of the contract, if the written objection contains an allegation that the termination or cancellation is based in whole or in part on improprieties concerning the award of the contract.

punitive damages

Those damages awarded to the plaintiff over and above what will barely compensate for his or her loss. Unlike compensatory damages, punitive damages are based on an actively different public policy consideration, one of punishing the defendant or of setting an example for similar wrongdoers.

purchasing

The outright acquisition of items, mostly off the shelf or catalog, manufactured outside the buyer's premises.

quality assurance

The planned and systematic actions necessary to provide adequate confidence that the service performed or good supplied will serve satisfactorily for the intended and specified purpose.

quotation

A statement of price, either written or oral, which may include a description of the product or service; the terms of sale, delivery, or period of performance; and payment. Such statements are usually issued by sellers at the request of potential buyers.

reasonable cost

A cost that, in its nature and amount, does not exceed that which would be incurred by a prudent person in the conduct of competitive business.

request for information (RFI)

A formal invitation to submit general or specific information concerning the potential future purchase of goods and services.

request for proposals (RFP)

A formal invitation that contains a scope of work and seeks a formal response (proposal), describing both methodology and compensation, to form the basis of a contract.

request for quotations (RFQ)

A formal invitation to submit a price for goods and services as specified.

request for technical proposals (RFTP)

A solicitation document used in two-step sealed bidding. Normally in letter form, it asks only for technical information; price and cost breakdowns are forbidden.

revenue value
The monetary value of an opportunity.

risk
Exposure or potential of an injury or loss.

sealed-bid procedure
A method of procurement involving the unrestricted solicitation of bids, an opening of the bids, and an award of a contract to the lowest responsible bidder.

selling, general, and administrative (SG&A) expenses
The administrative costs of running business.

severable contract
A contract divisible into separate parts. A default of one section does not invalidate the whole contract.

several
A circumstance when more than two parties are involved in the contract.

single source
One source among others in a competitive marketplace that, for justifiable reason, is found most worthy to receive a contract award.

small business concerns
An independently owned and operated business that is not dominant in its field; a business concern that meets government size standards for its particular industry type.

socioeconomic programs
Programs designed to benefit particular groups. They represent a multitude of program interests and objectives unrelated to procurement objectives. Some examples are preferences for small business and for American products, required sources for specific items, and minimum labor pay levels mandated for contractors.

solicitation
A process through which a buyer requests, bids, quotes, tenders, or proposes orally, in writing, or electronically. Solicitations can take the following forms: request for proposals (RFP), request for quotations (RFQ), request for tenders, invitation to bid (ITB), invitation for bids, and invitation for negotiation.

solicitation planning
The preparation of the documents needed to support a solicitation.

source selection
The process by which a buyer evaluates offers, selects a seller, negotiates terms and conditions, and awards a contract.

Source Selection Advisory Council
A group of people appointed by the source selection authority and responsible for reviewing and approving the source selection plan (SSP) and the solicitation of competitive awards for major and certain less-than-major procurements. The council also determines which proposals are in the competitive range and provides recommendations to the source selection authority for final selection.

source selection plan (SSP)
The document that describes the selection criteria, the process, and the organization to be used in evaluating proposals for competitively awarded contracts.

specification
A description of the technical requirements for a material, product, or service that includes the criteria for determining that the requirements have been met. Generally three types of specifications are used in contracting: performance, functional, and design.

stakeholders
Individuals who control the resources in a company needed to pursue opportunities or deliver solutions to customers.

standard
A document that establishes engineering and technical limitations and applications of items, materials, processes, methods, designs, and engineering practices. It includes any related criteria deemed essential to achieve the highest practical degree of uniformity in materials or products or the highest practical degree of interchangeability of parts used in those products.

standards of conduct
The ethical conduct of personnel involved in the acquisition of goods and services. Within the federal government, business shall be conducted in a manner above reproach and, except as authorized by law or

regulation, with complete impartiality and without preferential treatment.

statement of work (SOW)
That portion of a contract describing the actual work to be done by means of specifications or other minimum requirements, quantities, performance date, and a statement of the requisite quality.

statute of limitations
The legislative enactment prescribing the periods within which legal actions may be brought upon certain claims or within which certain rights may be enforced.

stop work order
A request for interim stoppage of work because of nonconformance, funding, or technical considerations.

subcontract
A contract between a buyer and a seller in which a significant part of the supplies or services being obtained is for eventual use in a prime contract.

subcontractor
A seller who enters into a contract with a prime contractor or a subcontractor of the prime contractor.

supplementary agreement
A contract modification that is accomplished by the mutual action of parties.

technical factor
A factor other than price used in evaluating offers for award. Examples include technical excellence, management capability, personnel qualifications, prior experience, past performance, and schedule compliance.

technical leveling
The process of helping a seller bring its proposal up to the level of other proposals through successive rounds of discussion, such as by pointing out weaknesses resulting from the seller's lack of diligence, competence, or inventiveness in preparing the proposal.

technical or management proposal
That part of the offer that describes the seller's approach to meeting the buyer's requirement.

technical transfusion

The disclosure of technical information pertaining to a proposal that results in improvement of a competing proposal. This practice is not allowed in federal government contracting.

term

A part of a contract that addresses a specific subject.

termination

An action taken pursuant to a contract clause in which the buyer unilaterally ends all or part of the work.

terms and conditions (Ts and Cs)

All clauses in a contract, including time of delivery, packing and shipping, applicable standard clauses, and special provisions.

unallowable cost

Any cost that, under the provisions of any pertinent law, regulation, or contract, cannot be included in prices, cost reimbursements, or settlements under a government contract to which it is allocable.

uncompensated overtime

The work that exempt employees perform above and beyond 40 hours per week; also known as competitive time, deflated hourly rates, direct allocation of salary costs, discounted hourly rates, extended workweek, full-time accounting, and green time.

Uniform Commercial Code (UCC)

A U.S. model law developed to standardize commercial contracting law among the states. It has been adopted by 49 states (and in significant portions by Louisiana). The UCC comprises articles that deal with specific commercial subject matters, including sales and letters of credit.

unilateral

See *bilateral contract.*

unsolicited proposal

A research or development proposal that is made by a prospective contractor without prior formal or informal solicitation from a buyer.

variable costs

Costs associated with production that change directly with the amount of production, such as the direct material or labor required to complete the build or manufacturing of a product.

variance

The difference between projected and actual performance, especially related to costs.

vertical exchange

A marketplace that is specific to a single industry.

waiver

The voluntary and unilateral relinquishment by a person of a right that he or she has. See also *forbearance.*

warranty

A promise or affirmation given by a seller to a buyer regarding the nature, usefulness, or condition of the goods or services furnished under a contract. Generally, a warranty's purpose is to delineate the rights and obligations for defective goods and services and to foster quality performance.

warranty, express

A written statement arising out of a sale to the consumer of a consumer good, pursuant to which the manufacturer, distributor, or retailer undertakes to preserve or maintain the utility or performance of the consumer good or provide compensation if there is a failure in utility or performance. It is not necessary to the creation of an express warranty that formal words such as "warranty" or "guarantee" be used or that a specific intention to make a warranty be present.

warranty, implied

A promise arising by operation of law that something that is sold shall be fit for the purpose for which the seller has reason to know that it is required. Types of implied warranties include those of merchantability, of title, and of wholesomeness.

warranty of fitness

A warranty by the seller that goods sold are suitable for the special purpose of the buyer.

warranty of merchantability

A warranty that goods are fit for the ordinary purposes for which such goods are used and conform to the promises or affirmations of fact made on the container or label.

warranty of title

An express or implied (arising by operation of law) promise that the seller owns the item offered for sale and, therefore, is able to transfer a good title and that the goods, as delivered, are free from any security interest of which the buyer, at the time of contracting, has no knowledge.

web portals

A public exchange in which a company or group of companies list products or services for sale or transmit business information.

win strategy

A collection of messages or points designed to guide a buyer's perception of a seller, the seller's solution, and the seller's competitors.

Work Breakdown Structure (WBS)

A logical, organized, decomposition of the work tasks within a given project, typically using a hierarchical numeric coding scheme.

World Trade Organization (WTO)

A multinational legal entity that serves as the champion of fair trade globally, established April 15, 1995.

Bibliography

Atkinson, William, "Beyond the Basics," *PM Network,* May 2003 (Project Management Institute).

Badgerow, Dana B., Gregory A. Garrett, Dominic F. DiClementi, and Barbara M. Weaver, *Managing Contracts for Peak Performance* (Vienna, VA: National Contract Management Association, 1990).

Bonaldo, Guy, *Interview with Business 2.0 Magazine*, Business Intelligence, February 2003.

Barkley, Bruce T., and James H. Saylor, *Customer Driven Project Management: A New Paradigm in Total Quality Implementation* (New York: McGraw-Hill, 1993).

Bergeron, Bryan, *Essentials of CRM: A Guide to Customer Relationship Management* (New York: John Wiley & Sons, Inc., 2002).

Bossidy, Larry and Ram Charan, *Confronting Realty: Doing What Matters to Get Things Right* (New York: Crown Business, 2004).

Bruce, David L., Marlys Norby, and Victor Ramos, *Guide to the Contract Management Body of Knowledge (CMBOK)* (Vienna, VA: National Contract Management Association, 2002).

Charan, Ram, Stephen Drotter, and James Noel, *The Leadership Pipeline* (San Francisco, CA, Jossey-Bass, 2001).

Cleland, David I., *Project Management: Strategic Design and Implementation* (New York: McGraw-Hill, 1994).

Cleland, David I., and William R. King, *Project Management Handbook,* 2nd ed. (New York: Van Nostrand Reinhold, 1988).

Collins, Jim, *Good to Great: Why Some Companies Make the Leap...and Others Don't* (New York: Harper Collins, 2001).

Coulson-Thomas, Colin, *Creating the Global Company* (New York: McGraw-Hill, 1992).

Covey, Stephen R., *The Seven Habits of Highly Effective People* (New York: Simon and Schuster, Inc., 1989).

Fisher, Roger, Elizabeth Kopelman, and Andrea K. Schneider, *Beyond Machiavelli: Tools for Coping with Conflict* (Cambridge: Harvard University Press, 1994).

Foti, Ross, "Louder Than Words," *PM Network*, December 2002.

Forsberg, Kevin, Hall Mooz, and Howard Cotterman, *Communicating Project Management* (New York: John Wiley & Sons, Inc. 2003).

Forsberg, Kevin, Hal Mooz, and Howard Cotterman, *Visualizing Project Management* (New York: John Wiley & Sons, Inc., 2001).

Freed, Richard C., Joe Romano, and Shervin Freed, *Writing Winning Business Proposals* (New York: McGraw-Hill, 2003).

Garrett, Gregory A., "Achieving Customer Loyalty," *Contract Management,* (August 2002).

Garrett, Gregory A., *Performance-Based Acquisition: Pathways to Excellence* (McLean, VA: National Contract Management Association, 2005).

Garrett, Gregory A., *World-Class Contracting: How Winning Companies Build Successful Partnerships in the e-Business Age,* 3d. ed. (Chicago: CCH Inc., 2003).

Garrett, Gregory A., *Managing Complex Outsourced Projects* (Chicago: CCH Inc., 2004).

Garrett, Gregory A. and Ed Bunnik, "Creating a World-Class PM Organization," *PM Network,* September 2000.

Garrett, Gregory A., and Reginald J. Kipke, *The Capture Management Life-Cycle: Winning More Business* (Chicago: CCH Inc., 2003).

Garrett, Gregory A. and Rene G. Rendon, *Contract Management Organizational Assessment Tools* (McLean, VA: NCMA, 2005).

Gates, Bill, *Business @ The Speed of Thought: Using a Digital Nervous System* (New York: Warner Books USA, 1999).

Harris, Phillip R., and Robert T. Moran, *Managing Cultural Differences* (Houston: Gulf Publishing Company, 1996).

Horton, Sharon, "Creating and Using Supplier Scorecards," *Contract Management* (September 2004): 22-25.

Jones, Kathryn, "The Dell Way," *Business 2.0,* (February 2003).

Kerzner, Harold, *In Search of Excellence in Project Management* (New York: Van Nostrand Reinhold, 1998).

Kirk, Dorthy, "Managing Expectations," *PM Network,* (August 2000).

Liker, Jeffrey K. and Thomas Y. Choi, "Building Deep Supplier Relationships," *Harvard Business Review* (December 2004): 104-113.

Manz, Charles C. and Henry P. Sims, *Super-Leadership* (New York: Berkley Books Inc. 1989).

Maxwell, John C., *The 21 Irrefutable Laws of Leadership* (Nashville: Thomas Nelson Inc., 1998).

Monroe, Kent B., *Pricing: Making Profitable Decisions,* 2d ed. (New York: McGraw-Hill Publishing Company, 1990).

Moran, J. and M. Riesenberger, *The Global Challenge* (New York: McGraw-Hill, 1994).

The National Contract Management Association, *The Desktop Guide to Basic Contracting Terms,* 4th ed. (Vienna, VA: NCMA 1994).

O'Connell, Brian, *B2B.com: Cashing-in on the Business-to-Business E-commerce Bonanza* (Holbrook, Massachusetts: Adams Media Corp., 2000).

Ohmae, Kenichi, *The Borderless World: Power and Strategy in the Interlinked Economy* (New York: Harper Collins Pubs., Inc., 1991).

Ohmae, Kenichi, *The Evolving Global Economy* (Boston, MA: Harvard Business School (HBS) Press, 1995).

Patterson, Shirley, "Supply Base Optimization and Integrated Supply Chain Management," *Contract Management* (January 2005): 24-35.

Pennypacker, James, "Center for Business Practices: Survey on Project Complexity," *PM Network* (May 2003).

Pennypacker, James S. and Kevin P. Grant, "Project Management Maturity: An Industry Benchmark," *Project Management Journal* (March 2003).

Peters, Tom, *Talent: Develop it, Sell it, Be it* (London: DK Publishing Inc. 2005).

Project Management Institute Standards Committee, *A Guide to the Project Management Body of Knowledge* (Upper Darby, PA: Project Management Institute, 2001).

Reichheld, Frederick F., *The Loyalty Effect* (Boston, MA: Harvard Business School Press, 1996).

Tichy, Noel, *The Leadership Engine* (New York: Harper Business Press, 1997).

Webster's Dictionary, The New Lexicon of the English Language (New York: Lexicon Publications, Inc., 1989).

Welborn, Ralph, Interview with *Business 2.0,* Business Intelligence, February 2003.

About the Authors

Gregory A. Garrett

Gregory A. Garrett, is a respected international educator, best-selling and award-winning author, dynamic speaker, and practicing industry leader. He has successfully led more than $30 billion of high-technology contracts and projects during the past 25 years. He has taught, consulted, and led contract and project teams in more than 40 countries. He has served as a lecturer for The George Washington University Law School and the School of Business and Public Management.

He currently serves as the chief compliance officer for the U.S. Federal Government programs and chairman of the Program Management Center of Excellence for Lucent Technologies.

With Lucent Technologies since 1997, Mr. Garrett has also served as: vice president, Program Management, North America, Wireless; chairman, Lucent Technologies Project Management Leadership Council, representing more than 2,000 Lucent project managers globally; and director, Global Program Management Platform at the company headquarters.

At ESI International, Mr. Garrett served as executive director of Global Business, where he led the sales, marketing, negotiation, and implementation of bid/proposal management, project management, commercial contracting, and government contract management training and consulting programs for numerous Fortune 100 multinational corporations, government agencies and small businesses worldwide, including: ABB, Dell, BellSouth, Boeing, IBM, Inter-America Development Bank, Microsoft, Israel Aircraft Industries, Lucent Technologies, Motorola, NCR, NTT, Panama Canal Commission, SBC, United States Trade Development Agency, United Nations, and the United States Department of Defense.

Formerly, Mr. Garrett served as a highly decorated military officer for the United States Air Force, awarded more than 17 medals, badges, and citations. He completed his active duty career as the youngest acquisition action officer in the Colonel's Group Headquarters USAF, the Pentagon. He was the youngest division chief and professor of contracting management at the Air Force Institute of Technology where he taught advanced courses in contract administration and program management to more than 5,000 people from the Department of Defense and NASA.

Previously, he was the youngest procurement contracting officer for the USAF Aeronautical Systems Center, where he led more than 50 multi-million dollar negotiations and managed the contract administration of over $15 billion in contracts for major weapon systems. He served as a program nanager at the Space Systems Center, where he managed a $300 million space communications project.

Mr. Garrett is a certified purchasing manager (CPM) of the Institute for Supply Management (ISM). He is a certified project management professional (PMP) of the Project Management Institute (PMI) and has received two prestigious international awards: PMI Eric Jenett Project Management Excellence Award, and the PMI David I. Cleland Project Management Literature Award. He is a certified professional contracts manager (CPCM), a Fellow, and member of the Board of Advisors of the National Contract Management Association (NCMA). He has received the NCMA National Achievement Award, NCMA National Educational Award, the Charles J. Delaney Memorial Award—for contract management literature, and the Blanche Witte Memorial Award for outstanding service to the contract management profession.

A prolific writer, Mr. Garrett co-authored the book *Managing Contracts for Peak Performance* (NCMA, 1990), authored the best-selling books *World-Class Contracting* (Third Edition CCH, 2003), *Managing Complex Outsourced Projects,* (CCH, 2004), *Contract Negotiations* (CCH, 2005), and co-authored the book *The Capture Management Life-Cycle* (CCH, 2003), and *Contract Management Organizational Tools* (NCMA, 2005). Mr. Garrett's newest book *Performance-Based Acquisition: Pathways to Excellence* (NCMA, 2005) is rapidly on its way to becoming another best-seller! Plus, during the past 19 years, he has authored more than 60 published articles on bid/proposal management, supply chain management, contracting, project management, and leadership.

He resides in Oakton, VA, with his wife, Carolyn, and children—Scott and Jennifer; his oldest son Christopher is studying business at The College of William and Mary.

William C. Pursch

William C. Pursch is president of Pursch Associates; a continuing studies faculty member of Villanova University; and professor emeritus and former head of the department of contracting management of the Air Force Institute of Technology at Wright-Patterson Air Force Base, Ohio.

With more than 30 years of teaching and consulting experience, Dr. Pursch specializes in contract management, materials management, and the development of purchasing systems, and has taught over 10,000 students in government agencies and Fortune 500 firms worldwide. He has performed reviews of purchasing and contracting systems for numerous commercial firms worldwide. Since 1999, he has been an active member of Committee E53 on Property Management Systems for the American Society for Testing and Materials.

As a warranted contracting officer for the United States Army, and a corporate purchasing specialist for Robbins and Myers, Inc., Dr. Pursch has experience in both government and commercial contracting management systems. As a retired lieutenant colonel from the U.S. Army he served in various logistical assignments in Germany, Vietnam, and Okinawa. His military decorations include the Legion of Merit, Bronze Star, Defense Meritorious Service medal, two awards of the Meritorious Service medal, and two Army Commendation medals. He is also a retired senior civilian (GM-15) from the U.S. Air Force and was awarded the Meritorious Civilian Service Award.

Listed in the 23rd edition of *Who's Who in the Midwest,* Dr. Pursch previously chaired the Board of Advisors for the purchasing and materials management degree for Sinclair Community College, Dayton, Ohio, and was the former chairman of the Board of Advisors for the National Property Management Association. A member of numerous professional associations, he currently sits on the Board of Advisors for, is a Fellow of, and is a oast national president of the National Contract Management Association (NCMA). He served as a co-leader of the 1986 NCMA People-to-People International Contract Management Delegation, and as leader of the 1989 Contract Management Educators' Delegation to the People's Republic of China. In 1990, he was awarded NCMA's highest honor—honorary life member.

Dr. Pursch received his Bachelor of Arts Degree from Gettysburg College; a Master of Science Degree from the University of Southern California; and a Doctor of Philosophy Degree from The Ohio State University.

Dr. Pursch resides in Bradenton, Florida, with his wife, Lenore.

Index

Page references followed by t and f denote tables and figures, respectively.

A

B

C

D

E

F

G

H

I

L

Q

T

U